GREAT CITIES OF THE

# WORLD

# GREAT CITIES OF THE
# WORLD

Marshall Cavendish London & New York

# CREDITS

Editor: Nicolas Wright
Designer: Kris Flynn
Picture Researcher: Kathy Brandt

LONDON: written by Tony Aldous
MOSCOW: written by Deana Levin
NEW YORK: written by Chris Maynard and Gail Rebuck
PARIS: written by Bill Garnett
ROME: written by Michael Gibson
TOKYO: written by Mitsuaki Usami and Cheung Hon-Chung of Chinatech Limited, London

Commissioned Photography:
London: Robin Bath
Moscow: Deana Levin
New York: Peter Semler
Paris: Bill Garnett
Rome: Anne-Marie Erhlich

Produced by Theorem Publishing Limited,
71/73 Great Portland Street, London W1N 5DH
for Marshall Cavendish Books Limited.

Published by Marshall Cavendish Books Limited,
58 Old Compton Street, London W1V 5PA.

ISBN 0 85685 514 6

Printed in Great Britain

The following sources have contributed photographs to this title:

All-Sport Photographic Ltd; Barnaby's Picture Library; Robin Bath; British
Tourist Authority; J. Allan Cash Library; Colorsport; Cooper-Bridgeman
Library; Daily Telegraph Colour Library/Burton, M. Hardy, K. Kirkwood, C. C.
Lim, P. Morris, D. Redfern, L. L. T. Rhodes, R. Rynning, J. Sims, E. Wilkins;
Douglas Dickins; Ann-Marie Erhlich; K. W. Faulkner; French Government
Tourist Office; B. Garnett; A. Georges/Chase Manhattan Bank; Habitat
Designs Ltd; Robert Harding; M. Hind; M. Hodgson; Italian State Tourist
Office; Japanese Airlines; Japanese Information Service; Japanese National
Tourist Office; Keystone Press Agency; Deana Levin; London Transport;
Mansell Collection; Mary Evans Picture Library; New York Convention &
Visitors Bureau; Novosti Press Agency; Popperfoto; port of London
Authority; Stuart Robinson/Royal Opera House, Covent Garden; Mick Rock;
Royal Shakespeare Theatre, Stratford-upon-Avon (by kind permission of the
governors); Peter Semler; N. Skelsey; Society for Cultural Relations with the
U.S.S.R; Spectrum Colour Library; R. Twinn; R. Updegraff; Veronese; ZEFA.

# Introduction

The world is full of cities. Each is unique. Each has its own history; its own culture; its own tradition and – above all – its own people. No matter the name of the city; no matter its location, its architecture or its climate, it is the people living and working there who make one city so completely different from another.

This book takes six such cities: London, New York, Paris, Rome, Moscow and Tokyo and describes, in a compelling series of picture essays, their quality and flavour. It looks at the familiar and the not so familiar; the beautiful and the bizarre.

Each section is introduced by a detailed and fascinating account which places the city in its historical and geographical setting. Learn why London was founded on the banks of the River Thames; why New York attracted those in search of a better life and why Paris is considered by many to be the world's most romantic city. Read about the cultural heritage with which Rome endowed western civilization; discover the artistic treasures stored in Moscow's Kremlin and see how east meets west in Tokyo's complex society.

This book captures the essence of these six great cities. Informed, succinct and expertly written text, coupled with a stunning collection of photographs, will give the armchair traveller a rare insight into what makes a city. Not only do the pages cover the magnificence of, for example, a state occasion in London, but they also linger over the often unnoticed and obscure, the minutiae of the streets such as a forgotten statue or a flower in bloom. People are seen at work and at play; grand buildings are given no more prominence than a market or a park.

In short, this book shows cities as they really are: vibrant and exciting; mellow and unhurried.

# Introduction to London

Thirty years ago the school textbooks used by London children boasted that their blitzed and blackened city was 'the greatest' in the world. Greatest meant biggest in population; it meant biggest in area; and it implied also that London was still then the heart of a great and glorious empire.

Today London is no longer 'greatest' in any of these senses. The British have given away most of their empire; London's population, partly as a result of deliberate policies, has fallen from its 1950s peak of nearly eight and a half million to fewer than seven million; and half a dozen cities in Asia and the Third World have far outstripped it in numbers and area.

Yet London remains in many ways the outstanding 'world city'. It may no longer rule an empire, but it remains a formidable commercial force. The expertise of its commodity markets and its international insurance and banking organisations give its historic commercial centre, 'The City', a rare status.

Another way in which three decades have transformed London is in mood. It is altogether livelier and more attractive. People visit it not, as in its imperial heyday, because they felt compelled to, they come because they like the place.

And this stems only partly from the informality and innovation that won 1960s London its 'swinging' reputation. There is much more to it than that. Many American visitors say they find London the most 'livable' of the world's big cities. You can still walk about the streets comfortably and securely. It has its share of new tower blocks, new highways and restless, fast moving traffic. But they have not destroyed its unique character and atmosphere.

It is still possible to wander in spacious parkland so lush that traffic noise is a forgotten, distant rumble; to stroll through elegant 18th and 19th-century streets where rectilinear steel, plate-glass and concrete seem not to exist. A block away, round a couple of corners, they reappear in a comfortable, convenient tourist hotel — but for the most part not too obtrusively.

Perhaps this is the key to London's popularity. It retains great diversity. It is cosmopolitan, so that the visitor does not feel isolated. It is on the whole friendly — Londoners will generally take time and trouble to help a stranger. And when it comes to things to do, the richness of what it has to offer in fields like theatre, music, museums, art galleries, and sport, withstand challenge from any other city anywhere in the world.

Despite the bulldozer, despite too many motorcars, despite the stops and goes of an erratic economy, London has flourished and blossomed with an amazing richness. It was a Scotsman, William Dunbar, who wrote nearly 500 years ago, 'London, thou art the flower of cities all!'. Its 1970s bloom is richer than ever.

REGENTS PARK

EUSTON RD.

TOTTENHAM COURT RD.

BAKER ST.

1

3

OXFORD ST.

BAYSWATER RD.

HAYMARKET

HYDE PARK

PARK LANE

THE SERPENTINE

PICCADILLY

ROTTEN ROW

THE MALL

GREEN PARK

ST. JAMES'S
PARK

KNIGHTSBRIDGE

BUCKINGHAM
PALACE
GARDENS

BIRDCAGE WALK

2

SLOANE ST.

4

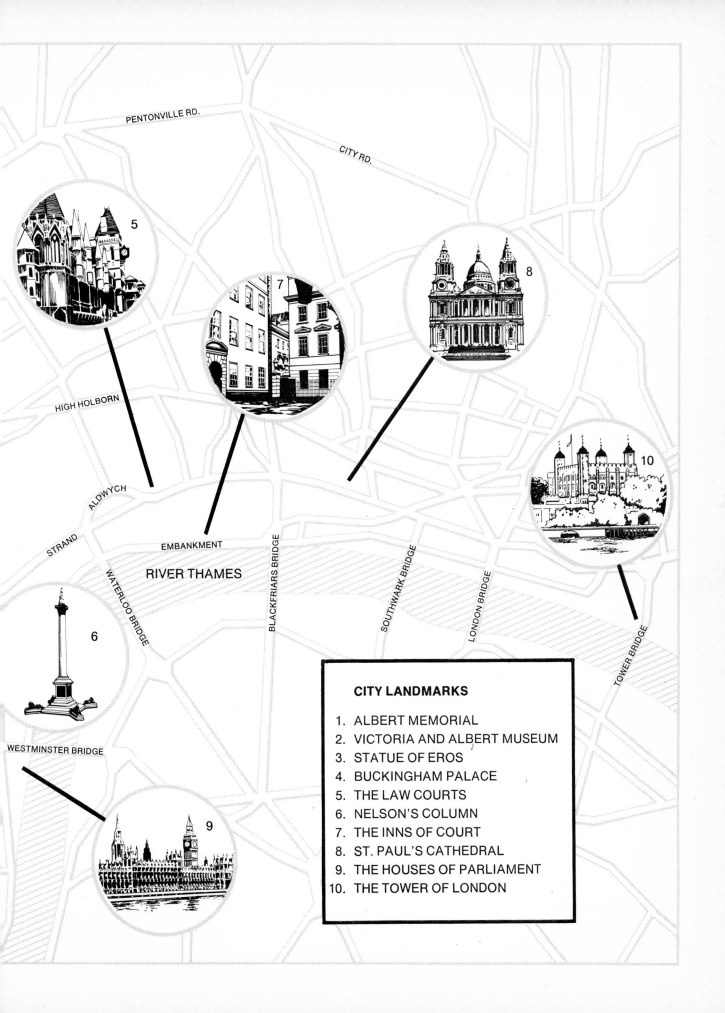

PENTONVILLE RD.

CITY RD.

HIGH HOLBORN

ALDWYCH

STRAND

WATERLOO BRIDGE

EMBANKMENT

RIVER THAMES

BLACKFRIARS BRIDGE

SOUTHWARK BRIDGE

LONDON BRIDGE

TOWER BRIDGE

WESTMINSTER BRIDGE

**CITY LANDMARKS**

1. ALBERT MEMORIAL
2. VICTORIA AND ALBERT MUSEUM
3. STATUE OF EROS
4. BUCKINGHAM PALACE
5. THE LAW COURTS
6. NELSON'S COLUMN
7. THE INNS OF COURT
8. ST. PAUL'S CATHEDRAL
9. THE HOUSES OF PARLIAMENT
10. THE TOWER OF LONDON

# London As It Was

London first became a city under the Romans, following a successful invasion of southern Britain by the Emperor Claudius in AD 50. A kind of settlement had already grown up there because this was the lowest point at which the Thames could be easily forded.

The Romans were quick to realize the site's potential and built the first London Bridge. From this early wooden structure radiated their roads: Watling Street south-eastwards to the Channel ports and north-west towards Chester; Ermine Street north towards York and south to Chichester; Ealde Street eastwards to Colchester, then a much more important town than London.

The original Roman town, Londinium, was also wooden until, in AD 60 Boadicea, Queen of the Iceni, rebelled against Roman rule. She burnt and pillaged both Colchester and London before the legions could be recalled from the north to suppress the revolt. After that the Romans rebuilt Londinium in stone.

Because of its position as crossroads and crossing place as well as a port, Londinium became the largest city in the western part of the Roman Empire. But after the Romans left in AD 410, the city entered the Dark Ages: its grand buildings fell into disrepair and the settlement that remained suffered sacking and burning at the hands of successive waves of invaders from continental Europe. Yet, if Greater London, the present city of almost seven million people, is essentially a city of villages, then most of those villages owe their origin to bands of marauding Saxons who decided to settle down.

London, from the fifth to the 11th centuries, was not England's capital city. Indeed there was no England until a Saxon King, Alfred the Great of Wessex, united the Saxons and pushed the Danes back in AD 877 into the northern and eastern parts of the country. His capital was Winchester. The city of London and most of its surroundings were strongly Saxon; but the eastern parts of what is now Greater London, north of the Thames, lay inside the Danelaw, on Danish territory.

Under Alfred, London rebuilt its walls, formed a militia, and began to establish the makings of civic independence. The later Saxon kings were mostly crowned at Kingston (the King's town), 12 miles south-west from London Bridge but today also in Greater London. The city within its walls, however, grew more and more prosperous and powerful. By 1042 when Canute died and the Witan (or council of wise men) met to decide on a successor, representatives of the City of London had a dominant voice in the proceedings that restored the Saxon line, with Edward the Confessor as king.

Edward's reign saw the rebuilding of an abbey one-and-a-quarter miles west of the walled city. Alongside this abbey, the West Minster, he built a royal palace. Thus began the twin centres of modern London: the City, the business capital; Westminster, the royal and administrative capital. Indeed for another six centuries the two

Tower Bridge, despite its gothic appearance, is a 19th-century steel-framed structure. It still opens to let large ships go up river.

remained physically separate, with only a sprinkling of palaces and grand houses overlooking the strand in between. And, although London is today for strategic purposes administered by the Greater London Council, the traditional duality of its centre is still reflected in the names of two of its local authorities: the City of London and the City of Westminster.

In 1066 England was successfully invaded for the last time by a foreign army: the Normans under their duke, William. He defeated Harold, whose succession he disputed, at Hastings on the south-east coast and marched to London. If he expected the citizens to fling open the gates in joy, he was mistaken; and walled London beyond the Thames was sufficiently formidable a fortress for him to turn away at Southwark and cross the Thames higher up.

By the time he came back that Christmas on the eve of his coronation, their attitude had changed. Norman rule was now an indisputable fact; perhaps there had been some parleying? The city proclaimed him king, and in return for their support and loyalty, its inhabitants received all the civic privileges and more that they had enjoyed in good King Edward's day.

But William the Conqueror was also William the prudent! He set about building a stone castle adjoining and looking over the city's eastern wall. It stands today. Known as the White Tower, it forms the central keep of that impressive, noble, three-ring concentric fortress, the Tower of London.

Throughout most of the medieval period, London was twice as populous as any other English city and many times richer. While feudal power held sway in most of England, London's Lord Mayor and aldermen administered their own courts and maintained a formidable armed force in the city's trained militia. During the 12th-century civil war between King Stephen and his rival for the crown, Matilda, that queen gave the Constable of the Tower rule over the city. He found he could not enforce it, was soon Stephen's prisoner and had to cede the Tower in ransom. Stephen promptly restored all the city's rights.

In the 12th century when Richard I was crusading in the Holy Land, his regent, who had made the Tower his headquarters, provoked the citizens to revolt in favour of Prince John, the king's brother. John led the city militia to the Tower, besieged the regent and forced him to surrender the fortress. However, in 1215, when John had become king, he found the city's boot was on the other foot. The Mayor and merchants of London joined the barons in extorting from him that

historic guarantee of rights and privileges, *Magna Carta.* One factor that persuaded the king was the likelihood that, if he did not agree, the citizenry would once again seize the Tower.

Increasingly, too, London's wealth told. Its merchants, no doubt, were only common men, who must bow, doff caps and show all respect to the landed nobility, but unlike landed magnates, they disposed of substantial liquid assets—not great estates—but gold and silver. So if the king lacked cash to pay an army or build a palace, he looked to London; London, respectfully but firmly, insisted on its price, often in new commercial privileges. In consequence, it grew steadily richer and more powerful.

By Shakespeare's day in the 16th century the city had spread westwards well beyond its walls; so had the authority of the Lord Mayor and aldermen. At Temple Bar a barrier set up across Fleet Street marked the limit of their jurisdiction. A later arch, designed by Sir Christopher Wren and dating from 1672, was moved to ease traffic congestion in the 1870s. It stands, now much decayed, at Theobalds Park, north-east of London. However, because it symbolizes constitutional freedom and the rule of law in both England and America, moves are afoot to restore and reinstate it in the City of London, perhaps on a site near St Paul's Cathedral. When the Queen visits the City, she still halts at its boundary with Westminster, where Temple Bar stood. The Lord Mayor proffers her the City's ceremonial sword which she accepts but hands back into his safekeeping—symbolizing the City's ancient independence under the Crown.

*Left:* The Houses of Parliament from the Thames. The big tower is the Victoria Tower; the clock tower is popularly known as 'Big Ben' after its bell.
*Top:* A Yeoman of the Guard, popularly known as a Beefeater, one of the guardians of the Tower of London, in his 16th century uniform.
*Right:* Temple Bar, which used to mark the entrance from Westminster into the historic City of London.

11

London, in Shakespeare's time, had also spread to Southwark on the south bank. In 1550 its jurisdiction was extended to most of this area. London's purchase of lands from the church did not, however, include two areas known as the Liberties of Clink and Paris Garden. That is why many pleasure gardens, places of entertainment and, above all, theatres flourished there, outside the grasp of the City Corporation.

The bridge itself, many times destroyed and rebuilt since the Romans' original wooden structure, was by this time the 13th-century London Bridge of Peter de Colechurch—a stone construction of 20 gothic arches, almost 600 feet long and more than 20 feet wide. It had a double drawbridge, raised to let ships sail up river and keep intruders out of the city. On it, and cantilevered outwards, Londoners had built their houses of three, four and more storeys. Skewered on spikes at its Southwark end, the heads of traitors and criminals stood as a warning to the populace to be loyal and law-abiding.

Two later London bridges have followed: Rennie's graceful five-arch affair of 1831, whose stone façades at least now adorn a bridge at Lake Havasu City, Arizona; and the present, efficient but uninspiring structure opened in 1973.

Seventeenth-century London, though it had spread beyond the walls, was packed tight. The wealthier citizens might take to living in country villages like Kensington, coming in by carriage or on horseback. The poor, lacking any public transport, or the time or money to indulge in it had it existed, lived crammed together within or close under the walls. The importance then of living near your business is well demonstrated by the legal profession. Its private walled city, the Temple, stood on the eastern edge of the City of London, close both to trade and to the Court, Parliament and royal courts at Westminster. By the end of Queen Elizabeth's reign in 1603, 300000 people lived within or close to the Square Mile of the walled city. Sixty years later, when Samuel Pepys was writing his diary, the population and overcrowding had grown immeasurably, and were a contributing cause of the Great Plague of 1665. So too had congestion grown. Today's Londoners may complain of the occasional traffic jam in the Strand; they experience nothing like the total standstills which encouraged Pepys to take to the river as the fastest way of commuting between Westminster and the City.

By Pepys's time London had ceased for practical purposes to be a walled city. In the Civil War which culminated in Parliament's victory over Charles I, and ultimately the king's trial and execution, the Lord Mayor and aldermen had significantly ordered construction of a ring of defensive earthworks to protect both the City *and Westminster.*

The Great Plague of London and the Great Fire which followed it in 1666 demonstrated that bursting medieval London could no longer safely support all the activity crammed into it. Overcrowded wooden houses harboured the rats that carried the plague-spreading fleas. The plague virtually stopped the city's heart and by September 1665 the weekly death toll had reached 7000.

Fortunately the colder winter weather all but ended the plague and commercial life returned to normal — for a while! The next autumn those same wooden houses—crowded together in narrow lanes and alleys, their overhanging upper storeys often almost touching—caught a spark from a baker's oven in Pudding Lane, near London Bridge. The wind fanned the flames; citizens struggled to save their own possessions rather than quell the fire; and by the time the king's brother, the Duke of York, intervened by blowing up houses to make a fire break, four-fifths of London within the walls had perished.

The tragedy of the fire seemed to offer an opportunity to rebuild a spacious new City of London. Plans were not lacking. In reality, however, 17th-century London and England possessed neither the money nor the legal and administrative machinery to rebuild London in a new mould—least of all in the midst of an expensive war with the Dutch. The best it could do was rebuild on the old street lines, but in brick or stone rather than wood, with taller houses only on the wider streets and some street widening.

The great architect, Sir Christopher Wren, contributed to the rebuilding with a new St Paul's Cathedral and 49 city churches, most of which still survive today, though in some cases tucked away behind large new office blocks.

Seventeenth-century London also saw other significant changes. Thanks to a far-sighted citizen and engineer, Sir Hugh Myddelton, it

gained, in the 38-mile-long New River, an aqueduct able to provide plentiful supplies of pure water in place of increasingly polluted Thames and well water.

The appearance of London was also changing. Inigo Jones's Whitehall Banqueting House and his Queen's House at Greenwich had given Londoners their first bemused taste of classical architecture instead of gothic. Now Wren and his contemporaries modified but reinforced the new fashion. For almost the next two centuries London's architecture—whether described as Jacobean, Queen Anne, Georgian or Victorian, and though usually a decade or two in advance of the rest of Britain—remained basically classical in style.

London continued to grow. The 17th century had seen planned development on the estates of the Earls and Dukes of Bedford at Covent Garden (originally the garden of a convent), the Earls of Southampton (Bloomsbury) and in the St James, Piccadilly and Soho areas. In the 18th century came the 'West End' — the planned and spacious Georgian grid development of Mayfair and Marylebone, culminating in the Regency period of the early 19th century with John Nash's grand design for a triumphal route via Regent Street and Portland Place, cutting through London to the landscaped green spaces and splendid stucco terraces of Regent's Park. Queen Anne's Gate, one of the prettiest and most complete 18th century streets in London, dates in part from 1704.

This century also did its best to improve the capital's road system. Westminster Bridge (1750) provided a second river crossing; Blackfriars (1769) and Battersea (1771) soon followed. The 'New Road' — along the line of what we now call City, Pentonville, Euston and Marylebone Roads—provided the city with its first major bypass and facilitated the rapid extension of the West End.

This was the London that prompted Dr Samuel Johnson (whose house you can still visit in Gough Square, just north of Fleet Street) to remark, 'When a man is tired of London, he is tired of life; for there is in London all that life can afford'.

And so there was for the rich, or even the tolerably well off. For the poor — ill-housed, ill-fed, constrained to exist in the ill-favoured areas where they could scratch, beg or steal a living — there was no escape until the railways came. For in the 19th century it was a transport revolution that produced the most dramatic changes of all in London's history. From the 1840s onwards the railways as well as horse omnibuses and later electric trams gave first the lower middle classes and then the working man, too, the chance to live in decent surroundings, with trees and gardens, rather than in overcrowded and improvized tenements.

*Below:* Boadicia, Queen of the Iceni, rose against her Roman oppressors in AD 60 and captured and destroyed London. Her statue stands on the Victoria Embankment near Westminster Bridge.
*Below right:* Piccadilly Circus with traffic swirling round the statue of *Eros.*

The march of bricks and mortar went now at a phenomenal pace. In 1801 the population of London stood at about 800000; by 1851 it was more than two million; by 1901, four and a half million. By that time the fast-spreading underground railway system further encouraged commuting and in the 1920s and 1930s electrified suburban railways and surface extensions of the underground actually preceded and made possible the outward suburban sprawl. It had eaten up most of the historic county of Middlesex before any government cried halt. In 1931 the area we now call Greater London sheltered eight million people — more than one-sixth of the total United Kingdom population.

By this time London — commercial and political heart of a great empire — had developed a local government system to suit its size. First, in 1855, Parliament created the Metropolitan Board of Works to look after the needs of London outside the narrow boundaries of the historic city; then, in 1888, it set up the London County Council, covering some 74000 acres including the City. At the end of the century it added 28 metropolitan boroughs responsible, alongside the City Corporation, for more local matters.

The story of London in the 20th century has been of a pond with ever widening ripples. First London swallowed country villages like Islington; developers turned them into more or less favoured residential areas; their inhabitants then moved onward and outward, as better transport enabled then to commute further in pursuit of the receding countryside. Districts like Islington, Hackney and Camberwell lost favour and declined. Their grander houses were sub-divided; industry moved in. Congestion again threatened to choke the centre.

But already in the 1930s the London County Council had been buying agricultural land for a 'Green Belt' to halt the spread of the built-up areas. After the Second World War these policies were given legal effect as part of Britain's new planning system. But at the same time governments recognised that London was now too fat to be healthy. For the 30 years following the war they prescribed for the capital a deliberate 'slimming' regime. A ring of new towns beyond the Green Belt were built, to tempt industry and its workers to leave the capital, moulded on the example set by Ebenezer Howard's Welwyn

*Left:* The hotel front of St Pancras Station, high-watermark of 19th-century gothic architecture. An historic building protected by law, the station still functions as a main line terminus.
*Above:* How London's rapid 18th and 19th-century expansion appeared to one contemporary observer: 'The March of Bricks and Mortar' by George Cruishank.

Garden City of the 1920s. Londoners were entitled to the English
dream of an individual house with its own garden, said the planners.

The policy worked, partly because of the sticks and carrots of
government policy; partly because Londoners and London employers
were deciding to move out anyway to pleasanter and more profitable
pastures. In the last 20 years Greater London's population has fallen
from a peak of eight million to less than seven million. Partly because
of this, the city is a pleasanter place in which to live. Other factors that
make today's London more attractive to residents and visitors alike are
the cumulative effects of the 1956 Clean Air Act and other anti-
pollution measures; the cleaning up of the once badly polluted River
Thames, so that some 60 varieties of fish now live comfortably in its
waters; two new underground lines — The Victoria Line (completed
1971) and the Fleet Line (first section opened 1977); and a
computerised traffic control system which will eventually control
traffic lights at more than 1000 road junctions.

London's planners believed 15 years ago they could improve the
city's environment by bold and drastic change: ambitious new
highways cutting through the city; new flats in high white towers in
place of the Victorian brick terraces; people moved whether they liked
it or not from their familiar if substandard habitats to what the experts
thought best for them.

*Right:* The new Port of London is concentrated down-river, on wider, deeper reaches of the Thames, and uses modern cargo handling facilities like these at Tilbury.

That philosophy is now dead. London has neither the money nor the wish for large-scale drastic change. Conservation and gradual, cautious renewal are the watchwords. People's tastes have changed: affluent professional families have found that 19th-century inner suburbs like Islington offer roomy houses, attractive environments and short journeys to work and entertainment. Parts of the inner city are blooming.

But only parts. Departing industry has left uncomfortable gaps. The Port of London has, quite predictably but rather suddenly, moved down river to deeper, wider reaches of the Thames which can accommodate the new large bulk carrier ships. Much industry, often with the encouragement of government grants and inducements, has gone to other parts of the country where workers were more plentiful and communications less congested.

As a result, London and central government have once again changed their tune. They are now promoting the development of the inner city, and especially the 5000 acres of redundant dockland east of the City of London. One industry has, however, been booming: tourism. The capital now welcomes more than eight and a half million overseas visitors a year. Most of them arrive by air, either at Heathrow on the western edge of Greater London now linked by an underground extension with a train every four minutes, or to Gatwick in the south (already on a fast railway line) or to smaller airports at Luton, Stansted and Southend.

The main London airport, Heathrow, lies some 15 miles west of central London, to which it is joined by a spur from the main M4 London-South Wales Motorway. Heathrow was first developed as a civil airport in 1946, to replace the pre-war Croydon Aerodrome in south London whose runways were too short for modern aircraft. In the three decades since its foundation, Heathrow has never ceased growing, with some part or other of its huge area always the scene of building operations. Its central area, reached from the motorway by twin tunnels, now boasts three terminal buildings; a separate cargo terminal on the airport's southern edge connects to the centre by a second tunnel; while a third tunnel brings in an extension of the Piccadilly Line underground train to the newly completed Heathrow Central station. In peak summer periods the airport handles almost 1000 aircraft movements a day, with a plane landing or taking off every 1–2 minutes. Some 23 million passengers use Heathrow each year — the lion's share of the 32 million who pass through all five airports serving London.

*Below:* One of the best vantage points for sightseeing in London is the top deck of a double-decker bus– seen here passing a mounted sentry at The Horseguards in Whitehall. *Right:* The statue of Sir Winston Churchill, war-time Prime Minister and statesman, in a characteristic pose overlooking Westminster.

The London they come to absorbs them remarkably well, even if natives sometimes complain that English is scarcely spoken in summer on No. 11 buses passing Westminster Abbey. London today is a cosmopolitan place; native Londoners increasingly have black, brown or yellow skins rather than white or pink. But immigrants are nothing new. In Spitalfields, just east of the City of London, stand 18th century houses that first gave shelter to Flemish weavers; the nearby building that started as a Lutheran church later served as a synagogue and is now a Bengali mosque. It all makes for vitality and diversity, if also a degree of friction. Dr Johnson's remark about London providing all life can offer, rings even truer today. You can live a lifetime here and still go on discovering something new. As for the ten million tourists — they seem to be able to find more than enough in London to occupy themselves with.

19

# Royal and Traditional London

London is still a royal city, a city of palaces. But for more than two centuries now, British kings and queens have reigned rather than ruled, acting only on the advice of elected governments. London's best-known royal palaces symbolize that constitutional fact. Buckingham Palace, where the Queen lives when in London (if she is there, you see the Royal Standard flying), is, despite a new and grander façade added in 1913, totally eclipsed in grandeur by the Palace of Westminster. And that 19th-century gothic pile between the Thames and Parliament Square, though technically still a royal palace, was built to accommodate the legislature.

There, every autumn, the three branches of Britain's law-making body — Commons, Lords and Sovereign — assemble under one roof for the ceremonial opening of a new session of Parliament. The Queen sits high on her throne; the Lords (some hereditary, some appointed for life) occupy their own benches; the Commons stand. But the speech the Queen reads is written by her Prime Minister, who comes from and commands the support of the elected house, the Commons.

Every year, just before the ceremonial opening, the Serjeant-at-Arms of this still royal palace, in a quaint and symbolic ceremony, leads an armed search of its cellars. He thus recalls the discovery, on November 5th 1605, of kegs of gunpowder in these same underground vaults, intended to blow up King James I, his Ministers and his Parliament. The British custom of bonfires and fireworks each November 5th — Guy Fawkes Day — takes its name from one of the conspirators.

A little more than 600 yards away in Whitehall stands the sole relic of another royal palace, the Palace of Whitehall — its Banqueting House, designed by Inigo Jones and dating from 1622. Here James's son, Charles I, having lost a civil war and been tried for treason, stepped to his execution on a scaffold which was erected just outside these high first-floor windows.

Westminster is royal because the saintly Saxon king, Edward the Confessor, built Westminster Abbey there. The first of the Normans, William the Conqueror, was crowned there in 1066, as has been every crowned British monarch since. The abbey was rebuilt by Henry III (1216-1272); he and five other kings and queen lie buried behind the high altar. When Henry VIII dissolved the monasteries in 1540, the church became a 'Royal Peculiar' independent of any bishop or diocese. Legend has it that John Bradshaw, who pronounced the death sentence on Charles I, haunts the deanery.

Other palaces in central London include St James's — a basically 16th-century building with state apartments by Wren — from whose balcony the Garter King of Arms, England's chief heraldic officer, proclaims new monarchs: Clarence House, home of the Queen Mother; Marlborough House, which accommodates the

The Queen has two birthdays: her actual birthdate, April 21st which is a private and family affair, and her official birthday, in early June, when she reviews her soldiers at the Trooping of the Colour.

Commonwealth Secretariat; and Lancaster House, now a conference centre. Here Chopin played to Queen Victoria and Prince Albert; and so grand is the interior that the Queen once told her hostess, the Duchess of Sutherland: 'I have come from my home to your palace!'

Royal ceremonies which the public can see in London include the Changing of the Guard on most days, outside Buckingham Palace and the Horse Guards; the annual Trooping the Colour on the Queen's official birthday in June, when she takes the salute on horseback; and the procession, from Buckingham Palace via the Mall, the Horseguards and Whitehall, for the State Opening of Parliament. Two buildings at Buckingham Palace are open to the public — the Royal Mews, and the Queen's Gallery, which exhibits, in rotation, selections from the interesting and extensive royal art collection.

Ancient and curious ceremonies surrounding the monarchy apart, the most fertile soil for strange and venerable traditions lies in the so-called 'Square Mile' of the City of London. The Lord Mayor, for instance, owes his election not to the Court of Common Council, the elected body which carries out the City's ordinary local government functions, but to the Liverymen of the City Companies — its ancient craft guilds such as Goldsmiths, Fishmongers, Vintners, Cordwainers, Tallowchandlers and 70 or 80 others, some of whose livery halls are among the City's outstanding historic buildings.

These liverymen foregather in Guildhall each Michaelmas Day (September 29th) in quaint and colourful costume including medieval fur-trimmed gowns, and select two aldermen from whom the City's Court of Aldermen (a sort of municipal senate, appointed for life) makes the final choice. Then on the second Saturday in November follows the Lord Mayor's Show, when the newly sworn-in Lord Mayor — in a four-ton 18th-century coach pulled by six horses and with a guard of pikemen in breast plates and helmets — drives to the Law Courts in the Strand to present himself to the Lord Chief Justice.

The Lord Chief Justice represents the Queen; and indeed Lord Mayors used to go by river to Westminster to see the sovereign personally. But now their route lies through crowded City streets, and this symbolic journey has long since become the occasion for a gargantuan procession of tableaux and displays on mobile floats, representing different aspects of City life and centering on a theme nominated by the incoming Lord Mayor.

Another City occasion which combines traditional ceremony with practical, present-day politics is the Lord Mayor's Banquet at Guildhall — one of a number of such occasions every year when guest speakers may include the Prime Minister or the Chancellor of the Exchequer and provide an important opportunity for public exchange of views between the business community and the government of the day. The Lord Mayor in his year of office needs both a fat purse and a strong constitution. He eats countless dinners and delivers more than 1000 speeches in the twelvemonth.

Most famous of his predecessors was Sir Richard Whittington, who as plain Dick Whittington, a lad not yet in his teens, was leaving London when, on Highgate Hill, he heard Bow Bells telling him 'Turn again Whittington, three times Lord Mayor!' In fact he held office four times, and is the popular archetype of the poor boy made good in business. During his year of office the Lord Mayor has precedence within the City boundaries over all save the monarch.

Another ancient tradition, honoured this time just outside the City boundaries, is the Ceremony of the Keys at the Tower of London. When the guard of Yeomen Warders has locked the Tower's outer gate

*Left:* The King's Troop, Royal Artillery, fire a salute in Hyde Park on the Queen's Birthday.
*Above:* Judges in their wigs and ceremonial robes walk in procession to the Royal Courts of Justice in the Strand at the start of the Legal Year.

each night, returning they meet a sentry. 'Halt, who comes there?' he challenges. 'The keys', replies the Chief Warder. 'Whose keys?' demands the sentry. 'Queen Elizabeth's keys', is the reply. At which the the guard presents arms, the Chief Warder doffs his red and black Tudor bonnet and pronounces, 'God preserve Queen Elizabeth!' 'Amen!' cry the guard, and march on to lodge the Queen's keys in the Queen's House, safe within the Inner Ward.

A Thames tradition, Doggett's Coat and Badge, dates from 1715. In that year Thomas Doggett, actor manager of Drury Lane and a regular commuter by river from Chelsea, was caught in a storm when he wanted to go home. A young and impecunious waterman got him there, so Doggett in gratitude endowed a rowing race for watermen just out of their apprenticeship. First prize is still 'a Coat of Orange Livery', a silver badge and a cup. The race takes place in late July or early August.

The Inns of Court represent a major stronghold of bizarre tradition — those four walled and gated precincts where barristers, the senior branch of the English legal profession, who wear wigs and gowns in court, work together in shared 'chambers', and have their libraries and dining halls. The Benchers of the four inns — Inner Temple, Middle Temple, Lincolns Inn and Grays Inn — are judges and senior barristers, and still exercise the sole right to 'call to the Bar' students who have qualified for entry into the profession. Examinations apart, a bar student must still 'keep his terms' by eating so many dinners in hall each legal term for a number of years. The student who fails to observe the complex etiquette of these occasions may be fined a bottle of wine if his neighbour at table challenges his conduct before the benchers. One bottle of wine for every four students is normally provided with the meal.

*Below:* The White Tower, central keep of the Tower of London, was begun by William the Conqueror soon after he took the English throne in 1066.

*Right:* Ancient customs bring a splash of colour to the workaday city: Life Guards leaving the Mall to return to their barracks after guard duty.

*Left:* The Queen leaves Buckingham Palace to drive to the annual ceremony of the Opening of Parliament. Her speech, though delivered with the Lords seated and the elected Commons standing, is written for her by the Prime Minister with majority support in the elected house.

*Below:* The Lord Mayor's Show. The incoming Lord Mayor drives in procession through the Square Mile of the City.

*Right:* The Chelsea Flower Show – an annual riot of colour.

*Left:* Chelsea Royal Hospital on Founder's Day.
*Above:* One of the inmates, a Chelsea Pensioner, in his traditional scarlet uniform.

# London by Water

London's major highway was traditionally the Thames. That is why two of its greatest palaces, Greenwich and Hampton Court, as well as Westminster and Whitehall, stood on the banks. Greenwich today is not a palace. The splendid group of buildings by Wren, Vanbrugh and Hawksmoor which transform this loop in a generally workaday river have served most of their 250-odd years first as a 'hospital' for naval pensioners, then from 1873 onwards as the Royal Naval College.

Their central vista leads the eye to Greenwich's finest building, Inigo Jones's Queen's House of 1616 — a vista which Wren preserved only on royal insistence. Two colonnades link it to the flanking wings of the National Maritime Museum, of which it now forms part — as does Wren's pretty Flamstead House, built on the hill above for the first Astronomer Royal, Sir John Flamstead.

At this hilltop observatory later Astronomers Royal made the observations which put Greenwich on the map as the Prime Meridian — 0 degrees of longitude—the dividing line between east and west.

By the riverside below stand two famous sailing vessels in a permanent dry-dock: *Cutty Sark,* last of the great clippers that brought tea from the Indies; and *Gypsy Moth,* in which in 1966–1967 Sir Francis Chichester sailed alone round the world.

In central London the great 19th-century granite embankments, added to steadily by new riverside walks, give public access to the Thames; and at two points, Westminster and Charing Cross, river launches, the summer bus service of the tideway — offer regular services downstream to Greenwich, and upstream to Kew, Richmond and Hampton Court. Similar services also run from Tower Pier. They are the best way for a visitor to discover the river. But strollers along the Victoria Embankment can also take pleasure in the growing flotilla of historic vessels permanently moored there. These include Scott's Antarctic exploration ship *Discovery;* a paddle-steamer turned pub, the *Old Caledonia;* and, down river opposite the Tower, *HMS Belfast,* grandly grey, last survivor of a vanished line of steel-hulled, big-gunned 20th-century warships.

One of the delights of a boat trip on the river is its procession of bridges: 27 of them between the Lower Pool, where the docks begin, and Teddington Lock, where the Thames ceases to be tidal. Outstanding among them must be counted Tower Bridge, Victorian gothic on a steel frame and with a central section which still opens for the occasional larger craft; Waterloo, white and clean of line from the 1930s; and Albert, despite its newly inserted central prop, still the prettiest suspension bridge on the tideway. Back below Tower Bridge, St Katharine's Dock, with its old Nore lightship, yacht harbour and splendidly restored ivory warehouse, shows that docks and dock buildings, left redundant by changes in port operations, can yet prove a rich asset to a city.

Further upstream, as the river narrows, come a dozen Thames-side towns and villages, parks and grand houses, preserving their diverse

Despite the movement of port trade down river, the Thames in central London still has its ships — moving and moored. Training ships for sea cadets, Scott's *Discovery*, floating public houses, restaurants, museums and art galleries.

identities in the midst of the London that now surrounds them —
Hurlingham, Fulham Palace, Strand-on-the-Green and Kew; Syon
House; Richmond, Marble Hill and Kingston; Hampton Court and
Molesey — each with its own particular charms and hidden delights.

But London has, apart from the Thames, another and yet more
secret waterway — the Grand Union and Regent canals, constructed in
the late 18th and early 19th centuries to connect the expanding canal
system of the Midlands with the Thames and its docks at Limehouse.
Its best known and most visible stretches are at Little Venice and
alongside the Zoo; also now at Camden Lock. But the Regent canal
mostly hides behind high walls and in deep cuttings — a marvellously
tranquil and attractive 19th-century world which you can explore on
foot along its towpaths (tunnels apart, there is now public access for
most of its length), or better still by boat. Canal 'narrow-boats' of
traditional design offer trips both from Little Venice and Camden Lock;
you can go to the Zoo by boat from Little Venice; and several
restaurant boats offer meals afloat, either moored or moving.

*Below:* Albert Bridge, between Chelsea and Battersea – arguably London's prettiest bridge.
*Right:* Ornate Victorian ironwork also gives its own character to the Victoria Embankment at Westminster, but copies of these lampstandards have also been installed on new stretches of river walk on the South Bank.

# Lively London

London in the 1970s is an altogether livelier and more cosmopolitan city than anyone could have imagined in the 1950s. The 1960s brought an *avant-garde* consciousness in pop music, pop art and pop fashions in clothes from which the long-standing foreigner's view of England as dull and conventional could never recover.

This 'Swinging London' has continued and grown from strength to strength at at least two focal points. The Carnaby Street area on the Regent Street side of Soho, now freed from traffic and given a psychedelic face-lift by Westminster City Council, offers shoppers a more informal, 'liberated' and, it must be said, noisier alternative to the big department stores of Regent Street and Oxford Street. In Chelsea, the King's Road from Sloane Square westwards into Fulham, full of boutiques, outrageous fashions, roaringly exotic and noisy eating places, *is* an experience — no, an adventure, rather — even for those who go to stare rather than buy.

The informality and non-conformity encouraged by the Swinging 1960s has spread, in a diluted, less garish form, into every aspect of London life. Matching it is the incredible cosmopolitanism of the city. In the London of the 1930s, the first Italian restaurant seemed, to the insular citizens of those days, exotic and suspect. Now in central London you can find Japanese, Hungarian, Burmese, Mexican, Scandinavian, Greek, Spanish, French, Italian, Dutch and many other nationalities of eating places; while almost every suburb has its Chinese and Indian take-aways and kebab-houses.

Londoners, too, are now a cosmopolitan crowd. China Town, originally in Limehouse, has now established itself round Gerrard Street in Soho — the district which still possesses the biggest and most polyglot concentration of exotic eating places, even if now marginally threatened for space by the spread of the blue film and pornography merchants.

Camden Town and Kentish Town have long been the Greek Cypriot quarter; New Cross is strong in Turks; Bengalis have colonised Spitalfields, as European Jews and Flemish weavers did before them; and Brixton and Notting Hill are the most notable centres of London's big West Indian population.

Each celebrates its distinctive customs and festivities — paper dragons and fire crackers in Soho; colourful saints' day processions at St Cyprians, Kentish Town; and — biggest, gayest but sometimes unhappily tinged with minority violence — the intensely colourful and noisy carnivals of the Caribbean communities.

London is on the whole an easy-going city. Policemen do not arrest you for crossing the road when the traffic light says 'Wait' to pedestrians. It's left to your good sense. Park keepers do not pursue you for walking or lying on grass. That, they say, is what it's there for — unless they have just resown it with grass-seed, in which case they'll fence it off.

Greek Street in Soho. Soho is still London's most cosmopolitan village, offering the most exciting range of places in which to eat out, and still has the best streets in London for food shops.

Londoners don't like their town to be *too* tidy, as indeed town
planners discovered when public opinion killed successive schemes
for 'redeveloping' the cheerful visual anarchy of Piccadilly Circus.
Sensible improvements like the pedestrianizing of Leicester Square,
with its extra benches, trees and flower-beds, they applaud.

Young London often seems a city in blue jeans. The town has its
elegant streets and quarters, but for the most part people prefer it to
be, not smart and conformist, but interesting and agreeable.

*Above:* London has always been a centre for music of all kinds. 'The Ants' are a New Wave band seen here playing at the Royal College of Art.
*Right:* Slightly less avant-garde musicians, Garth Hewitt and Kenny Marks at The Upstream Club in Waterloo.

Pearly Kings and Queens are a long established tradition. Originally they were a typical Cockney device to bring colour and gaiety to drab, impoverished London streets. Nowadays they help raise money for charity.

*Far left:* Carnaby Street was a focal point of 1960's 'Swinging London'. It helped London become a rival to Paris in the fashion markets of the world, and is still a Mecca for overseas visitors.

*Left and below:* The West Indians, who migrated to London in the '50s and '60s, brought a new vitality and sense of colour which they express in the now annual Notting Hill Carnival.

# Cultural London

The English traditionally distrust 'culture' as a concept and avoid using the word cultural. But that has not stopped their capital city from offering a more extravagant cultural banquet than almost anywhere else in the world.

One very richly laden platter is the South Bank riverside complex. Here stand three concert halls: the Royal Festival Hall, the Queen Elizabeth Hall and the smaller, more intimate Purcell Room; three theatres: Olivier, Lyttelton and Cottesloe, all part of Sir Denys Lasdun's exciting and impressive National Theatre building; two cinemas: the National Theatre's NFT One and NFT Two showing a variety of foreign, classic and off-beat films not usually seen in the commercial cinema; and for limited-period art exhibitions, the Hayward Gallery.

Central London's theatre-and-cinema-land also offers a remarkable feast. The two London evening newspapers regularly list some 70 theatres and as many central area cinemas. The heart of theatreland remains Shaftesbury Avenue and Covent Garden; most theatres there mount whatever plays or 'shows' producers think can make money. But in addition to the subsidized National Theatre, we find several other 'non-commercial' repertory companies — outstandingly, the Royal Shakespeare company at the Aldwych, but also the Royal Court in Chelsea's Sloane Square; the Mermaid, built in the shell of a Thames Warehouse at Puddle Dock, Blackfriars; the St George's, Tufnell Park, a Victorian church skilfully converted into a theatre of Shakespeare's day, and such local companies as Greenwich, whose high standards ensure that many of its productions transfer to the West End.

Art galleries and museums, too, offer themselves in profusion. The National Gallery in Trafalgar Square is pre-eminent in old masters; the Tate in impressionists; the Victoria and Albert, that rich and varied treasure-house in South Kensington, must not be missed by any devotee of the decorative arts. The Royal Academy at Burlington House, Piccadilly, stages regular definitive exhibitions on individual artists and subjects; hidden behind it in Burlington Gardens is the not-to-be missed Museum of Mankind.

South Kensington is London's traditional 'museum-land', established with the profits of the 1851 Great Exhibition. As well as the 'V & A', here stand the imaginatively presented Geological Museum; the Science Museum (really more a museum of technology); and, with its great halls full of whale and dinosaur skeletons, the British Museum of Natural History. South Kensington, grandly Victorian in architecture and in earnest pursuit of knowledge, also contains the Royal Albert Hall — London's most magnificent if never its best concert hall; and the Albert Memorial once abused by the 1950s 'anti-uglies', but now an object of affectionate wonder.

Kenwood House, its landscaped grounds merging with Hampstead Heath, was rebuilt by Robert Adam in the 1760s. Left to the nation by the Earl of Iveagh, it provides a splendid setting for a valuable collection of paintings and art treasures, as well as for concerts and recitals.

Further east, in Bloomsbury, stands the greatest treasure-house of all, the British Museum. Between it and Kings Cross, where a new British Library building is to be constructed, lies the academic precinct of London University. In the City, the Barbican Arts Centre is slowly taking shape, in a bombed quarter where new homes and new cultural ferment are intended to lighten the dead hours and days when the Square Mile's office workers have almost all fled to the suburbs.

*Left:* The new Museum of London at Barbican houses the combined collections of the former Guildhall and London museums. This cell, from an 18th century prison is one of the exhibits.

*Above:* A scene from the Royal Shakespeare Company's revival of 'Wild Oats', a 19th century comedy by John O'Keefe.

*Overleaf:* A magnificent scene from the Royal Ballet's production of 'Swan Lake' at the Royal Opera House, Covent Garden.

*Left:* The concrete and glass conglomeration of London's cultural centre on the South Bank of the Thames. Here there is a cinema complex, an art gallery and three concert halls. The futuristic landscape was also the birthplace of skateboarding in England, where young enthusiasts found the architect's concrete dream was perfect for their new sport.

*Below:* Sunday's open-air art exhibition along the park railings at Lancaster Gate.

# London's Green Spaces

Air passengers passing over central London often express surprise at how much green there is in the city below them. For London is generously if patchily endowed with parks, squares and gardens and more than one-tenth of its 390000 acres is public open space, or almost 6 acres for every 1000 of its resident population.

This generous endowment of open space is in part the result of Tudor monarchs' hunting habits. The chain of royal parks (public, but administered for the Crown by the Department of the Environment) were mostly in origin places to hunt deer. Stuart and later monarchs had them landscaped into parks in our modern sense and then threw them open to their subjects.

The Royal Parks include not only St James's with its lake and ornamental ducks, geese and wildfowl; Green Park, an oasis of verdure behind the traffic maelstrom of Hyde Park Corner; Hyde Park, with its riders in Rotten Row and its boating and swimming at the Serpentine; and Kensington Gardens with its Round Pond and elfin oak; but also Regents Park, bordered by Nash terraces and its adjunct to the north, Primrose Hill.

The Greater London Council also provides some fine expanses of parkland, outstanding among them Hampstead Heath and its associated open spaces, with picture galleries, open air concerts and a duelling ground at Kenwood; kite flying on Parliament Hill; and on the heath itself fairs, pleasant walks and the illusion of endless countryside. Other parts of London enjoy a profusion of smaller parks commons and woods open to the public. These include Blackheath, above Greenwich; and Clapham and Wimbledon Commons in the south. To the south-east the GLC also maintains a chain of upland woods and commons leading down to the Thames at Lesnes Abbey, the ruins of an Augustinian foundation, which now look out over London's own riverside new town of Thamesmead. In Abbey Woods bloom daffodils said to be descendants of those planted there by the medieval monks.

Two of London's largest and most popular open spaces are, paradoxically, maintained by the City Corporation outside not only its own narrow boundaries but those of Greater London – Burnham Beeches in Buckinghamshire; and Epping Forest, which is largely in Essex – a long chain of forest jutting into north-east London.

One special open space is the London Zoo, straddling the Regent Canal on the northern edges of Regent's Park. It holds 7000 wild animals; is administered by the Zoological Society of London; and in recent years alongside the original charming animal houses of the 1820s and 1930s stand larger modern buildings, functional and with exciting rooflines, such as Lord Snowdon's aviary and Casson, Condor & Partners evocative elephant houses.

Richmond Park is perhaps the most rural of the great Royal Parks, though by no means the only one with a herd of deer.

*Left:* The statue of Peter Pan, the boy who never grew up, created by the author J. M. Barrie and a firm favourite with children even today.
*Below:* A favourite pastime of Londoners is feeding the ducks in the park. London's Royal Parks are the accidental heritage of a series of royal hunting forests.

*Below:* The perfect escape from the hectic city rush; boating in Regent's Park, only minutes from the West End.
*Below right:* Polar bears are just one of the multitude of creatures to be found in London Zoo, which skirts Regent's Park on its north side.

*Left:* Rotten Row, traditionally the fashionable London ride along the southern edge of Hyde Park, is now paralleled by a new cycle path.
*Right:* Speaker's Corner, near Marble Arch is the traditional venue for the Englishman to exercise his right of freedom of speech. Here an anarchist preaches his esoteric gospel.
*Below:* The many-pinnacled Whitehall/Westminster skyline seen from St James's Park.

# Old London

London the 20th-century workaday city has much that survives from previous centuries – but in different degrees and at different levels. At one extreme we can find individual buildings – a City livery hall or a Wren church here, a 17th-century merchant's house there – whose form and fabric seem to have survived virtually unchanged. Then come bigger pockets or islands of antiquity where, again, the 20th-century scarcely seems to encroach. Narrow, traffic-free Goodwins Court, an almost hidden alley off St Martin's Lane with its unaltered 200-year-old shop fronts and houses, is one example.

A group of houses at Smithfield, 39–45 Cloth Fair provide, scarcely a butcher's hook away from the bustling modern meat market, the momentary illusion that we are in 17th-century London; Westminster Hall within the Houses of Parliament, with its great hammer-beam roof and stone austerity of floor and wall, still half seems to echo with the legal Latin and Norman French phrases of Tudor judges. New Square in Lincoln's Inn, spacious, tranquil and 17th century in its rhythms of stucco and brick, could be the place where Charles Dickens worked as an office boy.

In the Temple, to the south across Fleet Street we find a whole series of courts and lanes, halls, houses, chambers and chapels which look a good 300–400 years old even where the Benchers have had to patch and adapt.

Mostly, though, London's oldness is more diluted: antiquity has had to come to terms with the modern city. At this level whole quarters of London clearly rank as 'old' both for their architecture and, also, for a sense of style, an atmosphere which somehow survives tarmac road surfaces, motor vehicles and modern street lighting. Outstanding are the great landed estates developed in a spacious, well-mannered way in the 18th and early 19th centuries – St James, Bloomsbury, Belgravia, Mayfair and Marylebone among them.

The pattern the Georgians and earlier Victorians preferred was a largely rectilinear street plan softened by squares and crescents, planted with trees and shrubs but carefully railed and gated against the vulgar *plebs*. It is these squares and gardens – some now public, others still reserved for residents – which, with their well proportioned classical architecture and their welcome greenery are the chief glory of large swathes of Inner London.

For the devotee of Pepys or Johnson or even Dickens, a pilgrimage in pursuit of the famous shade is indeed a will-o'-the-wisp undertaking. Most of the houses they lived in have vanished, though Dr Johnson's House at Gough Square survives (a fine and interesting building in itself), as does Dickens' home from 1837–1839 in Doughty Street, Holborn, where he worked away at at least three major novels: *The Pickwick Papers, Oliver Twist* and *Nicholas Nickleby.* The George and Vulture in the City still provides the venue for a latter-day Pickwick Club; and across the river in Southwark, the George gives a glimpse of the kind of galleried courtyard typical of the many now-vanished coaching inns.

The bas-reliefs at the foot of Nelson's Column. Erected in 1839-42, the Column is made of Devon granite, and is 170 feet tall. It is topped by a 16 foot statue of Admiral Nelson.

Back across London Bridge the Monument is worth the labour of climbing its 311 steps for the view it still gives over Thames and City. It is 202 feet high, and marks the distance from the spot in a baker's shop in Pudding Lane where the Great Fire of London began in 1666. The lanes and alleys to the east, round Lovat Lane and St Mary-at-Hill, form one of the few surviving fragments of the old merchant City.

*Left:* St Martin's-in-the-Fields'
church was once just what its name
suggests – in the fields beyond the
western boundary of the City of
London. Now Gibb's classical 18th
century church is a focal point of
Trafalgar Square, the official centre
of London from which road-sign
distances are measured. The statue
in the foreground is the Duke of
Wellington.
*Above:* The Whitehall skyline as
seen from Trafalgar Square.

*Left:* The Royal Courts of Justice in the Strand, usually called simply 'The Law Courts'. This 19th century gothic group of buildings designed by G. E. Streek houses only the High Court's civil cases. Criminal cases are heard at the Old Bailey.

*Below:* Henekey's Long Bar, next to the gateway of Gray's Inn, is a favourite haunt of lawyers and law students.

*Right:* St James's Palace includes some of the 16th century buildings which Henry VIII constructed on the site of 'the Hospital of St James for leper maidens'.

*Below:* Admiralty Arch is the ceremonial gateway from Trafalgar Square into the long processional route of the Mall up to Buckingham Palace – all a memorial to Queen Victoria.

*Right:* The cloisters of Westminster Abbey, which date from the 13th century.

*Below right:* The beautifully vaulted cloister roof.

# London Villages

When we talk of London villages, we may mean any one of a number of different things. First there is the picturesque surviving village centre, church and churchyard, winding high street, charmingly crooked group of cottages and perhaps stately manor house, embedded in the fabric and life of a busy suburb when once it stood amid fields and woods.

Charlton in south-east London is a good example of this type of village, though its surroundings are now marred by the oppressive presence of large, barrack-like blocks of municipal flats on the hillside below. Still, thanks to the efforts of an active local civic society, Charlton is now looking very pretty. It has its 17th-century brick church, whose churchyard has lately been given a discreet facelift; its high street with a charming pub, the Bugle Horn; mounts an annual Horn Fair, revived after a century or so; and a stately Jacobean manor house, now used as library and community centre, whose Dutch gabled stable-block has recently been restored and converted to office and community use.

Charlton is not famous among London villages; one and a half miles beyond Greenwich, it is off the tourist track. It lacks the social cachet of Hampstead, Highgate, or Blackheath. These, with Chelsea in the central area, and Dulwich and perhaps Wimbledon to the south, represent a second kind of village: one whose ancient village centre is physically preserved, but where fashion has wrought a profound social and commercial change.

Restaurants, antique shops and boutiques have gradually taken over from less profitable, but from the residents' point of view, often more useful, shops; the place is a-bustle not so much with local people as with visitors who come to eat, drink, explore the antique shops and boutiques and generally just stroll about and enjoy agreeable surroundings and a stimulating atmosphere.

More numerous is the ordinary run of villages, local centres with shops and cinemas, churches, libraries and often a town hall or community centre. Frequently the commuter station is the focus. Other London villages such as Kew have two distinct centres, the village round the green, and the Victorian village centre built in the 1860s and 1870s round the station.

Some local centres are recognizably 'towns' rather than 'villages'. Woolwich, for instance, or Uxbridge, on the western edge of London. And then, close to Uxbridge we find, finally, a fourth type of village.

Harefield, set in the green belt and still workaday and agricultural, has never been fashionable. It is a 'mud-on-your-boots' village rather than a pretty, pink-gin commuter village. Much of the land hereabouts is actually owned by the Greater London Council, and at least one GLC tenant farmer opens his farm to the public several days each year.

Townsmen who live cheek-by-jowl with the countryside, he says, need to be shown how it works so that they respect it. The GLC agrees and encourages such farm open days.

The city still has its fragments of riverside villages, tranquil and unspoiled oases amidst the rush and roar of modern London. Here, Strand-on-Green, with its boats, pubs and attractive waterside houses.

*Left:* Gentleman's Walk, Enfield – an elegant district.

*Right:* Bedford Park, a model suburb laid out in later Victorian times for middle-class families with artistic pretensions and glorying in leafy tree-lined avenues and stylish red-brick houses by such architects as Norman Shaw.

*Below:* Highgate Village, with its hilltop high street, has kept its character and identity despite being split, for municipal purposes, between three different boroughs.

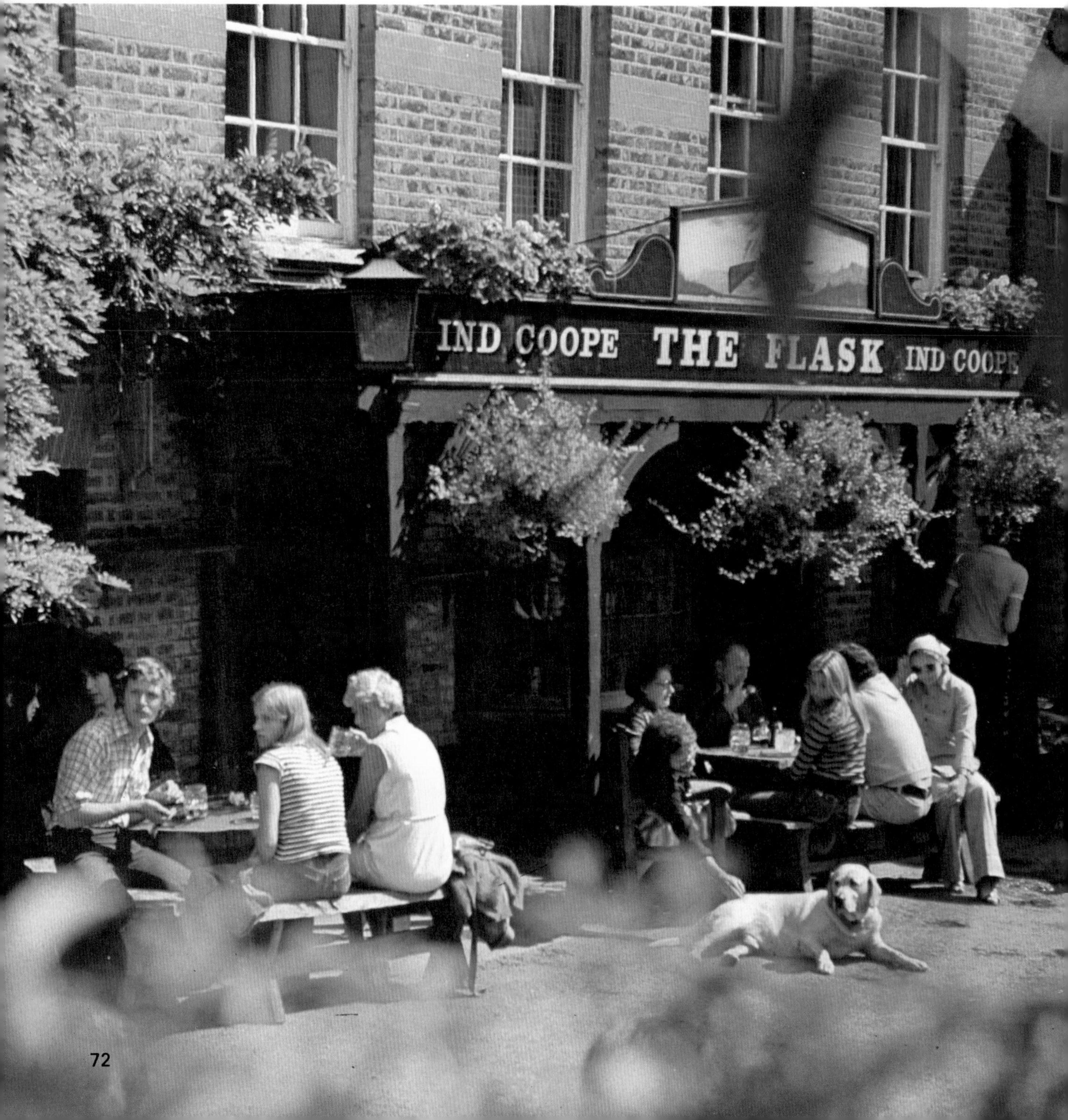
IND COOPE THE FLASK IND COOPE

Highgate and Hampstead are twin villages on the Northern Heights, with the carefully cultivated 'wildscape' of Hampstead Heath between them.
*Left:* open-air drinkers at the Flask public house in Highgate Village.
*Right:* Hampstead Fair, a regular Bank Holiday event for Londoners.
*Below:* One of the many ponds which give the Heath much of its character. Who would think this scene is only 15 minutes or so by the Underground from the heart of the West End?

# Markets and Emporiums

Shopping in London runs the whole gamut from the elegant and expensive specialist shops of Bond Street, St James, and Saville Row to bustling Cockney street markets like Petticoat Lane and Chapel Market in Islington.

One of the prettiest and most elegant places to shop is Burlington Arcade. It is sedately 1820s in style, covered against the rain and very expensive. There is still a uniformed beadle who restrains anyone tempted to do so unseemly a thing as *run*. Legend has it that some years ago he effectively restrained a public-spirited citizen running in pursuit of a thief.

Saville Row, the street of tailors, has this same aura of expensive elegance, as does Old Bond Street with its jewellers and picture galleries, and St James with its old-established wine merchants and shoe-makers, exclusive and urbane behind their inviting, yet ostentatious, 18th-century shop-fronts.

Harrods, of course, is the best known of the great emporiums – a department store whose boast is that it will sell you almost anything. Most Londoners prefer the less expensive stores such as John Lewis, Selfridges, or for clothes Fenwicks, Austin Reed or one of the large stores of Oxford and Regent Streets.

For design and quality, Liberty's behind its 1920s half-timbering, and Heal's are among the leaders; for 'with it' household goods and furnishings the various branches of Habitat are beyond compare. For high quality edible English goodies Jackson's in Picadilly and its neighbour Fortnum & Mason (with a miniature Mr Fortnum and Mr Mason as bellboys to strike the hour for the clock outside) beckon compellingly. In Jermyn Street behind them, Paxton & Whitfield stocks a range of cheeses to throw the gourmet into ecstasies. For umbrellas (also sword-sticks and shooting sticks), James Smith & Sons on the corner of New Oxford Street and Shaftsbury Avenue is *the* place.

As for street markets, the two most famous are Petticoat Lane, the traditional and longstanding Sunday morning general and rag-trade market held in Middlesex Street, near Aldgate on the eastern edge of the City; and Portobello Road, the antique and junk Mecca frequented by wealthy tourists, in north Kensington.

London's wholesale markets can also be fun to look at, though in the interests of efficient operation they increasingly discourage outsiders. Covent Garden, trading fruit and vegetables across the pavement in the heart of the West End, used to be the great draw, full of noise, bustle and the smell of decaying cabbage; but the New Covent Garden Market at Nine Elms is enclosed, mechanized, efficient, and excludes the public altogether. At Spitalfields and the Borough, trading still spills out of doors across pavements; as it does at Smithfield (meat) and Billingsgate (fish).

But trade involves retail as well as wholesale. Thus a large area of north London is learning to appreciate the advantages of motorized, one-stop shopping at Brent Cross, a huge brick box at the intersection of the M1 motorway and the North Circular Road, surrounded by car parks and containing branches of many major stores. As enclosed shopping centres go, this is quite a good one, with attractive 'open' cafés in the main shopping mall and some interior sense of style and atmosphere. Not as lively as a street market, but useful.

Souvenirs for tourists bring colour and vitality to the pavements of London.

Antiques, 'sub-antiques', junk – the whole business of second-hand goods with the attraction of age has boomed in London in recent years.
*Above:* Portobello Road, Mecca of the popular antique world.
*Right:* A busker with an unusual line in entertainment.
*Far right:* 'Be a dear and raise your hats to the readers!'

*Left:* Harrods, which will supply almost anything, at a price.
*Below:* Wray's Lighting Emporium has 'rubbed up' the traditional shop-front character of the King's Road admirably.
*Below right:* Habitat is one of the new Aladdin's Caves of the London retail scene.

# Sporting London

London as a centre for spectator sports has much to offer. In the football season there are a dozen professional clubs to choose from: Arsenal and Tottenham Hotspur in the north; Brentford, Chelsea, Fulham and Queen's Park Rangers in the West; Crystal Palace, Millwall and Charlton in the south; Leyton Orient and West Ham United in the east; and Watford on London's northern fringe. Wembley Stadium, which holds 100000 spectators under cover, is the venue for international matches and for the top domestic fixture, the Cup Final.

What Wembley is to soccer, Twickenham is to Rugby Union. Harlequins, who play there, are one of 11 leading Rugby Union clubs in London. The English national summer game of cricket has its headquarters at Lord's in St John's Wood, headquarters of both the ruling body, the MCC, and of a leading county, Middlesex. The other main cricket ground in London is the Oval, where Surrey plays.

The Mecca of lawn tennis is, of course, Wimbledon, where the All England Club have recently opened a fascinating museum of the history of the game; just as Hurlingham is the sedate and private headquarters of the game of croquet.

For athletics, the national and international venue is now, for the most part, the National Sports Centre at Crystal Palace. It is set in a park which surrounds the site of Paxton's revolutionary iron-and-glass exhibition building of 1851 – alas, burnt down in 1936. Big boxing matches usually take place at either Wembley or the Royal Albert Hall; horse racing in season at Sandown Park, Kempton Park, Epsom Downs and Windsor.

Participatory as distinct from spectator sport is well catered for in two ways: clubs and public facilities. Swimming pools abound; there are tennis courts in almost every public park. In fine weather the lakes in Regent's and Hyde parks are covered with boats.

Recent years have, however, seen a certain change of emphasis, with deliberately growing provision for the 'non-joiner'. Thus the Lee Valley Regional Park Pickett's Lock Centre, with swimming pool and covered and open-air sports facilities, seeks specifically to encourage informal recreation, especially in family groups, rather than conventional competitive sports.

The Lee Valley Park, spread over 19 miles of the neglected, down-at-heel flood plain of the River Lee in north east London, aims to improve all manner of recreational facilities for that traditionally under-provided sector of London. With its expanding provision for boating, swimming, horse-riding, walking, running, and indeed just sitting and dreaming in pleasant surroundings, it is London's most ambitious recreational experiment to date.

Of all the London race meetings, Royal Ascot – which the Queen and members of her family traditionally attend – is the most fashionable. Grey top hats, strawberries and cream, and much pomp and circumstance is the order of the day. The thousands of more ordinary racegoers who gaze at the occupants of the Royal Enclosure, do so these days more with amused tolerance than with envy.

*Below:* To the casual observer, croquet often seems a game of unruffled tranquillity. However, it does have its moments of viciousness and its times for vengeance.

*Right:* Veteran motor cars cross Westminster Bridge at the start of the annual London to Brighton Rally.

*Right:* One of London's top class
football teams, Queen's Park
Rangers, playing at their home
ground against Manchester City.
*Top, far right:* Borg and Nastase
battle it out at the Wimbledon Tennis
Championships.
*Bottom, far right:* The Mile field
slogging it out at the Crystal Palace
sports centre.

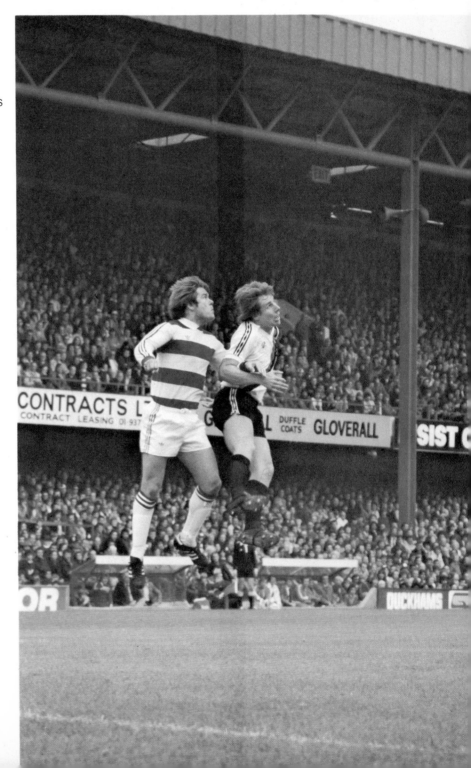

# Changing London

In one sense, London has changed more in the last 25 years than in all its 20 centuries. It has changed in vertical scale. Firm planning policies have indeed stopped its sprawl. Instead of growing outwards it has grown upwards. The City of London has sprouted a score of tall towers, bursting the 100 foot height limit long maintained by the old London County Council, swamping that incomparable skyline of Wren spires, and in effect shrinking St Paul's whose dome no longer dominates as it did for 250 years.

In the West End, the illusion the royal parks once fostered that you were in the heart of the countryside, has gone. Elegant though it may be, the Knightsbridge Barracks tower blows one more hole in that illusion, first damaged by the early 1960s London Hilton.

The Post Office Tower, that cheerfully vulgar symbol of a changing West End (bulging with radio link transmitters for our telephone system and a revolving restaurant), is now challenged for height by the new National Westminster Bank tower rising above the City. We have to look hard now for poor old St Paul's.

All this, of course, is an expression of the commercial City seeking to modernize and expand its working space within the tight limits of the Square Mile. However, the developers do not have their own way the whole time. Even late Victorian and early 20th-century commercial buildings are now statutorily protected and occasionally, despite the millions of pounds at stake, Government Ministers, on the advice of public inquiry inspectors, rule that they are too precious and have too much historical importance to demolish.

Conservation and concern for good environment now dominate the thinking of London's town planners. Architects tend more and more to favour sympathetic infill development rather than brash or arrogantly modern design to fill gaps in an older townscape. The paving over of Leicester Square and many other sections of street in both central London and the suburbs represents a new sensitivity to the needs of pedestrians as against motorists.

During the early 1970s London's voters effectively stopped for good the building of large-scale, expensive and ruinously destructive urban motorways in inner London. An outer ring, the M25 orbital motorway, is however pressing ahead at a radius of some 12–15 miles from the centre, aimed at taking the bulk of bypassable traffic, especially heavy container lorries from the industrial Midlands to the Channel ports, out of the streets of London.

That and new measures to revitalize the more down-at-heel inner city areas are the biggest changes currently taking place. For now London clearly perceives that 'quality of life' depends on more than simply concrete, steel and glass, or bricks and mortar. Reasonable prosperity and a stable, pleasing environment are now recognized as the cornerstones of contentment.

The tunnel of the new Fleet Line underground railway during construction. This is the first stage of the new line running from Charing Cross to Baker Street, where it links with the existing Stanmore branch of the Bakerloo Line.

*Below:* The redevelopment of the north side of Victoria Street in the 1960s was a disaster of dullness. The total opposite is the '70s development on the south side by architects Elsom, Pack and Roberts, who have brought a distinctive and mildly jokey character to enliven the scene.
*Right:* One of an epidemic of large new hotels encouraged by generous government grants in the 1960s.

*Above:* The Nash terraces formed the traditional delicate backcloth to Regent's Park, until the arrival of the new London Mosque and Islamic Centre designed by Sir Frederick Gibberd and sited at Hanover Gate.
*Right:* The interior of the new Brent Cross shopping centre, showing the ornamental fountain and spectacular coloured glass roof.

*Above:* The Hilton Hotel in Park Lane – at first regarded by Londoners as an out-of-scale intruder; now almost an old friend.

*Right:* The old and the new rub shoulders, the Old Curiosity Shop, said to have links with Charles Dickens, in a side street between Lincolns Inn Fields and the London School of Economics.

*Far right:* The new glass facades of London offices tower above the more friendly equivalent of a past era.

# London Excursions

The best way to reach Kew is by boat up river from Westminster or Charing Cross piers. Kew began as a park surrounding a royal palace, but unlike other such royal parks never became a *public* open space. Instead it forms the Royal Botanic Gardens, whose prime purpose is to advance the science of botany.

The gardens contain some 45000 different trees and plants. The Herbarium, not ordinarily open to the public, is, in effect, a huge filing cabinet containing some seven million dried plants and herbs.

Exotic buildings as well as exotic flora beguile your wanderings through the gardens – the pagoda, the Palm House, the Temperate House and the charming little Kew Palace or Dutch House of 1631, with its newly created Elizabethan herb garden behind it.

By the same boat as to Kew you can normally reach Hampton Court, the 16th-century palace built by Henry VIII's rich and powerful chancellor Thomas Wolsey. Its very grandeur accelerated Wolsey's downfall, which the gift of Hampton Court to the king failed to avert. Henry added to it as did other monarchs after him: Wren added the fountain court and state apartments for William and Mary. Hampton Court Park and the adjoining Bushy Park spaciously accommodate Versailles-like vistas. The palace's attractions include its Tudor kitchens, state apartments, the Great Vine, the Maze, and the huge and finely decorated 16th-century Astronomical Clock above Anne Boleyn's Gateway.

Another Tudor palace in all but name is Knole, the ancestral seat of the Sackville family since 1603 – though its earliest buildings date from 1456. Now owned by the National Trust, it is said to contain a room for every day of the year and a staircase for every week.

Knole's main drive runs about half-a-mile straight out of the centre of the charming Kentish town of Sevenoaks; the extensive park with its herds of deer then stretches to the edge of the wooded Greens and hills. With its great ragstone walls and curling Tudor chimneys, its outbuildings housing granaries, bakery, brewery, blacksmith's and stables, Knole is more like a self-contained medieval town than a mansion. Walks in the park are a delight. Sevenoaks is about 35 minutes by rail from Charing Cross or Victoria.

Brighton, only 55 minutes by train from Victoria, is London's most popular and stylish seaside resort. Not to be missed are the curiously oriental Royal Pavilion, the stately terraces of Kemp Town and Hove and the Lanes, a network of narrow shopping streets between the town centre and the seafront.

North of London on the edge of the Chiltern Hills lies Whipsnade, more spacious country branch of the London Zoo. Here the animals are, so to speak, in the open, in wide paddocks; the visitors confined to the spaces in between. Sometimes humans and other mammals are allowed to mix, as on the downland edge of the zoological park where wallabys hop wild as well as other smaller creatures. A minibus service provides transport for those unable or unwilling to walk around this extensive park.

Windsor Castle, a medieval fortress turned into a royal residence. Its hunting forests are now wonderfully landscaped parks open to the public. The castle is seen here from the Long Walk.

Windsor Castle, farther up river from Hampton Court, is the Queen's chief country residence, built originally by William the Conqueror but much added to over the centuries. St George's Chapel, with its stalls of the Order of Knights of the Garter and fine fan-vaulted roof, stands within the castle. To its west and south stretch the twin expanses of Windsor Home and Great parks; close under its walls on the east is the town of Windsor with its 17th-century Guildhall, stately houses and attractive riverside. Across the now pedestrians-only Windsor Bridge lies Eton's narrow and historic high street and Eton College, founded by Henry VI in 1440. The Royal Windsor Horse Show takes place each Spring; Windsor Safari Park lies two miles to the south-west.

North of London, 30-40 minutes by train from Moorgate or King's Cross, lies Hatfield House, built in the 17th century for Robert Cecil, first Earl of Salisbury. It is Jacobean architecture at its most sumptuous. Here the second Marquis, around 1850, welcomed the railways, unlike most other landed proprietors of that era, but required the Great Northern Railway Company to lengthen its platform at Hatfield Station and provide him with a private waiting room.

*Left:* the Royal Horticultural Society's gardens at Wisley, just south-west of London.
*Below left:* Brighton's bizarre Royal Pavilion, built for a Prince Regent.
*Below:* Epping Forest, a chain of woodland penetrating right into east London, where the visitor can actually escape on two legs from the tyranny of four wheels!

*Left:* Kew Gardens, an unrivalled collection of trees and plants in a landscape dotted with beautiful and bizarre buildings, like this 18th-century pagoda.
*Right:* Epping Forest is wilder. Queen Elizabeth's Hunting Lodge recalls Tudor times when it was a royal hunting forest rather than a Londoner's playground.
*Below right:* Hampton Court, too, began as a Tudor palace, but the landscape gardening is of a later, more elegant age when French influences were strong. This shows the Sunken Garden.

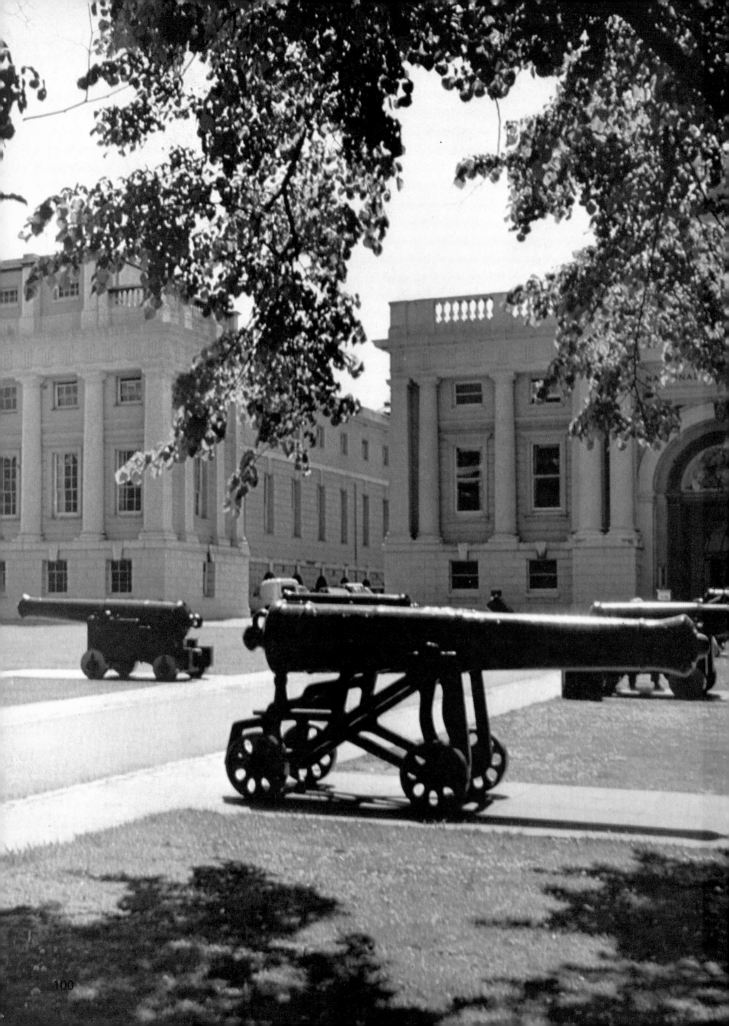

# Introduction to Moscow

There is always a fascination in going to an entirely new place, but there is an extra fascination in going to Moscow for the first time, sometimes even, a slight feeling of mystery. Is there really an 'iron curtain'? Once there, however, it is clear that apart from the customs there has been no barrier to cross! The streets full of people, all with a sense of purpose; the colourful onion-like domes of the city's numerous little churches; the greenness of the squares; the boulevards and the courtyards behind the blocks of houses. These are some of the sights which introduce the visitor to this different world.

The Kremlin, the heart of the city, and the towers along its walls, can be seen from many points. The gate into the Kremlin is open and anyone can stroll in freely, roam its streets and gardens, enter a church or cathedral or look over the parapet wall down to the river below.

The Kremlin wall also forms one side of Red Square, another famous landmark in Moscow. No traffic is allowed here at any time, night or day. There are crowds of people, foreigners and Muscovites, who wander up and down, looking at the extraordinary Cathedral of St Basil, at Lenin's marble mausoleum, or at the windows of the large store known as 'GUM' which stretches along one side of the square.

The Moscow river, the Moskva, curves round in great sweeps and one can take a trip either on a swift hydrofoil or on a more leisurely river 'tram'. From the river there is a lovely view of the Kremlin domes and towers, with the Bell Tower of Ivan the Great rising above them all. Further up the river is the high bank covered by woods, and the Gorky Park. A walk up by paths through the woods leads to a platform at the top from which there is a panoramic view of the city, the loop of the river and the huge sports complex.

It is interesting to note that there are no private names over the shops. Instead, the inscriptions read 'Fruit and Vegetables', 'Food Shop', or 'Books'. Some of the clothes shops have names such as 'Svetlana', and a chain of children's shops is simply called 'Children's World'. There are also highly specialized shops like 'Cheese' or 'Tea and Coffee'.

There are no commercial advertisements in Moscow. Posters are put up on special boards showing the programmes of cinemas and theatres, or announcements of various exhibitions.

Russians love to eat ice creams at any time of the year and they are sold from stalls or kiosks along the streets as well as in cafes and restaurants. When the temperature is well below zero, the ice cream stalls are just as busy as in the summer.

The city looks very different in winter. For about five months there is not a spot of green anywhere. The snow comes down and the frost moves in and the bare trees look black against the sky. It is true that the snow ploughs keep the roads clear and the pavements are swept. The traffic moves freely, but the parks and gardens are covered and in the parks many paths are flooded and turned into skating rinks. In May the snow begins to melt and in no time at all the leaves are out.

Moscow is the capital of a vast country consisting of 15 republics. It is the gateway to many other interesting places, such as Samarkand in Central Asia or Lake Baikal in Siberia. So when you have seen Moscow it is easy to fly further and explore other parts of the U.S.S.R.

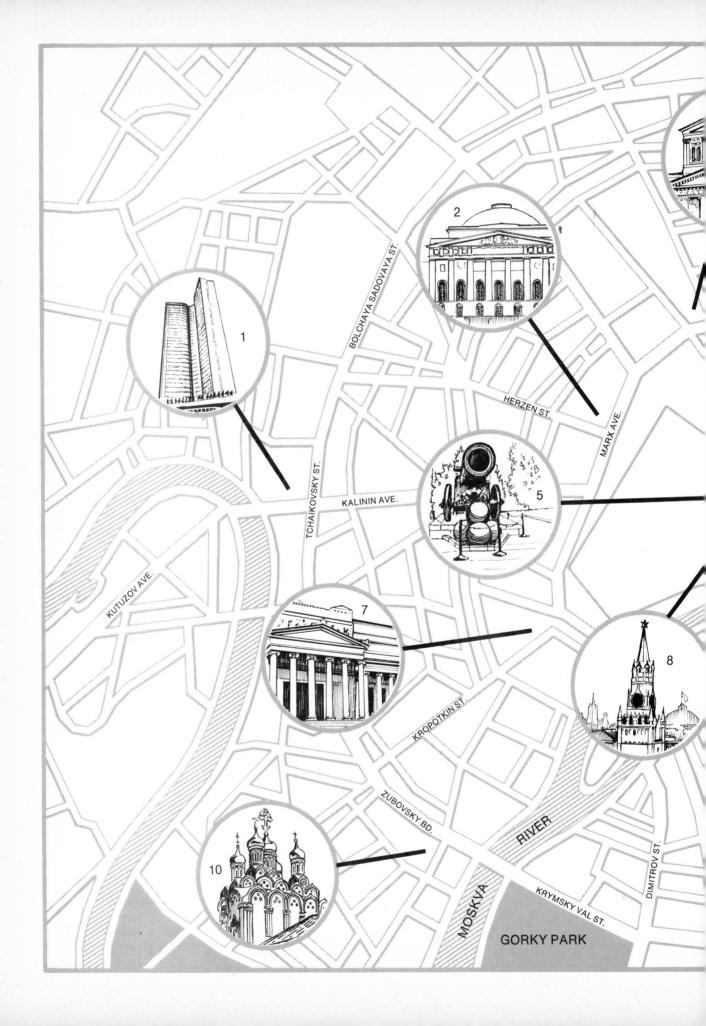

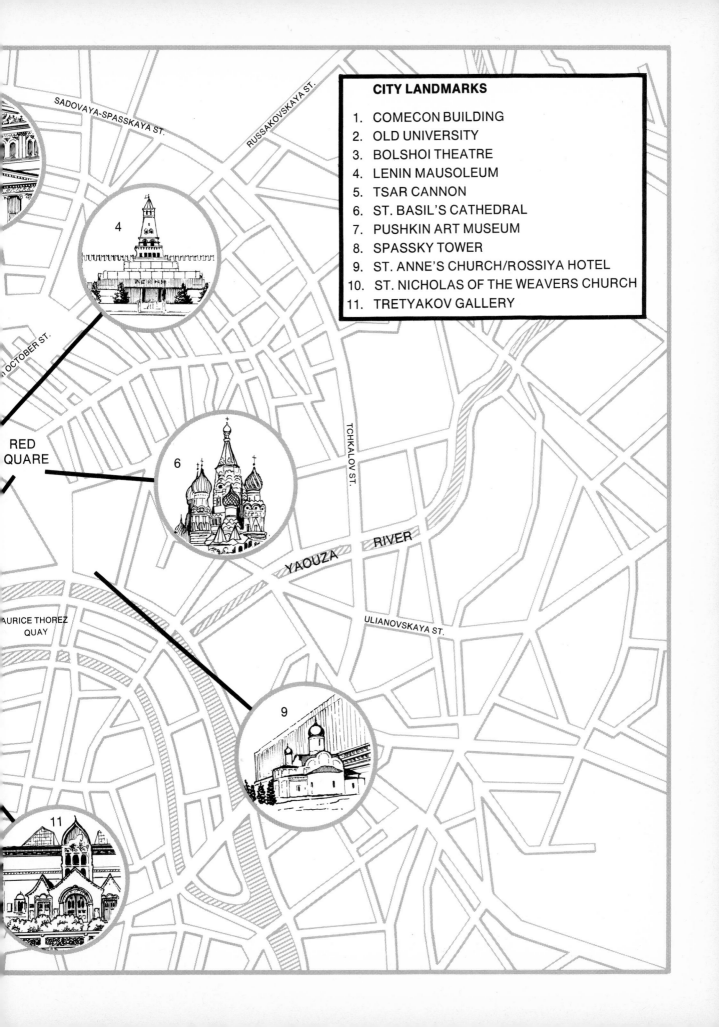

**CITY LANDMARKS**

1. COMECON BUILDING
2. OLD UNIVERSITY
3. BOLSHOI THEATRE
4. LENIN MAUSOLEUM
5. TSAR CANNON
6. ST. BASIL'S CATHEDRAL
7. PUSHKIN ART MUSEUM
8. SPASSKY TOWER
9. ST. ANNE'S CHURCH/ROSSIYA HOTEL
10. ST. NICHOLAS OF THE WEAVERS CHURCH
11. TRETYAKOV GALLERY

SADOVAYA-SPASSKAYA ST.

RUSSAKOVSKAYA ST.

OCTOBER ST.

RED QUARE

TCHKALOV ST.

YAOUZA RIVER

MAURICE THOREZ QUAY

ULIANOVSKAYA ST.

# Origins and Growth

Moscow is one of the youngest capitals in Europe. It was first mentioned in an old chronicle in 1147 and this date has been officially taken as its foundation. The chronicle records that Yuri Dolgoruky (Yuri Longarm) sent an invitation to his relative, Prince Sviatoslav, to visit him in 'Moscov', where he had an estate. In 1156 Yuri fortified Moscow, which was situated on a hill between the Moskva River and the small, swift Neglinnaya River; Slav tribes had lived in this area for centuries as it was well placed for waterways and trade routes.

Archaeological finds have confirmed that in the twelfth century Moscow was a well established settlement with the fortress as its centre and the homes of artisans and traders outside the walls. Other discoveries of pots, ceramics and a seal of Kiev origin, from the same period, show that Moscow had contacts as far away as the Ukraine.

The first Kremlin walls were built of wood and enclosed wooden houses, a small wooden church and stables. Beyond the settlement were pine forests. In 1238 the Mongol-Tartars invaded Moscow and burnt it down. But it was rebuilt and became the capital of a small principality.

By the 14th century Moscow was the capital of a much larger area, that of the principality of Vladimir. Its growing importance was reflected by the fact that the head of the Russian Orthodox Church, the Metropolitan, moved to Moscow from the town of Vladimir.

In 1339 Prince Ivan Kalita, nicknamed Moneybags, extended the Kremlin, building new walls of oak. More traders, artisans and boyars (aristocrats) lived both within and outside it, on both sides of the river. Inside the Kremlin the first stone churches were built.

Around Moscow land was cleared of forest and planted with crops. Trade expanded and many of the great rivers were used, joined by porterage pathways; in this way it was linked to the Azov and Black Seas and to many inland cities such as Kiev.

From the time of Ivan Kalita, Moscow's rulers took the title of Grand Prince. Political and economic power increased and by the 15th century the city became the centre of the Russian people's struggle against the Mongol-Tartars.

In 1367 the wooden walls of the Kremlin were replaced by walls of white stone and fortified monasteries were built at strategic points near the city to strengthen its defences. The settlements outside its walls consisted mainly of artisans such as blacksmiths, potters, tanners, and armourers. At the end of the 15th century the stone walls were replaced by brick ones and extended still further. Eighteen towers were placed at the corners and along the walls of the triangular shaped fortress so that there were seven protecting each side. The walls were nearly 15 feet thick and they stand to this day.

Inside the Kremlin the cathedrals and churches were rebuilt and a new cathedral, the Cathedral of the Assumption was used for the crowning of the Grand Princes. Two palaces were also built.

The Spassky Tower on the Kremlin wall and St Basil's Cathedral from the back. The other side of the cathedral faces Red Square.

As the settlements of artisans and traders spread further, they were very vulnerable to attack. Towards the end of the 16th century stone walls were built around these settlements, forming a second encircling ring. There were towers and gates through which radial roads led outwards beyond the city. Later, earth ramparts were thrown up beyond this ring; they were surmounted by wooden walls and towers. Some of the fortress monasteries were along this line of fortifications. A number of them still exist and are used as museums. The Inner Boulevard Ring and the Sadovoye Ring in present-day Moscow run where the second and third lines of fortifications were built. Parts of the second wall have been preserved; it was wide enough for a horseman to ride along it.

It was at this period that Ivan the Great's Bell Tower was built inside the Kremlin, and St Basil's Cathedral in Red Square. (Incidentally, the name Red Square is a mistranslation for Beautiful Square.)

As the city expanded, its unique circular shape developed. Radial roads ran in all directions from the centre, intersecting the ring roads which followed the lines of the walls.

*Left:* Kolomenskoye Cathedral. Part of the outdoor museum on a former large estate on the bank of the Moskva River.
*Below:* Moscow fathers looking after their babies, enjoying the fresh air and their newspapers. Women's Lib. in action – Russian style.

During the centuries Moscow was not only attacked many times by the Mongol-Tartars, but also by the Poles and Lithuanians who plundered and burnt it in the 17th century, and by Napoleon, who invaded Russia in 1812. He was forced to retreat, however, when the Muscovites set fire to the city, having destroyed food supplies. When retreating, Napoleon's army destroyed buildings in the Kremlin and damaged the walls and towers. These were all restored later.

In the 18th century Peter the Great gave orders for the improvement of Moscow. He prohibited the building of new houses in the back yards of existing ones, ordering instead that they should be in lines facing the street. Stone pavements were to take the place of wooden walks and the whole city was to be 'modernised'. But as Peter became more and more engrossed in the building of what was to be the new capital, St Petersburg, not much of this plan was carried out.

Russia's first university, however, was founded in Moscow in 1775 by Lomonosov, the famous scientist after whom it is named. Theatres, as well as other educational institutions, were also built at this time.

Many street names and the names of squares in present-day Moscow still retain their connection with the people who lived there long ago. They recall the armourers, the potters, the cannon foundry, the cauldron makers and others. Some squares are named after the gates that once led into the old city through the towers on the fortification walls.

*Above:* The Tsar Cannon stands in the Kremlin grounds. It was cast by Andrei Chokhov, master of the cannon yard, in 1586.

*Right:* Friendship House, Kalinin Prospect was built at the end of the 19th century by the millionaire Morozov, who sent his architect to Portugal to study style there. There is a story that, when the house was finished, Morozov invited his mother, who lived in the country, to come and see it. When she looked at it, she is reported to have said: 'Till now, only I knew you were a fool. Now the whole world will know it'.

At the beginning of the 18th century Peter the Great transferred the capital from Moscow to St Petersburg. Moscow remained the industrial and commercial centre. Most of the nobility and the rich merchants moved to the new city and development in Moscow slowed down. Some of the nobility remained, however, and built themselves beautiful palaces in huge estates and laid out parks and gardens with grottoes, fountains, statues and pavilions. Many of these buildings stand today and are used by public organisations: for example, the former Pashkov Mansion is now part of the Lenin Library, almost in the centre of the city; others are used as the headquarters of the Academy of Sciences, the House of the Trade Unions (formerly the Noblemen's Club), and the Sklifosovsky Casualty Hospital.

In 1741 new city limits were defined by the building of the Kamer-Kollezhsky ramparts with 16 gates at which internal customs duties

*Below:* Some restored old churches near the Rossiya Hotel, near the bottom of Red Square.
*Right:* The Education Pavilion at the Economic Achievements Exhibition.

were levied on all through traffic.

By the end of the 18th and the beginning of the 19th centuries Moscow had a population of 275,000 and there were about 300 factories, many of them for textiles. After the defeat of Napoleon the reconstructed city grew even larger. It was at this time that the Bolshoi and Maly theatres were built. By the mid-19th century, when serfdom was abolished, artisans producing handicrafts were replaced by factory industries, though textiles still predominated.

Because Moscow's geographical position was so much better than that of the capital, St Petersburg, it was the centre of the development of the railways. Its population increased faster and it spread well beyond the Kamer-Kollezhsky ramparts, forming a new industrial ring. The 1897 census figures showed that the population was nearly a million strong.

The middle classes built themselves taller and bigger houses, four or more storeys high, near the centre of the city; these houses dominated the one and two storey wooden houses round them. The architectural style was very mixed, neo-classical, Romanesque, Gothic, pseudo-Russian and modern. The pseudo-Russian style imitated in stone the old wooden architecture. Compared with the dignified pillared mansions of the nobility of the earlier period, these are far less attractive than the buildings they emulate.

By the end of the 19th century the autocratic tsarist empire began to crumble and there was great unrest. The 1905 revolutionary uprising was crushed, but during the First World War, when Russia was losing, the poorly equipped soldiers were demanding an end to the fighting. They were asking for peace 'with their feet'. In 1917 the workers of Moscow joined with their brothers in St Petersburg and seized control. A year later the capital of the new Soviet state was moved to Moscow.

*Left:* The Church of St Simon Stylites, built in the 17th century, on Kalinin Prospect, holds its own among the tower blocks all around. It is now a museum belonging to the All-Russia Nature Conservation Society.
*Above:* Three young Muscovites in their courtyard.

In the early years after the revolution the country was torn by civil war, by wars of intervention and by terrible famine. Moscow, with the rest of the Soviet Union, remained little changed in its structure. Hundreds of lanes and little streets were still cobbled. The only way to house people with the greatest need was to put them into large flats abandoned by those who left the country, or in rooms considered surplus in large houses so that several families had to share kitchen and toilet facilities. Transport was limited, trams went through the centre of the city and choked the main streets when there was a power failure. Shop windows were empty. Everything — including food — was in short supply.

Plans were made for the future development of the city. The main radial roads had to be widened. As a preliminary measure to improve the housing situation, houses which were solid enough to stand it had extra storeys added.

It was found that behind the houses of what is now Gorky Street there was ample space to build new blocks of flats. Certain buildings of historic value were moved back by a method of underpinning. The present Moscow Soviet building (the equivalent to a local authority's headquarters) for example, was moved back 15 yards by this method. Subsequently it had two floors added on top. When the new blocks of flats in the yards were completed, the people in the houses in front were moved into them, as well as others from further away (they were much larger). The old houses were then demolished, leaving plenty of space to make the street into a wide thoroughfare.

The clusters of wooden houses around the former mansions of the rich industrialists and merchants had no running water. It had to be drawn from standpipes in the street. Heating was by stoves fed with wood and food was prepared on oil cookers.

*Below:* The former Moscow Stock Exchange, is now used as the city's Chamber of Commerce.

By the mid-1930s material conditions were beginning to improve, food supplies were increasing and housing was going up all over the city. But another terrible blow was in store – the Soviet Union was invaded and devastated by the Second World War.

The German army was so sure of capturing Moscow that they even transported marble with them to build new headquarters for Hitler in the capital! (This marble was later used to face a new building in Gorky Street.) But the people of Moscow built barricades across the approaches to their city and withstood the onslaught. By their heroic stand they won one of the greatest victories of the war.

The post-war period has been marked by large building projects. At first, fairly large blocks of flats were built, often with a certain amount of ornamentation on the outside; also the eight enormous wedding-cake skyscrapers, including the new university which dominates the city on the Lenin Hills, and the Ministry of Foreign Affairs. Then many five storey blocks, built around large courtyards and without lifts, were put up at great speed, often made of prefabricated parts which were assembled on the sites. More recently the City Soviet (Moscow's local government organ) decided to build upwards, and now tower blocks of varying heights are going up, especially in the new districts in the outer suburbs.

The small wooden houses are vanishing fast, their residents moving from their ill-equipped homes into modern flats with hot and cold running water, central heating and other amenities. In many places the only indication that a village once existed are the fruit trees and other old trees which have been incorporated into the greenery of the courtyards of the new blocks of flats. One of the first things that people do when moving into new places, is to plant trees and flowers in the yards; they also put up apparatus for small children and position seats where anyone may rest and enjoy the fresh air.

The Moskva River now has more than 20 bridges and is enclosed by granite embankments many miles long. Its water had been increased enormously by the building of the 80 mile long canal which links it to

*Below left:* The tomb of the Unknown Soldier is under the Kremlin wall just inside the Alexandrovsky Gardens. A perpetual flame burns in his memory.
*Below:* A sledge, or troika, as it is called, drawn by three horses. This one is used for joy rides in the grounds of the Exhibition of Economic Achievements.

the Volga, with pumping stations to ensure a regular supply.

The Neglinnaya River has long since been imprisoned in a conduit and runs underground into the Moskva. The same has been done to other small rivers. The only other river of any size in Moscow is the Yauza. It is a tributary of the Moskva, and in 1937 the rubbish was cleared from either side, its width nearly doubled, and its banks lined.

There is a complete plan for the future development of Moscow. Since there is no private ownership of the land in the city, there is no reason why it should not be carried out. It is hoped to make Moscow a model city with good living accommodation for all its citizens and every amenity possible. New housing is going up rapidly, but even so it will be a real problem to keep up with the needs of Moscow's growing population, now estimated to be more than seven and a half million.

Moscow is now among the largest cities in the world. It lies at the centre of the European part of the U.S.S.R., and is connected with the rest of the world by railways going in every direction, by airlines flying from four airports, by ships sailing to and from its river ports and by 13 highways. The plane only takes three and a half hours from Moscow to London and there are flights from Moscow to New York, Tokyo, Havana, Colombo and many other cities of the world. Trains go across Siberia in one direction and across Europe to the Hook of Holland and Paris in the other. It is also possible to go by car or tourist bus from most European capitals to Moscow, crossing the seemingly endless North European Plain.

*Left:* The Space Monument, 312 feet high, is made from titanium that shimmers in the light. Leading up to it is an avenue lined with the busts of scientists and cosmonauts involved in the space project.

*Above:* This statue of a worker and a woman collective farmer dominates the entrance to the Exhibition of Economic Achievements.

Moscow is the capital of an enormous country. It is its planning headquarters, it determines the distribution of industry throughout the territory of the U.S.S.R; this involves transport, agricultural development, the building of new cities, the opening up of new areas. It is also the seat of COMECON, the common market of the socialist countries.

Thousands of tourists from foreign countries visit Moscow every year; it can compete with any other capital in what it has to offer, historical places, sport, museums, theatre and ballet, concerts, interesting walks and trips on the river.

# Traditional Moscow

With the sharp change in the political structure in 1917, old traditions were discarded and, over the years, new ones adopted. One that did remain, however, was the celebration of New Year; the kindly old man in a red, blue, or white robe, driving his reindeer through the air is called Grandfather Frost, but he behaves in the same way as Father Christmas does everywhere, bringing presents for both young and old and attending parties. His companion is a snow maiden.

Tall, decorated fir-trees are put up in many squares and other public places in the capital. The shops are decorated and sell special fare. Decorated trees appear in homes and at places of work; parties are held in schools, factories, clubs, homes . . . everywhere, just like other countries in Europe. Huge children's parties are held in the Kremlin and other large halls.

The Russian Winter Festival is held annually in Moscow from December 25th to January 5th. This is when the theatres and concert halls present special programmes for Soviet citizens and foreign visitors. The finest Soviet actors, ballet dancers and the most accomplished musicians are seen and heard during this period. As relaxation horse drawn troika rides are taken in parks, with hot tea from samovars provided on stalls along the way.

The other festival, the Moscow Festival of Stars, takes place in May. May Day and November 7th, anniversary of the Russian Revolution, are, of course, greatly celebrated. There are military parades followed by huge civilian demonstrations in Red Square and the whole city is decked with red flags and slogans. All the traffic stops until the evening and after the demonstrations people stroll leisurely through the main streets, buying snacks and ice cream at the stalls and enjoying family outings.

The first and last days at school now have their traditions firmly entrenched. On September 1st, (unless it is on a Sunday, when schools then start on September 2nd) around eight o'clock in the morning, hundreds of seven year old boys and girls may be seen walking along the streets with their parents, clutching large bunches of flowers. They are going to school for the first time and the flowers are a present for their teachers. Their teachers spend the first morning introducing the children to their new school. They are also welcomed by the top class, the tenth, whose members give each new pupil a gift, usually coloured pencils or some other useful objects.

The ceremony for school leavers involves the ringing of the 'last bell', when they officially hand over their responsibilities to the ninth class. There is then an evening dance and finally, at midnight, a walk in Red Square – the square is filled with young people in their party clothes strolling about until dawn.

Moscow's impressive October Revolution Parade demonstrates worker solidarity and the military muscle of the Soviet Union.

March 8th is International Women's Day, a day which in many countries is devoted to the question of gaining equality for women. As Soviet women have equal rights before the law, equal pay, equal opportunities in jobs and public life, its celebration is something of an anomaly. But as some of the old traditional attitudes of men towards women in the family still linger, the symbolic gestures made on this day towards women by men both at home and at work may be significant. Husbands, sons and brothers give presents and flowers to the women in the family, make the breakfast and wash up in the evening. At work, too, men present their women colleagues with flowers and there may be a festive cup of tea.

It is a custom for young people, after their wedding ceremony, to visit two places. They lay a wreath on the tomb of the unknown soldier in the gardens beneath the Kremlin Wall, and they go up to the viewing platform at the top of the Lenin Hills to look at the panorama of Moscow below. Then home to a big celebration party!

*Above and left:* The Lenin Mausoleum contains the embalmed body of Lenin. On the days when it is open to the public, queues of people line up to pay their respects. The top is used as a reviewing platform on May 1st and November 7th.

*Above:* Grandfather Frost with a school choir at a New Year celebration.
*Right:* Traditionally, on their first day at school, Moscow schoolchildren present their teachers with bunches of flowers.

# The Kremlin's Glory

Every visitor to Moscow must see the Kremlin. This fascinating complex contains a fabulously rich collection of art treasures, churches and palaces dating from different periods, starting at the 15th century.

The word Kremlin means a high fortified place. It is entered through the gates of the Kutafya and the Troitsky towers, with the bridge over the former moat between. The first building inside is the most modern, the Palace of Congresses, finished in 1961. This is the seat of the Soviet Parliament, but the hall is also used for concerts and for performances by the Bolshoi Ballet and visiting companies.

There are many historic buildings in the Kremlin; the former arsenal, completed in 1736, has the guns captured from Napoleon's army mounted on its high, thick walls; what was once the Senate House is now the seat of the U.S.S.R. Council of Ministers; the Bell Tower of Ivan the Great rises 265 feet into the air, it dates from the 16th century and is crowned with a gilded dome. At the foot of the tower is a bell, weighing 200 tons and cast in the 18th century. It was never hung and was badly cracked in a fire when a huge piece fell off.

But the most beautiful part of the Kremlin is the square, which seems full of cathedrals and palaces. They are now preserved as museums, and contain frescoes, murals, icons, the tombs of tsars, and the throne of Ivan the Terrible.

There is a pleasant garden with seats, fruit trees and flower beds and a view over the ramparts down to the Moskva River.

A beautiful and powerful view of the Kremlin at night, its lights enchantingly reflected in the river.

*Left:* The gold-coloured cupolas
give a fairy-tale look to the
Annunciation Cathedral.
*Above:* The equally extravagant
Assumption Cathedral.

*Left:* Some of the elaborate frescoes decorating the walls of the Granovitaya Chamber in the Kremlin.

*Above:* An icon of 'Christ All-Seeing Eye', from the 14th century, in the Kremlin Assumption Cathedral.

*Right:* The 16th century fur-trimmed crown of the Kazan Kingdom is made of gold and studded with precious stones and pearls. It is exhibited in the Kremlin Armoury and was once worn by Ivan the Terrible.

*Below left:* The Tsar Bell, weighing 200 tons, was cast in 1733 but never hung. It was cracked in a fire in 1837 and a piece weighing eleven tons fell off.
*Below:* Lenin's study in the building of the Council of Ministers in the Kremlin. He used it from 1918 to 1922.
*Right:* one of the many paintings of Lenin. This is entitled *Lenin's Return to Russia* and is by K. Aksyonov.

# Old Moscow

There are parts of old Moscow all over the city; some will vanish as reconstruction goes ahead; some will be preserved because of its historic and aesthetic value.

During the many battles and invasions in the history of Moscow, the houses, which were originally made of wood, were burnt down or gutted. Only the churches, which were of stone, remained to show the style and skill of the old Russian builders.

In addition to those in the Kremlin, there are numerous small and medium sized churches dotted around the city. Most of them have been completely restored and are often used as small museums. A certain number are still used for worship.

One of the oldest is the Church of Antipy, dating from the 16th century; the Church of Nikola-in-Pizhi is a fine example of 17th century Russian architecture, with a tent-like belfry and an ornate pyramid of rounded gables and domes. The Church of the Nativity-in-Putinki, near Pushkin Square, is an interesting 17th century church, built at the time of the stone fortifications around the city. It is impossible to walk in any direction without soon coming across one or other of the dozens of churches still standing.

Many of the great mansions which belonged to the aristocracy are now used as the headquarters of various organisations. They can be recognised by their porticos and the columns which support them. Merchants who wished to imitate the style were allowed only to have simulated columns fixed to the walls of their houses! (They did not always abide by this restriction, however.)

A few examples of this kind of architecture are: the present Rheumatism Research Institute, in the former house of merchant Gubin; and the Institute of Physical Culture in the former palace of Count Razumovsky, which was one of the few timber palaces which escaped the fires of 1812. It was built by an English architect. The Archive of Military History is kept in the palace of Franz Lefort, one of Peter the Great's admirals, and built at the end of the 17th century. Such buildings are found in all parts of the inner ring of the city. Their outside walls are still painted in the traditional colours, warm yellow, pale blue or pale green, often picked out with white.

As one would expect, the area near Red Square on the side away from the Kremlin, is full of old buildings. The street, now called 25th of October Street, was formerly part of Kitai-Gorod, inside the second line of fortifications and there is still a gate and part of the wall left. In the courtyard of number seven, there is part of the Monastery-behind-the-Icon; No 15 was the Printers' Yard, where the first printing press was set up in 1563. The first Russian newspaper was produced here in 1703. The building, with its lace-like carvings in white stone on the facade, is now the Institute of History and Archives.

Not far from this street are three squares next to each other, called New Square, Old Square and Nogin Square, with a very wide boulevard running along the side. At one end is the large Polytechnical Museum, which is a mixture of styles as it was put up between 1877 and 1907, parts being added at different times.

At the beginning of the boulevard is the Monument to the Grenadiers killed at Plevna during the Russo-Turkish war of 1877-1878. The Church of all the Saints-in-Kulishki, was built in 1380 to commemorate a victory over the Tartars, and was reconstructed several times, the last occasion taking place in the 17th century. Near by is the Church of the Trinity, also 17th century – beyond these squares, and all around the Hotel Rossiya are various churches which

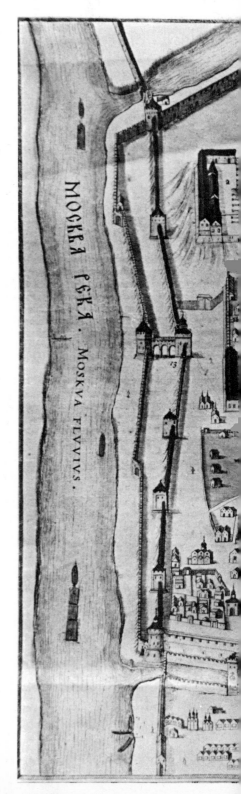

132

КРЕМЛЕН ГРАД.

KREMLENAGRAD,

CASTELLVM VRBIS MOSKVÆ

MAGNO DOMINO CÆSARI, ET MAGNO DVCI
ALEXIO MICHAELOVITS,
DEI GRATIA,
OMNIVM RVSSORVM AVTOKRATORI, VLADIMERSKII, MOSKOFSKII
NOVOGORODSKII: TZAR KAZANSKII, TZAR ASTOROCHANSKII, TZAR
SIBIERSKII: DOMINO PLESKOFSKII: MAGNO DVCI SMOLENSKII, IVERSKI
OVGORSKII, PERMSKII, VEATSKII, BOLGARSKII: ETIAM DOMINO, ET MAG
NO DVCI NOVOGORODI IN TERRIS INFERIORIBVS, TZERNIGOFSKII,
REZANSKII, POLOTZKII, ROSTOFSKII, IAROSLAFSKII, BELOZERSKII,
OVDORSKII, OBDORSKII, KONDINSKII ET TOTIVS SEPTENTRIONALIS
REGIONIS MANDATORI; ET DOMINO TERRARVM IVERSKYE,
KARTALINSKICHI, ET GRVZINSKICH CÆSARVM ET
TERRARVM KABARDINSKIES, TZERKASKICHI, IGORSKICH
DVCVM: ET MVLTARVM DITIONVM DOMINO
ET MODERATORI

Caſtellum cum tribus contiguis Vrbibus Moſkuæ, prout
ſub florenti Imperio, piæ memoriæ, Magni Domini Cæſaris,
et Magni Ducis Boriſſi Foedorovits, omnium Ruſſorum, &c.
ſitu, et dimenſu fuit; ſummâ ac debitâ obſervantiâ,
offertur, dicatur, conſecratur.

133

*Above:* A 17th century print by Vasnetsov showing the Kremlin's walled grandeur rising above the wooden houses of the city.
*Left:* A stone lion, part of the Spassky Tower's decorative features.
*Right:* The 16th century Church of St Anne. It stands near the river in front of the Hotel Rossiya and has been beautifully restored.

have been restored to their former beauty.

The Arbat is another area dating back to the old fortifications. Here there used to be a gate in the outer ring. In the 16th and 17th centuries artisans and craftsmen lived here and many of the still narrow and winding streets bear the names of their callings, such as silversmith, carpenter, bread and tables. In the 19th century aristocrats built their mansions in this district and many are now used by public bodies.

It is still possible to find wooden houses in some parts of Moscow, which, before the Revolution was known as 'the big village'. A few of historic value will be kept but the rest will vanish. Any traces of the villages that were engulfed as the city expanded will only be found in the names of the districts where they once stood.

*Left:* The intricately carved front gives this old Moscow farmer's house a distinctive appearance.
*Above:* A two-storeyed wooden house from another village now engulfed by the city. It will probably vanish as this part is rebuilt.

*Below:* A romantic view of Smolensk Cathedral situated in the Novo-Devichy district of the city of Moscow.

*Right:* One of Moscow's few remaining old buildings. Time has given it a crown of vegetation.

# Along The River

Trips along Moskva River start at the Kiev pier and go downstream. On the slower river trams it takes about an hour and a quarter to reach the end of the route, going round two great curves.

The first sight on the left bank is of the fortress walls of the former Novo-Devichy Convent. Its fine belfry rises above the cupolas of the churches inside the walls. The convent dates from the early 17th century and the belfry was built in 1690. It was in the convent cathedral that Boris Godunov was proclaimed tsar in 1598. Later the wife and sister of Peter the Great were imprisoned there for plotting against him. Many famous people are buried in the cemetery within the walls.

Next, on the same side of the river, is the sports complex of Luzhniki and opposite, the steep high slope of the Lenin Hills come down almost to the water. At this point there is a double-decker bridge carrying the underground and a road over the river. There is a station actually on the bridge, with escalators going up towards the top of the hill. At the top, dominating the skyline, is the giant building of the Moscow University.

As the boat rounds the first curve of the trip, the gardens at the foot of the Lenin Hills widen into the large territory of the Gorky Park. On the left bank, beyond the embankment road, are many new buildings.

A succession of bridges span the river, most of them either reconstructed or built since the Revolution. The Crimea Bridge, just below the park, is a very long suspension bridge, and beyond it the new huge picture gallery to replace the Tretyakov, is going up.

At this point, on the left bank, stands a two storeyed house with a quaint roof, a large balcony of brick and an ornamented facade. It was built in the late 19th century. During the Second World War it was used by the French Military Mission and there is a plaque on the wall in memory of 42 heroes. The French airmen fought with their Soviet allies on the front from Moscow as far as Germany.

The Drainage Canal, which branches off to the right, was built in 1786 along the former channel of the river, which it rejoins further down. On the left are the high diving boards of the Moskva swimming pool. A little further down, up on the hill, the whole wonderful panorama of the Kremlin palaces and churches with their golden domes bursts into view. It holds the eye and tends to distract attention from some of the interesting buildings on the other side. One is a rare survival from the 17th century, a boyar's house, and next to it a church which has been restored. The British Embassy is a short distance further down.

On the same side as the Kremlin, down the river, is the huge Rossiya Hotel which can accommodate several thousand visitors; many Muscovites regret its position as it spoils the view from Red Square towards St Basil's. In front of the hotel is a small church surrounded by young trees.

Like most great cities, Moscow was founded on the banks of a river and, as a result, grew in size and importance. The River Moskva flows through Moscow and a trip down it is an ideal way to see the city.

Soon the boat reaches the place where the River Yauza falls into the Moskva. New parts of Moscow can be seen on either side and the last stop is at the Novo-Spassky Bridge, near the Novo-Spassky Monastery. This is one of the fortress monasteries and its towers and belfry can be seen above the walls.

From the same starting point as for this trip there are boats going up-stream, in the opposite direction. The river curves a great deal and the excursion ends at Fili-Kuntsovo Park and a river beach.

A ride on a hydrofoil along the Moscow-Volga Canal starts at the river port, Rechnoi Voksal, which is actually on the Khimki Reservoir. The boat passes through the pleasant countryside around the city, with a number of stopping places where people picnic, swim or sunbathe. There are many bathing beaches, boating centres, quiet corners for fishing and interesting small towns along the route.

Large steamers pass on their way down the Volga and since the opening of the canal, cargo-carrying boats can reach five separate seas from Moscow.

*Below:* Hardy Muscovites taking a Sunday dip in the Moskva.
*Right:* A hydrofoil trip along the Moscow-Volga Canal is an exciting way to see the city and parts of the surrounding countryside. The hydrofoil has a wake which folds in on itself, thus safeguarding the banks.

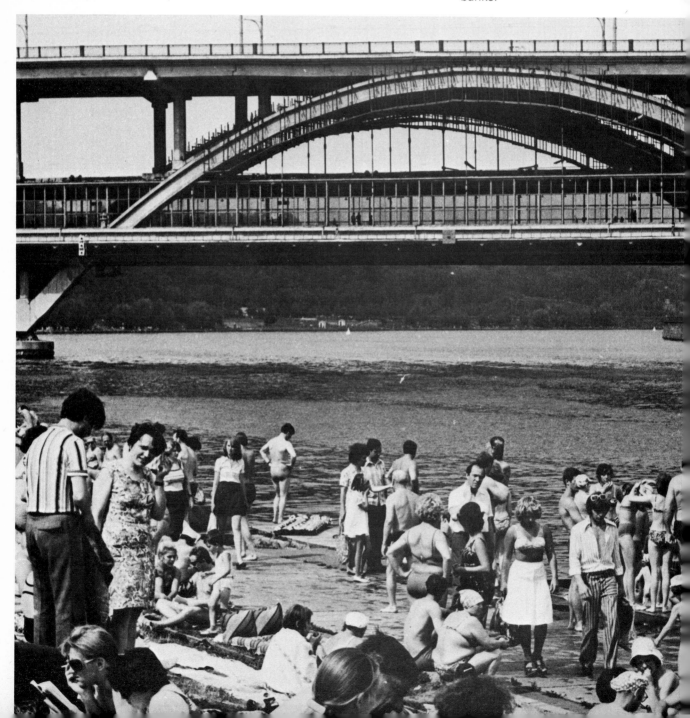

*Left:* Arkhangelskoye, near Moscow. Part of the estate is on the high bank of the Moskva River and has this kind of outlook.
*Below:* A view of the Lenin Stadium from across the river.

# Sporting Moscow

Muscovites, young and old, like most Soviet citizens, are very keen on sport and have excellent facilities for any kind they choose. Many organizations, factories and the university, have their own sports clubs and between them have built around 70 stadiums in the city. In addition to providing for football games, there are usually facilities for other sports at these stadiums. Under the grandstands are gyms and other sports' rooms, showers, changing rooms, and a first-aid post. Certain times during the week are set aside for children's sections, with coaching from experts.

In a wide loop of the Moskva River is the huge sports complex of Luzhniki. It occupies an area of more than 350 acres and provides for almost every type of sport, games and athletics, both in winter and summer. Its central stadium is the largest in Europe; one section seats 103,000, another 15,000. The Palace of Sport accommodates 17,000 and is used for a variety of competitions such as gymnastics and figure-skating, as it can be converted into an ice-rink. All the buildings and pitches are set in a well laid-out park, where, in winter, parts are flooded for skating.

Football is enormously popular and matches are always sure of a full crowd as well as a huge television audience. The climate, with five months when the ground is covered in snow, means that football is almost a summer game. Ice-hockey, said to be one of the fastest games in the world, is played mostly in winter.

Swimming can go on all the year round. There are beaches along the Moscow-Volga Canal, and there are many swimming pools, both indoor and out. The giant Moskva swimming pool and the smaller Chaika are open all the winter and are, of course, heated. One can see the huge cloud of steam rising into the air above the Moskva from a long distance and the swimmers have to move about in a mist! As in other countries, in winter there are those hardy types who like to break the ice and plunge into freezing water. Holes are made for them and they have a special gala swim on New Year's Eve.

Holes are also made in the ice for winter fishing. People, huddled in warm clothing, sit for hours on stools waiting for the fish to come up to the holes to breathe. It is an extraordinary sight: a long stretch of ice with black dots of figures sitting all over the place! Fishing is also a summer pastime for many, both young and old.

Skiing is another popular winter sport. It is hard to find any steep and long slopes anywhere near Moscow. Nevertheless there is ample flat space in several of the large parks in the city. At weekends people can be seen setting off for the railway stations with their skis over their shoulders, bound for the countryside. There are centres both in the parks and in the country where it is possible to hire skis and boots.

Olga Korbut, world champion gymnast, is the winner of many medals. She is known throughout the world for her vitality and lively personality.

One of the features of Moscow, as it is indeed for the whole of the U.S.S.R., is the encouragement given to children to take up sports. There is one sports complex which belongs exclusively to schoolchildren. Many courtyards are flooded in winter and used by the children living there for skating and ice-hockey. The click of the hockey sticks against the puck can be heard as one goes along the pavements. Children begin to skate at a very early age and can join figure-skating classes at most stadiums.

There are competitions (called Olympiads) in all sports at every level. In this way the Soviet Union produces many fine athletes, gymnasts, and football and ice-hockey players. The costs to the individual are minimal as the state gives heavy subsidies and every help and encouragement.

*Below:* Three girl swimmers, the Olympic medallists, Koshevana, Russanova and Jurchenia. Russia is world-renowned for the skill of its sportsmen and women.

*Right:* The Moskva Swimming Pool. This enormous pool is round and divided into sections. It is heated in winter and the steam rising from the water forms a warm, protective layer of air for the swimmers. The rising steam can be seen for miles. The pool is entered from the changing rooms through an underground tunnel.

*Left:* Faina Melnik, the discus thrower.
*Below:* The Lenin Central Stadium is in the sports complex of Luzhniki, by the river. Its large bowl seats 103,000 and the other bowl seats over 15,000. Under the grandstands of the large bowl there are several storeys which provide for gyms, massage, medical rooms, dressing rooms, showers, snack bars and other amenities.

*Left:* This courtyard belonging to a block of flats has been flooded and is used as a rink by the inhabitants. This is a very common occurrence all over the city during the winter.
*Above:* Muscovites leaving the city on what is known as a 'health train', one of many used for weekend excursions to the country.
*Right:* Valeriy Borzov, 100 metre champion of the Soviet Union and an Olympic gold medallist.

*Above:* A fencing match at the
World University Games.
*Right:* A team of Russian gymnasts
displaying their skills in a human
column.

# Shopping and Eating Out

Moscow shops, especially those near the centre, are so full of customers that it is difficult to get close enough to the counter to see what is on display. Tourists, if they wish, can buy souvenirs and other articles in their own currency, either at the special counters in their hotels (most of the big hotels have them) or in several special shops in the city, called Beryozka. The hotels also sell items in Soviet currency.

The quality and quantity of goods in Soviet shops is still not as good as those in, for example, London or New York, but some, such as books and gramophone records, are of good value. For those foreigners who do not know the language and wish to go shopping, there are always fellow customers pleased to help them over any difficulties they may experience.

The largest shop, or rather, shopping complex, is GUM (pronounced GOOM) in Red Square. This is a series of three parallel arcades on two floors, containing shops of every conceivable kind. In the centre of the middle arcade is a fountain, and here there is a very good souvenir shop selling handicrafts from different parts of the country: lacquered wooden articles, pottery, bone and wood carvings as well as many other items. Opposite, is a jewellery shop. The ice cream sold in GUM is delicious, as the number of people eating it proves!

TSUM is a large department store by the side of the Bolshoi Theatre. (TSUM are the Russian initials for Central Department Store.) On the ground floor there are several counters selling souvenirs. This shop also has branches further up the street, which is called Petrovka.

On Petrovka there is also a special shop selling traditional handicrafts of a very high quality and most attractively displayed. Kuznetsky Most is a street running into the bottom of Petrovka. It is full of bookshops.

Another good shopping centre is the new part of Kalinin Prospect, a wide street with very wide pavements. The street is lined with skyscrapers which hardly dominate because they are built somewhat back from the road. In this street is the largest bookshop in Moscow, a good record shop and a variety of other stores and also a number of restaurants.

Gorky Street was one of the first shopping centres in Moscow and is well worth a walk. Near the bottom is the Central Telegraph Office where the latest issues of the attractive Soviet stamps may be bought. Along this street there are some fine bookshops, many food stores, a Beryozka shop and shops selling clothes and materials.

In addition to the shops, on the pavements of the main streets there are numerous stalls and kiosks selling fruit, ice creams, newspapers, cigarettes and cheap souvenirs, kvass (a fermented thirst-quenching drink) in summer, theatre tickets, cakes and other things – they are often the overflow of shops, and, of course, they are all state-owned.

Beriozka shops can be found in most of the tourist hotels and in two districts of Moscow. They sell all sorts of goods, including souvenirs and handicraft items in exchange for foreign currency.

*Left and above:* GUM consists of three parallel arcades on two floors with a series of shops selling everything imaginable — food, materials, photographic supplies, clocks, records, haberdashery, stationery and, of course, ice cream which is delicious and rightly popular with the crowds who come to do their shopping here.

Every district in Moscow has a large covered market where collective farmers can sell their produce; the fruit and vegetables often come from their private plots. They travel from as far away as Central Asia with the kind of fruit that does not grow in a cooler climate, such as grapes, peaches and melons. There are also stalls run by state enterprises at prices found in the ordinary shops. Here in the markets are fruit, vegetables, milk products, meat, honey, plants and flowers. There is a big Central Market in Tsvetnoi Boulevard.

Moscow is not yet provided with enough snack and coffee bars, nor are there nearly enough quick service cafeterias, cafes and restaurants. Restaurants attached to hotels are usually open to non-residents. If one wants to have an evening meal in a restaurant, however, it is wise to go very early or to book by phone. When Russians go out for a meal it is with the intention of having a real outing, eating in a leisurely way, and dancing between the courses. They are apt to occupy their tables for the whole evening!

The restaurants of interest to foreigners are those providing food from the national republics; the best of these include the Aragvi, specializing in Georgian dishes, kebabs, spicy sauces with chicken, fish or cheese, and very good wine; the Uzbekistan, with special soups, its own kind of kebab, delicious flat bread and good wine. The Ararat serves Armenian food, the Baku, Azerbaijanian food and there are others serving foods from different republics.

*Left:* A Moscow bookstall, typical of many throughout the city. Stalls like these always attract large crowds.

*Below:* The interior of a large food store.

*Left:* The exterior of GUM, Moscow's largest store.
*Right:* Petrovka, a popular shopping street near the Bolshoi Theatre.
*Below:* Young people getting married have the choice either of a special ceremony in a wedding palace, where they can also celebrate in a special room with food and wine; or they can go to an ordinary registry office in their district. This is a last-minute-present shop in the palace itself.

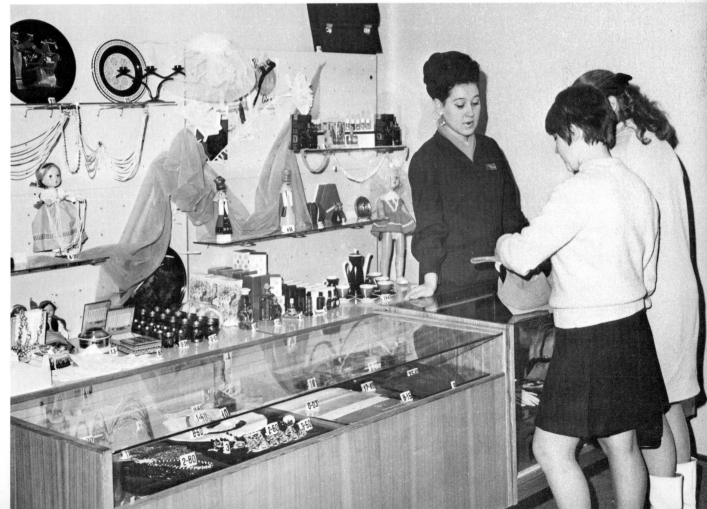

# Cultural Moscow

Moscow is a great cultural centre. There is far more than the world famous Bolshoi Ballet and the architectural riches of the Kremlin. The city has numerous museums, art galleries, theatres, cinemas, concert halls and historic sites, most of which are worth more than one visit.

The Tretyakov Art Gallery is based on a private collection presented to the city in 1892 by P. Tretyakov. The building looks like something out of a Russian fairy tale. It houses an enormous collection of Russian art, including the works of contemporary Soviet painters and sculptors. It is now far too small and a huge new gallery is in the process of construction near Gorky Park.

The Pushkin Gallery of Western Art contains a collection of classical and other sculptures, as well as many fine paintings, including early Italians, El Greco, Rembrandt, Constable, Corot, Picasso and van Gogh. The smaller Museum of Eastern Art houses carvings, jade ornaments, pottery and other handicrafts from China, Japan, India, Turkey, Iran and the Central Asian Republics of the U.S.S.R.

Many of the city's 28 theatres are of a very high order. The theatres have permanent companies, are heavily subsidized and work on a repertory programme. Some of them have their own acting schools. There are several theatres presenting ballet and opera; the Bolshoi has an opera company and two ballet companies, one of which performs in the Palace of Soviets in the Kremlin and the other in the Bolshoi itself. The Stanislavsky Theatre also has a ballet and opera company and its version of *Swan Lake* is different from that of the Bolshoi. The Moscow Art Theatre is well known for its presentation of Chekhov and other Russian classics while the Taganka Theatre has earned itself world fame for its experimental staging of a wide variety of plays.

The Central Children's Theatre next door to the Bolshoi, and the Theatre of the Young Spectator, as their names suggest, cater for different age groups of young people. The Central Puppet Theatre, with its intriguing facade, is popular with young and old alike.

Buying a ticket for almost any kind of production is difficult; Muscovites are keen theatre-goers, as is evidenced by the queues at the box offices. One feature of the theatre scene: all outdoor garments must be left in the cloakrooms. In the winter members of the audience bring shoes so that they can leave their thick boots outside and enjoy themselves in comfort.

Some of the 14 house museums are charming. These were the homes at different times of famous writers, composers, actors, artists and scholars, including Gorky, Tchaikovsky, Chekhov, Tolstoy and many others. These small old houses have been preserved intact amidst the tall new buildings.

There are other museums to suit all tastes: museums such as the History Museum on Red Square; the Lenin Museum nearby; the Museum of the Revolution on Gorky Street and the Museum of the History and the Reconstruction of Moscow, in the former church of St John under the Elm in Novaya Square. Part of the History Museum is in the former Novo-Devichy Convent, built in 1525, and enclosed by a crenellated wall with 12 towers.

This new section of Moscow University was completed in 1953. The central part of the building is 780 feet high, topped by a 200 foot spire. There are 37 buildings dotted about the 415 acres containing, among other amenities, 1,000 laboratories and 148 auditoriums. The library contains over one and a half million books. A large botanical garden and an observatory lie in the park which surrounds the university.

The Ostankino Palace Museum of Serf Art is unique. It was built in 1791-1797 in neo-classical style and is made entirely of wood. It was owned by the Sheremetov family, whose serfs, many of whom were superb artists and craftsmen, designed and built it. The moulded ceilings, the perfect proportions of the rooms, the chandeliers, the furniture and the parquet floors of rare woods are witness to their skill. The largest room in the house is the theatre, with a stage which could hold an entire company of 200 serf-actors. By a clever mechanism invented by one of the serfs, the seats in the auditorium could be moved in a few moments to clear the floor for dancing.

A number of former monasteries and churches are now museums of different kinds and several halls belonging to the Union of Artists hold temporary exhibitions of paintings and sculpture executed by contemporary artists.

The cultural scene in Moscow includes over 70 publishing houses, which produce millions of books yearly; cinemas; a fine circus; cultural clubs belonging to factories, enterprises and organisations, where their members can relax, join classes in folk dancing, singing, languages, or whatever interests them. They form many amateur dance groups, choirs and orchestras. The city is also a great musical centre, with a number of concert halls. The Conservatoire and several music schools produce some of the finest musicians in the world.

*Below:* The Rossiya Cinema on Pushkin Square.

166

*Left:* The Tretyakov Gallery contains a rich collection of Russian art. The pictures range from eleventh-century icons and mosaics, to contemporary paintings. There are also drawings, sculptures and engravings. The building was presented to the city in 1892 by P. Tretyakov, together with his private art collection.
*Below:* The impressive Ostankino Serf Art Museum.

*Left:* The Bolshoi Theatre is one of the oldest theatres in Moscow. It was founded in 1776 and can seat over 2,000. It was twice destroyed by fire and was finally restored in 1856. Its columned facade is topped by the famous quadriga of Apollo.

*Below left:* The auditorium of the Bolshoi Theatre.

*Below:* The Tchaikovsky Conservatoire, founded in 1866 by the musician Nicolai Rubinstein. Many famous Russian composers and performers were trained here and also taught here themselves. The large hall seats 2,000. A statue of Tchaikovsky stands in front of the building.

A typically colourful performance of
opera at the Bolshoi Theatre.

*Above left and left:* Georgian
national dancers give exciting and
colourful displays.
*Above:* The Moscow circus is one
of the finest in the world. Its
animals and clowns are highly
trained and perform many feats.
There is also a circus on ice where
bears, as well as humans play
hockey on skates.

# Moscow's Open Spaces

Moscow is a very green place, except in winter. This is mainly due to the many parks, gardens and other green spaces all over the city. There are three very large parks and eleven others, most of them accessible by underground or other transport.

Gorky Park is the best known and there are always streams of people entering its gates. Its 300 acres, however, easily absorb large numbers and its amenities appeal to a wide variety of tastes. The park stretches along the bank of the Moskva River for nearly two miles. The further one goes from the entrance, the wilder it grows, with paths winding up the Lenin Hills, among shady trees. These slopes are popular in winter among skiers.

The section nearer the gates is full of flower beds and flowering shrubs. The central path leads to the boating lake, with a cafe on its bank. There is an amusement park with a huge ferris wheel and a parachute jump. There are pavilions for exhibitions and an indoor dance hall. The open-air Green Theatre, with a large stage, can seat 10,000, and there are many other open-air stages for concerts and variety shows. There are dance floors for national and other dancing, cafes and restaurants, all kinds of stalls selling souvenirs, newspapers and ice creams, an outdoor library, chess corners, a rose-garden and seats everywhere.

There are five ponds, including one specially for swans. In winter large areas and paths are flooded to enable skaters to go quite long distances. There are also rinks for children, beginners, and experts.

Sokolniki Park provides many of the same facilities and occupies 1,500 acres. It takes its name from the Russian word for 'falcon' as it was once a hunting forest for the nobility. Large tracts are still wooded and untouched, except for well trodden paths where people come to breathe the fresh untainted air. Beyond the impressive fountain near the entrance is a group of pavilions where international commercial fairs are held.

The third large park is the Ismailova Park, more than 2,000 acres of woodland, streams and meadows. In addition to the usual facilities there is a riding stable and an archery field.

Ismailova was once the Moscow estate of the tsar's family and game was bred in it specially for hunting. Peter the Great spent time here when he was a child and used to sail on the pond.

Another park associated with Peter is Kolomenskoye, once a country residence of the princes and, later, the tsars of Russia. It is on the bank of the Moskva River and is now an open-air museum of Russian architecture. In a grassy meadow is the Church of the Ascension, built by an unknown architect in 1534, and the first Russian church to be put up in the 'tent' style. It is 190 feet high, of red brick and white stone.

A fountain in the attractively laid-out Exhibition Gardens.

Dotted about the park, among the old trees, are various buildings which have been moved from other places, including the 17th century wooden fortress tower from the shores of the White Sea; a tower from the old Bratsk jail in Siberia and a little wooden house from Arkhangelsk in which Peter the Great lived when he was young. At that period he also lived for a time in Kolomenskoye.

The Exhibition of the Economic Achievements of the U.S.S.R. is housed in more than 70 pavilions situated in a vast, well laid-out park. A little rail-less train plies from one end to the other, to save the feet of those who wish to see as many of the pavilions as possible. Throughout the grounds are stalls selling soft drinks, snacks, ice creams and other refreshments; there are also restaurants and cafeterias where full meals are served.

There are other smaller parks in various parts of the city. In addition to these are numerous squares and broad boulevards where seats are always to be found under the trees and by pleasant flower beds.

*Below:* Sokolniki Park is four times as big as Hyde Park in London. It was formerly a hunting estate for the tsars, who came here with their falcons — sokol means falcon in Russian.

*Right:* A number of Moscow parks have a special section for children where they can play games, see a puppet show, read or just enjoy the fresh air.

*Below right:* Playing dominoes in the open air is a popular activity for off-duty Muscovites.

*Below and below left:* Two of Moscow's beautiful fountains that decorate many of the city's public places.

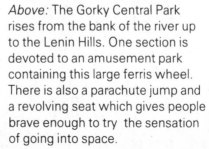

*Above:* The Gorky Central Park rises from the bank of the river up to the Lenin Hills. One section is devoted to an amusement park containing this large ferris wheel. There is also a parachute jump and a revolving seat which gives people brave enough to try the sensation of going into space.

*Left:* There are always crowds in Gorky Park, particularly on Sundays, but it is easy to go further into the park and lose sight of them.

*Below:* Gorky Park has five lakes and there are black swans on one of them. It is also possible to row on the river as there is a large boat-house on the embankment. In winter, vast stretches of the park are turned into skating rinks.

# Moscow Excursions

The Arkhangelskoye Estate is a few miles out of Moscow. Here there is a large palace built in the late 18th century; it belonged at one time to Prince Yusupov who was the director of the Hermitage Picture Gallery in St Petersburg. When buying art treasures all over Europe for the imperial collection, he also acquired many for himself. The palace, which is kept as it was when he lived in it, is still full of treasures, pictures by old masters, period furniture and china. The layout of the park was inspired by Versailles. In the park there are other interesting buildings, including a serf theatre, now a museum, and, on a high part of the river bank, a small church which has been beautifully restored. It contains a fine collection of icons.

Zagorsk, a little more than 40 miles from Moscow, is the centre of the Russian Orthodox Church. Priests are trained here and its churches and monastery are among the most famous in the country. The Sergius-Troitsky Monastery was founded in the first half of the 14th century and is an architectural gem. It was also at this time the cultural centre of old Russia. The monastery had an important library, and master icon painters, wood-carvers, silversmiths and other craftsmen had their workshops here. The collection of art treasures accumulated over the centuries can be seen in the museum.

There are numbers of other beautiful churches in Zagorsk, as well as a bell-tower, an old refectory, a hospital, fortress walls and towers, and, a modern touch, a museum of toys with 30,000 exhibits including dolls from many countries and of different periods.

Leninsky Gorky is about 20 miles from Moscow and is the centre of a flourishing collective farm. It is known for the house where Lenin lived at the end of his life and where he died. The house, now a museum, was built in 1830 and stands in extensive grounds. The rooms have been left as they were in Lenin's time. In the garage is the old Rolls-Royce motor car which was given to Lenin by a group of his English friends and admirers.

Although rather far, more than 100 miles, it is possible to visit Vladimir and Suzdal in one day. They are both interesting and beautiful places.

Vladimir was founded in the 12th century and most of it was built by the son of Yuri Longarm. It was enclosed by earthen and wooden fortifications with a Golden and a Silver Gate in them. Many of the cathedrals and churches within this city are standing today and have been fully restored. In the Cathedral of the Assumption there are remains of murals by Rublyov.

Suzdal is preserved as a museum town and contains marvels of old Russian architecture. In the Kremlin, built in the 12th and 13th centuries is the white stone Cathedral of the Nativity. The facade, facing the Kremlin Square, is richly carved and ornamented. Inside, the walls are covered with frescoes from the 13th to the 17th centuries.

The town itself has 36 lovely churches, each one unique in design. There are also many former monasteries and convents. A large tract of land has been turned into an open-air architectural museum. It features old buildings, houses, a well, and a wooden church built without the use of a single nail. They have been brought from many places and reconstructed here.

Two old wooden houses from Moscow have been brought here to form part of the Suzdal out-door architectural museum.

*Left:* Arkhangelskoye Palace was built in the 18th and 19th centuries and is now a museum that houses a collection of works of art, paintings, furniture and porcelain.
*Below:* One of the stone lions guarding the palace. These lions have almost human faces.
*Bottom:* A beautifully restored little church on the Arkhangelskoye estate on the high bank of the Moskva. There is a marvellous collection of old icons on view.

*Left:* The Pokrovsky Monastery in Suzdal, one of several which are now used as museums.
*Below:* Snow-covered, wooden houses left from the former village of Pionyskoye. There are still such houses standing in various parts of old Moscow, but they are disappearing fast, giving place to modern buildings.
*Right:* This old two-storeyed house in the Leningrad district may well be sacrificed to development too.

*Below, right and below right:* Three of the many monasteries within easy travelling distance of the city of Moscow.

# Changing Moscow

Of all the capitals in the world, Moscow has probably gone through the most drastic changes. Since the Revolution of 1917 and especially over the last 15 or 20 years, it has emerged as a modern city with clear outlines for its future development. More than half its population has been rehoused, broad new highways run from the centre, side roads have all been surfaced and one of the best transport systems serves the inhabitants.

Although its vast building projects depend on modern methods and are mainly functional, there have been changes in architectural design. The period when blocks of flats of prefabricated sections looked so monotonously alike, has given way to more variety in size, height, and colour. For example, no longer are all the balconies along a road the same colour. The former dull brown so much used has given way to varied shades. All flats except those on the ground floor have balconies or loggias. At one period in the 1950s five storey blocks, without lifts, were the norm. Now, tower blocks of nine, 12, 20 and more storeys bring variety to the skyline. As practically all the women work and many children are in nurseries and kindergartens until they go to school, the problems of loneliness faced by housewives in tower blocks in other countries rarely arise.

The radial and ring shape of the capital has been extended and developed; the new highways have green boulevards down the middle where people can walk and not suffer from the traffic. Further out they are lined with new modern buildings. The smaller roads off the rings and highways are being brought up to date, and the whole city has been enclosed by a circular bypass, over 67 miles in circumference. Beyond is a green belt, to be used for relaxation.

The first overall plan for the development of Moscow was made in 1935, and all the subsequent plans have been extensions of and improvements to, this plan. As there is no private ownership of land, the City Soviet (City Council) can go ahead without having to buy owners out, or obtain anyone's permission. The next plan was for the years 1951 to 1960, and now the 1971 plan aims to take Moscow into the 21st century, and, as the preamble says, make it a model city. The three zones will remain. The central zone is to continue as the heart of the capital, with many administrative buildings, historic architectural monuments, cultural amenities such as theatres, concert halls, museums and a shopping centre. People will continue to live here so there is no danger of it becoming 'dead'.

The second, middle zone, is still an industrial belt which grew up between the third line of fortifications and the Kamer-Kollezhsky ring during the industrial revolution after the emancipation of the serfs in the 19th century. Railway stations and the river ports are in this area as well as a number of villages and workers' settlements. According to the plan, some industries are to be removed: those which pollute the air or constitute other health or fire hazards. Small factories are to be combined, to leave more space. New shopping centres are being built and green areas planted.

The Panorama Museum contains the vast *Battle of Borodino* canvas — a full 377 feet long and 49 feet high — painted to commemorate the 1812 war. The statue is of the victorious general, Kutusov.

The outer zone extends to the peripheral bypass and occupies more than half the area of the city. It includes former small towns and rural settlements. Radial roads are being extended and with them, transport. The underground is being extended further and further out. Here there are many parks and green spaces. Factories, with residential blocks in the vicinity, are being built with the aim of reducing travelling time as much as possible. Many research institutes are going up, as they do not pollute the atmosphere.

It is hoped the plan will ensure that the population of Moscow remains stable by the end of the century at about eight and a half million; that there will be a better balance in the relation between the workplace and home, shopping and recreational facilities. Less industry and more people employed in the public service sector, will make life easier for Muscovites. More schools, hospitals, theatres and cinemas, shops, restaurants and green spaces will be provided. It is possible to believe that this will come to pass, when one sees the pace of development going on now.

*Above:* Modern apartment blocks now house many of the citizens of Moscow.
*Above right:* An unusual ring-house block of flats.
*Right:* One of the new housing estates in Moscow, showing the width of the roads and how the houses are separated from the road by wide verges of grass and trees, as well as by pavement.

192

*Left:* The new C.M.E.A. building
terminates the reconstructed radial
Kalinin Avenue.
*Above:* A modern Moscow street
lined with office blocks. But for the
styling of the cars, this street could
be in any major city in the world.

# Introduction to New York

Cities can be difficult places to come to grips with. Some require painstaking research and are best sampled in small doses; others seem to invite a more leisurely exploration. But not New York. Here is a city that requires no preliminary politeness, no careful reconnoitering before plunging in.

For visitors lucky enough to arrive by sea, like countless immigrants before them, the way to New York takes them directly past the 300 foot-high Statue of Liberty. The monument dominates the searoads and lets foreign travellers know that not only have they reached the New World, but that they have also arrived at a place where seemingly everything is done on a grand scale. A quick glance across the harbour is proof enough. The view ahead is of a sheer wall of concrete and glass—the towering skyscrapers of Lower Manhattan.

But the plunging canyons that intersect the buildings and lead the eye to the streets below are the key to another New York. The teeming streets tell a different story; the story of a city so diverse that it almost defies description. New York is the home of every kind of group, every kind of individual and manages to cater for every kind of taste.

Although the city is a conglomeration of five boroughs; the Bronx, Brooklyn, Queens, Staten Island and Manhattan, it is usually only the latter that people have in mind when they think of New York. In a very real way, Manhattan is indeed the heart and soul of the city. Here, like nowhere else, one is plunged into the excitement and exhilarating energy for which the city is renowned.

Manhattan is as easy to navigate as a sheet of graph paper. The majority of the city streets are laid out in a simple grid, each square of which is called a block, in which there are but two kinds of thoroughfares; streets (which run east to west) and avenues (which run north to south). The dividing line of east from west is Fifth Avenue which runs from Washington Square in Greenwich Village all the way to Harlem in the north. As a rough rule of thumb, north-south distances can be calculated by the fact there are 20 blocks to the mile.

Now for the exceptions: Broadway, which follows the path of an old Indian track and runs the entire length of Manhattan, meanders diagonally across the island from the southeast to the northwest. In the area south of 14th Street, New York's history triumphs over the logic of the grid system and the streets here become the jumble that most visitors from Europe used to the confusion of their own cities, will find familiar.

New York probably has a greater number of distinct neighbourhoods than any other city in the world. Not only can they be classified into categories such as working class, middle class and rich, or financial, shopping and entertainments, but also according to the dozens of different nationalities that live in the city. In Manhattan, the standard way to recognize that you have crossed from one ethnic neighbourhood into another is by the menus of restaurants. Nor are these the sort of menus you encounter in the rest of the United States, where a hamburger isn't fit to serve unless smothered in adjectives, and even the plainest slab of starch is qualified by at least a paragraph of ecstatic praise. New York menus are the genuine article, right down to the uncompromising spelling of unpronounceable ethnic dishes.

This book with its fascinating collection of hitherto largely unpublished photographs will show just what it is that makes New York America's most effervescent city and gives the place its world-wide reputation.

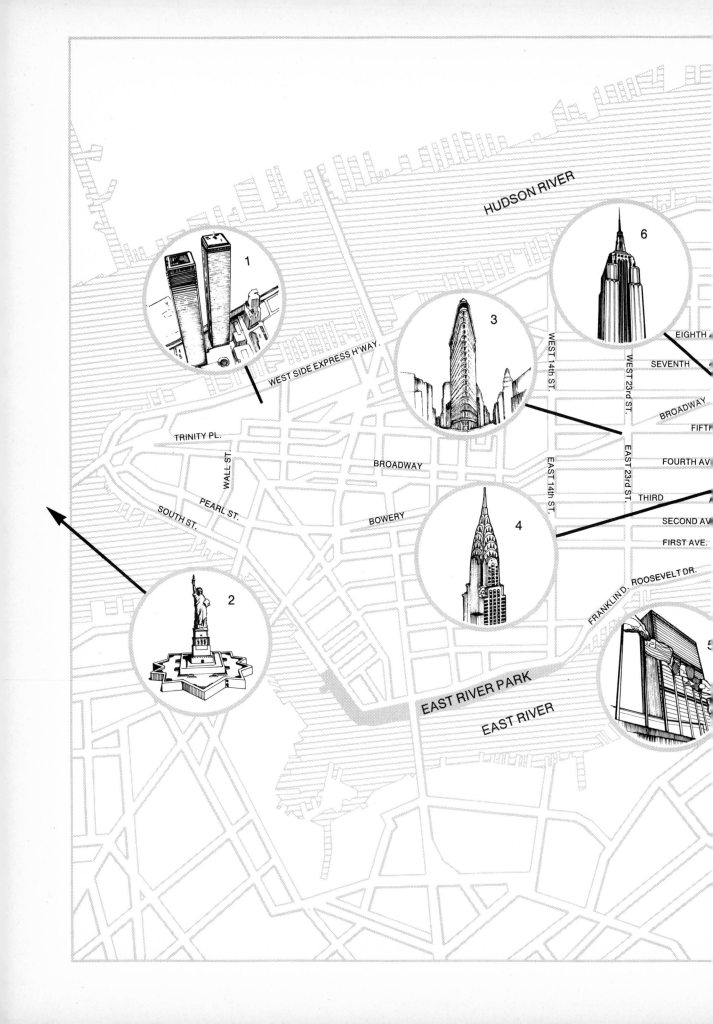

HUDSON RIVER

1

3

6

WEST SIDE EXPRESS H'WAY.

EIGHTH

WEST 14th ST.

WEST 23rd ST.

SEVENTH

BROADWAY

TRINITY PL.

BROADWAY

FIFTH

WALL ST.

EAST 23rd ST.

EAST 14th ST.

FOURTH AV

PEARL ST.

PEARL ST.

THIRD

SOUTH ST.

BOWERY

SECOND AV

FIRST AVE.

4

2

FRANKLIN D. ROOSEVELT DR.

5

EAST RIVER PARK

EAST RIVER

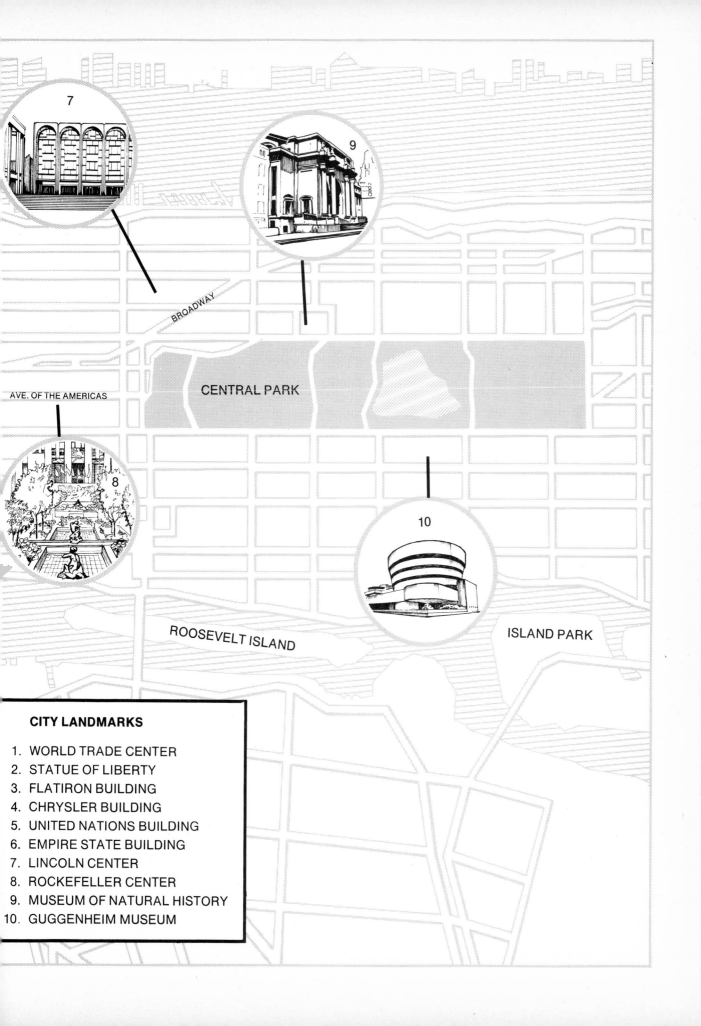

BROADWAY

AVE. OF THE AMERICAS

CENTRAL PARK

ROOSEVELT ISLAND

ISLAND PARK

**CITY LANDMARKS**

1. WORLD TRADE CENTER
2. STATUE OF LIBERTY
3. FLATIRON BUILDING
4. CHRYSLER BUILDING
5. UNITED NATIONS BUILDING
6. EMPIRE STATE BUILDING
7. LINCOLN CENTER
8. ROCKEFELLER CENTER
9. MUSEUM OF NATURAL HISTORY
10. GUGGENHEIM MUSEUM

# New York Past and Present

New York's history is very recent. The only great tradition is construction. Yet very little of the city's beginnings have been physically preserved for the place is continuously rebuilding itself. As the natives are fond of saying, 'New York would be a great place to live if they ever finished building it'.

New York owes its existence to the sea. It possesses the finest deepwater harbour on the east coast of America and has long been the principal port of the United States for both trade and immigration.

Though Italian and Portuguese explorers were already nosing around New York harbour as early as the 16th century, it was the Dutch who founded the first colony here. In 1629, they established a small settlement at the southernmost tip of Manhattan, on a plot of land they purchased from the Algonquin Indians for a mere 60 guilders (about 24 dollars).

From the outset, New Amsterdam, as the settlement was christened, was run as a commercial enterprise. Administered for the Dutch West India Company by a succession of governors, its chief reason for existence was profit through trade – a business maxim New Yorkers have faithfully clung to ever since.

The venture was a success and the steady flow of beaver and otter skins attracted an equally steady flow of new settlers. By 1660, some 300 houses had already been built and land speculation, still a contemporary practice, was rife.

From the start, the settlement attracted an unruly populace. Even the famous tyrannical governor, Peter Stuyvesant, was reduced to issuing futile directives decrying the excessive drinking and general low-life of his citizens. However, his task was abruptly terminated in 1664 when two warships under the command of the Duke of York, brother of King Charles II of England, sailed into the harbour. The resistance put up by the 10,000 colonists was anything but fierce and the English captured the city without firing a shot.

The colony was renamed New York in honour of James, the Duke of York, and the inhabitants settled down to being loyal British subjects: a fickle loyalty as events a century later were to prove.

Almost nothing survives to mark the original 17th-century Dutch colony save the cramped layout of the streets of Lower Manhattan and a few place names such as Brooklyn (coming from Breukelen or marshland), Harlem, Stuyvesant Street and the Bowery. This last name derives from the small Dutch farms called *bouweries* that once dotted the countryside to the north of Wall Street.

Wall Street itself marks the path of the wooden wall that ran from the East River to the Hudson and defended New Amsterdam from northern attack. However, it was never much of a deterrent to the Indians who preferred canoeing on the river to tramping overland. Anyway, the European settlers made a habit of ripping out sections for firewood! The wall was pulled down by the English in 1699 and

The pulse of New York is the thunder of its traffic. The restless energy reaches a fevered crescendo at major junctions, such as here at Times Square.

became a street. Nearly a century later, in 1792, a group of traders met here at the Tontine coffee house, establishing a regular market to facilitate the buying and selling of government securities. Like most historic sites, this first home of the New York Stock Exchange was pulled down long ago. Today it is commemorated by a wall plaque.

Perhaps the only real vestige of the Dutch presence in New York is the Bowling Green Park, a tiny plot of land at the foot of lower Broadway. The Dutch colonists paid a nominal rent of one peppercorn a year to graze their cattle here. Later, the site was turned into the city's first public park. A statue of George III stood here until the War of Independence when it was melted down into musket balls and aimed at his troops.

This was the third and last time that New York changed masters. Though British troops managed to occupy the city and drive out Washington and his army, mysterious fires during the time of their occupation razed at least a third of the city to the ground. When the British withdrew in 1783, they left a much ruined New York behind. It was rebuilt virtually overnight and for one brief year in 1785, even acted as the first capital of the United States.

There are still one or two relics of the revolutionary era of New York's history that remain intact. One, Dyckman House (Broadway & West 204th St), is the only surviving farmhouse on the whole of Manhattan. Although it was built in the 1780s it mirrors the style used by wealthy farmers of the century before, being a broad solid-looking structure of stone and wood with a peculiarly long, sloped roof.

During the years of the British presence in New York, most buildings were faithful copies of English Georgian styles. Almost all are long gone, victims of the city's notorious nonstop efforts to destroy its past, save for St Paul's Chapel, a very English-looking church built in 1766 at the corner of Broadway and Fulton.

At the time of the War of Independence, the population of New York was approximately 20,000 people. By 1800 it had risen to 60,000 and 20 years later, it reached 120,000 making it the biggest city in the United States. Sixty years after that it had multiplied another ten times. However, the greatest years of expansion did not even begin until the mid-19th century.

The city grew at an incredible pace, overflowing the crowded area of Lower Manhattan, spilling northward along the island. Today, as a general rule, older buildings are concentrated at the southern end of the city while the newer ones occupy the area above 14th Street, the geographical dividing line between Lower and Midtown Manhattan.

*Left:* Gracie Mansion, the official residence of New York's mayor, is set in the pleasant greenery of Carl Shurz Park. The mansion's 18th century elegance offers a marked contrast to the city jungle its occupants are elected to manage.
*Below:* This quaint wooden building at the tip of Battery Park is the landing stage of the Staten Island Ferry.

But like any rule, this one has exceptions. In the late 18th century, wealthy New Yorkers who sought to escape from the bustle of the city in the surrounding countryside, built themselves mansions further north on the island. At the far end of what today is East 88th Street stands Gracie Mansion. This large, white-frame building was built in 1799 and is the traditional home of New York's mayors. At the very northern tip of Manhattan, at 161st Street, stands the Morris-Jumel Mansion. Originally erected in 1765 and extensively restored around 1810, this house was once located deep in the country. Today, the two buildings are the sole remains of the great 18th-century country homes that were once scattered around Manhattan.

A rare sight in New York is a building with a history. This clapboard church is a reminder of the days when wood, not steel and glass, was the city's main building material.

*Left:* The looming pile of St Patrick's Cathedral, a design inspired by Cologne Cathedral, on Fifth Avenue was built between 1858 and 1879 to serve New York's growing Roman Catholic population.

The Fraunces Tavern at the corner of Pearl and Broad streets is one of the oldest buildings in the city with a non-religious history: it still serves food and drink today. The Tavern's original claim to fame was that George Washington wished his troops farewell from here after the War of Independence. They were deceived, for he returned a few years later to be the country's first president – and its new Commander-in-Chief.

Not far away is Trinity Church, a fully-fledged gothic cathedral erected in 1846 on the site of a church of the same name, which was cleared away to make room for the newer building. Today it is surrounded by a lush green churchyard occupying the block between Broadway and Trinity Place. The site is over-shadowed by the nearby skyscrapers of the World Trade Center and the Chase Manhattan Plaza. South of Trinity Church on Beaver Street is the city's oldest, and still one of its finest restaurants, Delmonico's. Its contribution to the stability of the Stock Exchange is as considerable as any financial institution in the neighbourhood.

As one moves uptown, the financial district gradually merges with the political administration of New York; not by any means an incompatible arrangement. Here, south of Foley Square, are City Hall, the Municipal Building (the office of the city's administration), and the main courthouses. The present City Hall (it is the third) between Broadway and Park Row dates from 1811. It was built in the classical European tradition, but later modified to suit simpler, more democratic New World tastes. This style has since become known as 'American Federal'. The nearby City Hall Park is an expanse of green with a very chequered history, having at various times been the scene of riots, a public execution site, a madhouse and a graveyard.

The City Hall dates from the start of a boom period in New York's history when ideas and styles of building were imported from Europe in a wholesale way. The steady stream of immigrants brought with them the traditions and styles they had known at home. While they, for the most part, were too poor to build for themselves, they provided a pool of skilled talent that could realize the extravagant dreams of the rich who during the early decades of the 19th century, were beginning to discover Europe and acquire a greed for all its cultural trappings.

*Right:* This view of Trinity Church has hardly changed in 80 years. It was nearly as closely framed by the canyon-like gorge that is Wall Street in the 1890s (*below*) as it is today (*above*).

New Yorkers returned home fired with the thought of building their own Italian palaces, French chateaux, neo-gothic follies and every conceivable variation of classical Greek, Roman (even Egyptian) masterpieces. Houses and public buildings of any and every style were erected; Roman next to Victorian, both facing something Venetian. Often all three were combined in the same building. With complete disregard for the centuries of history and the diverse cultures that were being sandwiched in this way, the rich of Manhattan set about building.

For reasons of their own, the rest of the city's population were not slow to join the rich in their never-ending task of transforming Manhattan. Repeated outbreaks of fire and yellow fever in the narrow, overcrowded streets of the older parts of the city were a tremendous incentive for people to move uptown to newer and more fashionable neighbourhoods. Also, newly arrived immigrants tended to settle in the old, low-rent areas and drive out the earlier inhabitants who were appalled at the prospect of living next door to babbling foreigners.

*Left:* The rich of late 19th-century New York, and there were plenty of them, lived in ostentatious splendour in massive brownstone mansions along Fifth Avenue – then dubbed 'Millionaire's Row'.
*Below:* The narrow, neo-Georgian houses of Greenwich Village lend it the colourfully chaotic charm for which it is renowned.

This pattern of ever-shifting neighbourhoods has been characteristic throughout New York's history. It continues to this day.

Greenwich Village and the Bowery sprouted during the 1820s to house the expanding population from downtown. However, the utterly unplanned growth of New York that had so far been the rule was at last coming to an end. In 1807 the City Councillors appointed a group of commissioners to tackle the problem of the city's growth. They eventually devized a geometrically planned grid system of avenues (running north to south) and streets (running east to west) on the basis of which the rest of the island was to be surveyed and laid out.

One not unconsidered result of the new grid system was an explosive real estate boom. In the ensuing speculation, numerous New Yorkers pocketed small fortunes, among them Jacob Astor, the millionaire, who is reputed to have claimed on his deathbed that, had he been able to relive his life, he would snap up every available inch of land in Manhattan.

The opening of New York's first railway, the Harlem Railroad, in 1831, contributed to the city's rapid expansion by linking such small outlying villages as Bloomingdale, Yorkville and Harlem with the lower portion of Manhattan and adding them to the list of potential development sites. By now, great sections of the island were being measured out in block lots that were being built on as quickly as men and material could be brought to the site.

The feverish activity was fuelled by an astonishing population growth that in the 30 years prior to 1850 saw the city more than quadruple in size. Every ship that arrived in the harbour seemed to disgorge a stream of immigrants. In one year in the mid-1820s, some 22,000 Irish alone disembarked.

The majority of the newly arrived were next to penniless. They settled either in the crowded and squalid slums of the old downtown areas or else squatted in marshy, mosquito-ridden land in shanty towns that stretched toward the area later to become Central Park. The contrast between their misery and the elegant town houses going up around Washington Square could not have been more extreme, yet it well reflects the air of confusion and social upheaval that marked New York's expansion.

Throughout the first half of the 19th century, the major buildings erected in New York were all copied from one kind of European design or another and were usually executed in marble or the much-loved brownstone. But by the 1850s, a new and more functional style of building began to appear. The real estate boom in the city created such perennial shortages and delays that speed was everything when putting up a building. If corners could be cut by building simply and keeping decorations down to a minimum, then they were sure to be taken. In any case, there seemed little reason why department stores, offices and warehouses had to be elaborately dressed!

*Above:* The heyday of Manhattan's docks is past. With the steady shift of port activity to New Jersey, great tracts of waterfront have been left to decay slowly. Where street traffic has been siphoned off by expressways, whole neighbourhoods have been isolated.
*Left:* The 'El', a steam train running on elevated tracks, was part of New York's first rapid transit system begun in the 1870s to ease downtown traffic congestion.
*Right:* In later years, the line was electrified.

Simultaneously, American love of gadgetry and labour-saving devices was being applied to building methods. In particular, prefabricated sections and cast-iron structural skeletons helped to make building techniques far more efficient. They also introduced a distinct native style of architecture, the cast-iron building. What perhaps most appealed to New Yorkers was that these buildings not only were easy to erect but could be just as easily dismantled and reassembled elsewhere.

Cast-iron construction caused a major revolution in architecture. It did away with the need for sturdy walls and massive supporting columns and allowed much wider and longer window spaces. One of the most famous of the new buildings was the Haughwout Building (1857) at Broadway and Broome Street. Supposedly the first-ever office building with elevators, it was a direct ancestor of New York's best-known invention – the skyscraper.

A reaction to Manhattan's pell-mell expansion set in during the years immediately prior to the Civil War. Led by the *Evening Post,* a growing section of the public began campaigning for a check to the mindless growth spawned by the grid layout of the city. Commercial building was felt to be devouring every last inch of the island without the slightest consideration for the people living there. The need for recreational amenities resulted in the establishment of a commission that included, among others, the writer Washington Irving and the newspaper editor and poet William Bryant.

The outcome of their work was the setting aside of some 840 acres of parkland right in the middle of Manhattan. Designed by Olmstead & Vaux, Central Park was begun in 1859 and finished 20 years later. It was laid out with painstaking attention to detail and when complete, included ponds, meadows, paths to ride and walk on and even a zoo.

*Above:* The advertisement that became a landmark; the inveterate chain-smoker of Times Square has been puffing away for years.
*Right:* In the building boom of the late 19th century, thousands of cheap apartment blocks were erected all over the city. To save money and space, iron fire escapes were slung over the front of the buildings.

*Right:* The Statue of Liberty, the symbol embodying the hopes and ideals of a young nation, stands facing out to sea in New York harbour.

*Far right:* The Staten Island Ferry, long famous as the cheapest ride in New York, offers a scenic cruise across the Upper Bay from the tip of Lower Manhattan, past the Statue of Liberty to the borough of Staten Island.

While the Civil War had a devastating impact on the south of the United States, for New York it was a time of unchecked growth. Property values doubled between 1861 and 1865, railroads and banks prospered and the Stock Exchange, ever a faithful barometer of the times, boomed. New buildings mushroomed and Fifth Avenue became transformed into a two-mile boulevard of mansions known locally as 'Millionaire's Row'.

By now, the crowding in Manhattan had generated enough pressure for the population to start spilling across the river to Brooklyn and Queens, areas which were fast losing their country status and becoming sprawling dormitory suburbs, although it was not until 1898 that Manhattan and the outlying boroughs of the Bronx, Staten Island, Queens and Brooklyn were joined to form Greater New York, now the largest city in the world. The need to link them with Manhattan was acute and a series of bridges across the East River was begun; the most famous of them all was the Brooklyn Bridge. Begun in 1867, it took 16 years to build. People at the time marvelled at its twin gothic towers of masonry and its single, cable-hung central span arching gracefully across the river; they recognized it with pride as being a symbol of America's enormous energy and enterprise.

As a centennial birthday gift from France to the United States, and a token of the longstanding friendship between the two nations, the idea of a gigantic Statue of Liberty, embodying the American ideals of democracy and freedom, was conceived. The French sculptor, F. A. Bartholdi, was sent to New York. One glance at the city's harbour decided his site. The statue was to be placed on a little island off Lower Manhattan but looking out towards the mouth of the harbour – a perpetual welcome to all who arrived by sea.

Bartholdi returned to France and cast the outer skin of the statue in copper sheeting; it was supported by an inner skeleton of steel designed by Gustave Eiffel (famous for the tower in Paris). In 1885 the statue was shipped to America and, in October of that year, officially unveiled by President Cleveland. The statue depicts the Goddess of Liberty clothed in flowing robes. Held high in her right hand is a torch symbolizing liberty while the left hand holds the Declaration of Independence inscribed on a tablet. At her feet lie broken shackles, symbols of defeated tyranny. The statue and its base stand more than 300 feet high and together weigh some 225 tons. Inside is an elevator and a set of stairs allowing access to the viewing platform in her crown. As an idea of the scale of the Statue, the length of the right arm alone is 42 feet.

Despite this grand statement, New York was still suffering from real and urgent problems. If the spread to the suburbs represented one solution to overcrowding, equally inventive alternatives were being found within the constricted area of Manhattan itself. The most significant innovation to deal with the city's housing shortage was the apartment block. First introduced in 1869 by Richard Hunt, the idea was an immediate triumph. One of the earliest and most successful apartment buildings was The Dakota, a sprawling luxury block with a deliberate Renaissance chateau-look, overlooking Central Park at 72nd Street and built in 1884. It has always been one of the most fashionable addresses in the city, particularly among noted people in the arts.

Apartments were a housing solution for the rich and middle classes; but for the poor a different sort of building was devised – the tenement. The first were erected as early as 1835. As Louis Mumford writes in his book *Sticks and Stones,* they were a means of 'producing congestion, raising ground-rents, and satisfying in the worst possible way the need of the new immigrants for housing'. By the late 1870s, a standardized tenement design, known as the dumb-bell, had emerged; shaped like a dumb-bell, the interiors were so narrow that the flow of fresh air was virtually impossible. Some survive to this day in the crumbling districts of the lower East Side and in the Bronx.

*Left:* Behind the glittering facade, acute social problems beset the city of New York. The extremes of wealth and poverty are never more than a few blocks apart.
*Right:* The scale of the past and of the present; scarcely a century ago St Patrick's Cathedral overshadowed mid-town Manhattan. Today, skyscrapers dwarf its ornate splendour.

214

By now, the transformation of the New York skyline was gathering momentum. The technique of erecting steel-framed buildings, combined with elevators and improved heating and ventilation systems, heralded a radically new concept in architecture. It provided the ideal solution to New York's chronic shortage of land, finding room in the sky where none existed on the ground. Although the idea of building tall was not new (complaints about the canyon-like streets of Lower Manhattan had been heard since the 1850s) technological limitations had previously restricted buildings to approximately five storeys. Now, with the advent of steel-frame buildings, the sky was quite literally the limit.

One of the first buildings to possess the characteristic slimness and soaring elegance of a skyscraper was the Flatiron Building, erected in

1902 on 23rd Street at the corner of Broadway and Fifth Avenue. Others soon followed turning the city into the forest of steel and concrete for which it is world famous.

Early skyscrapers, such as the Chrysler, Daily News and Woolworth Buildings, still kept a certain amount of decoration on their façades but since then, simpler and more stripped-down designs have become the rule. Today, the 'International Style' predominates. Its characteristic features are great unadorned rectangular slabs of glass and aluminium or steel.

Since World War II, New York's population has reached a plateau and now hovers fairly steadily around the figure of eight million. But this overall stability hides a tremendous shift in the make-up of the population. Throughout the 1950s and 1960s, a mass exodus from the inner city to the suburbs took place. Predominantly middle class and white familites moved away and their place was largely taken by a massive influx of poor southern blacks and Puerto Ricans. The results of this shift are very marked indeed, for the 1,700,000 population of Manhattan is now more than ever divided between the very rich and the very poor, each in their own ghettos.

The most visible signs of this imbalance are the grim decaying slum areas of Harlem, the south Bronx and parts of Brooklyn. Though unlikely to be visited by the average tourist, they serve as a stark reminder that New York is not all flashiness and glamour.

However, the problems that haunt New York are shared in some degree by many of the greatest metropolises. In New York they are significantly offset by the vibrantly cosmopolitan life the city attracts. Perhaps it is just a cruel paradox that a city with such seemingly insoluble social problems should also be one of the most alluring, vibrant and exciting places in the world.

*Left:* Nightfall, and the city becomes transformed into a world of glittering lights. The tempo of life picks up again after dusk and a new world of excitement beckons.
*Below:* A token will take you anywhere into the tiled underworld of New York's subway system; nowadays half-hidden beneath the fantastic hieroglyphics of spray-on graffiti.

# Reaching for the Sky

At the turn of the 20th century the combination of a massive
population explosion, rocketing real estate prices and revolutionary
developments in the construction industry (not to mention big
business's hunger for prestige) resulted in a breathtakingly simple
solution to the overcrowding problems of Manhattan. Americans
began building up higher and higher creating the world's most
renowned skyline.

The history of the skyscraper is hard to disentangle. An
acknowledged forerunner is the Haughwout Building (488 Broadway),
a department store built from prefabricated cast iron sections,
completed in 1857, and boasting the first fully operational 'elevator'.
One of the earliest and most distinctive skyscrapers is the Flatiron
Building (1902). Built to match exactly the tapering corner lot of
Broadway and Fifth Avenue, the aptly named Flatiron rises 20 storeys.
While the exterior has neo-rennaissance pretensions, the inner
construction, a firm steel frame, strikes a new note. This building
method set a new style to which there seemed to be no limits. Ten
years later, New York saw the towering 60 storey Woolworth Building
(233 Broadway) with its fancy neo-gothic style tiered crown, being
completed.

But the real boom in skyscrapers came with the roaring 1920s. The
stunning art deco style of the Chrysler Building (42nd St and Lexington
Ave) completed in 1930 and reaching 1048 feet to the tip of its spire is
proof enough. The steel used in its construction is said to be the
hardest ever forged. The 102 storeys of the Empire State Building (350
Fifth Ave), completed in 1931 with its seven miles of lift shafts and
floor space capable of housing 20,000 workers, remained unequalled
for nearly half a century. The 86th floor observation deck still gives a
memorable view of New York.

Skyscrapers were sprouting faster than anyone had imagined. No-
one disputed the force, power and energy of the single unit, its pride
and exalted attitude, but the maze of streets below was becoming a
living nightmare. In 1940, 14 years of planning came to fruition in the
Rockefeller Center (Midtown, between Fifth & Sixth Ave). Thirteen
buildings were erected around a central plaza on a 17 acre site. The
landscaped walkways and plazas set out to prove that the human
element could still be combined with a high rise, high density
commercial precinct.

But it was only after World War Two with the use of materials such
as glass and aluminium that the skyscraper became the delicate long
slim structure that we recognise today. No more mixing of outward
styles, but simply an elegant building standing alone, a symbol of the
efficient, no-trimmings modern world. The United Nations (First Ave
between 42nd and 48th St) completed in 1953, and designed by an
international group of architects, relies heavily on these principles.
Also noteworthy are the Manufacturers Hanover Trust Bank (510 Fifth
Ave), a steel structure completed in 1954, covered by a glass curtain
wall, revealing the inner workings to all passers-by; the Seagram
Building (375 Park Ave), a sheath of brown glass set back from the
street; and the stunning Number '9' West 57th St—a mirrored column
which begins with a curve from ground level.

There have been criticisms too—the Pan Am Building (200 Park Ave),
a 60 storey high slab of concrete with a now unused heliport on its flat
roof, is said to have added too much traffic to the Grand Central
complex without introducing any compensating amenities.

But perhaps the ultimate building in New York is the modestly

The view from the street in downtown Manhattan is one of soaring perspectives that threaten to overwhelm with their gigantic scale.

219

*Left:* The Flatiron Building takes its name from its resemblance to this widely used household utensil. Since 1902, it has been one of the most unusual-looking buildings in the city.

*Below:* The terraced central plaza of the Rockefeller Center is transformed from a skating rink in winter to an outdoor café in the summer.

*Right:* The name Rockefeller has never been synonymous with understatement. The statue of Atlas, here framed by the International Building – one of the 13 skyscrapers in the Rockefeller Center – might well be a symbol of the family's all-embracing business activities.

named World Trade Center with some nine million square feet of office space devoted to—world trade. Its twin, 1302 feet towers dwarf even the Empire State and from the observation deck there is a splendid view of the city and a panorama that, on a clear day, extends some 50 miles into the distance.

The New York skyline is certainly not a testimony to human responsibility and planning, but the sight of so many towers jostling to be seen cannot fail to take your breath away.

GRACE

*Left:* Since 1975, the World Trade Center has captured the prize of Tallest-Building-in-New York; and it goes without saying that that includes the rest of the world. Incredible as it may seem, a mountain-climbing enthusiast actually scaled the building in the summer of 1977 – and was arrested for trespassing!

*Above:* The sloping flanks of 'No. 9' West 57th Street make this stunning skyscraper one of the most beautiful in the city.

*Right:* Clearly visible in the burnished facade of one skyscraper is the reflection of its neighbour directly opposite.

*Far left:* The Woolworth Building is one of the city's oldest skyscrapers.
*Left:* A view of the top of the Empire State Building, once the world's tallest skyscraper.
*Below:* The third highest skyscraper in New York is the Chrysler Building ornately Art Deco in design.

# Serving to Please

No matter what you want to buy, no matter how obscure your tastes, you will be satisfied in New York. Although the city is tottering on the brink of bankruptcy, evidence of wealth and luxury abounds.

It might appear masochistic to have your competitors all around you, but New York shopkeepers seem to have a marked preference for this kind of set up. 'Diamond Row' (along 47th St) is the market for 80 per cent of the entire US trade; the shops are simply furnished though crammed with spectacular jewels. The Flower Market (along 28th St) houses more than 1,000 florists, while a third of all the clothes sold in the US are manufactured in the Garment District (a 30 block area between Fifth & Seventh Ave, 28th & 38th St). The traffic here is a nightmare of overloaded clothes rails whizzing past, driven by young apprentices. The Fur District handles 90 per cent of America's furs.

For books and handicrafts visit Greenwich Village – although the midtown bookstores of Brentanno's, Scribners and Doubleday should not be missed; small art galleries abound and crowd the ten block area of Madison Avenue around the Whitney Museum.

For curios and exotic spices visit Chinatown; for pastas, Little Italy on the East Side. New Yorkers have an obsession about food; the city is a gourmet's paradise of delicatessens – don't miss Zabars (Broadway & 80th St) for a cornucopia of cheeses and cold cuts.

But the wholesale districts and neighbourhood shops are only one side of the picture. In New York, everything is big, the variety is stunning, and ease of access is of the utmost importance. Hence the popularity of the department store, a style perfected in New York, gigantic complexes which offer a wealth of top quality goods.

Bloomingdales (Lexington Ave, 59th St) is famed for its superlative household department and food store. For women's clothes, visit Saks (Fifth Ave, 50th St) to find boutiques devoted to all the great names in design; for bargain hunters, try Alexanders (next door to Bloomingdales). Macy's (Broadway, 35th St) with its excellent toy department, is the biggest store of them all – and in New York being biggest is just as important as being best. FAO Schwarz (Fifth Ave, 58th St) carries nothing but toys; Abercrombie & Fitch (Madison Ave, 45th St) excels in sporting equipment; for men's clothes, visit the renowned Brooks Bros (Madison Ave, 44th St). But for gimmicks, extravagances, and outrageous gadgets (the world is surely a better place since the invention of the square egg maker!) drop into Hammacher Schlemmer (145 E 57th St).

From the great shops to the grand hotels, size and opulence still predominates. A private luxury bathroom, water or vibrating bed, colour TV, air conditoning and special iced water taps and bar are standard features in most top class hotels. The Plaza is perhaps the grandest in the city, run in the European tradition, where the staff remember the guest's name. Traditional sumptuous decor enjoyed by the élite who stay there also characterizes the St Regis Sheraton. The renowned Waldorf Astoria and elegant Regency Hotel with its Louis XIV style suites both rank among the greats. Newcomers, such as the New York Hilton, with its 2150 rooms built in an international luxury style, exist side by side with the famed Algonquin, steeped in the culture of the 'Round Table' dinners, where 'personalities' still enjoy cocktails in the pannelled lobby.

But just as vast department stores exist alongside the smaller shops, so the grand hotels vie with the smaller establishments. The Chelsea Hotel breathes an air of gentility from another age with its fancy wrought iron balconies and fading gothic style.

The greatest shopping street of them all, Fifth Avenue, is crowded with exclusive boutiques, expensive department stores, bookshops, jewellers and toyshops.

Food has the status of a minor religion in this city; and for many New Yorkers, paradise is the neighbourhood 'deli'. Wherever you go, there are people talking food, thinking food, selling food and, above all, eating it. For many, the ultimate in *al fresco* dining is at a street corner vending cart.

*Below:* The jostling weekday crowds on Fifth Avenue make leisurely window shopping a nightmare. A quiet Sunday stroll is the only way to take in the sights at a relaxed pace.

*Left:* The Waldorf-Astoria on Park Avenue, with a guest list straight out of *Who's Who,* is the ultimate in the grand hotel tradition.
*Below:* The Lexington, with more than 800 rooms, epitomizes a modern, unpretentious style of hotel.
*Right:* The magnificent Plaza Hotel, overlooking the southern end of Central Park, recreates a grand European tradition with its imposing, chateau-style atmosphere.

*Left:* Neighbourhood restaurants may be as simple as this diner; but the tradition of fast food, served in huge portions, survives even here. *Below* and *right:* Shopping in New York ranges from the grand – Tiffany's is one of the most fashionable jewellers in the city – to the cheerful stalls of a street market. Orchard Street on the Lower East Side is a mecca for Sunday bargain hunters.

# The Almighty Dollar

If there is any truth in the saying 'money makes the world go round', then New York wins an uncontested prize for the rate of its spin.

Although the city itself is in dire financial straits, nobody finds it strange that one of the greatest concentrations of wealth in the world should also be found here. Roughly one fifth of the 500 biggest businesses in America have their headquarters in New York. The financial district around Wall Street is a hive of banks, trust companies, insurance corporations, public utilities, railway and shipping concerns, stock brokers and exchanges. So great is the prestige of a Wall Street address that companies are willing to endure crippling rents of up to 600 dollars a square foot; the highest in the world as any superlative-loving New Yorker will hurry to let you know.

Here, in Lower Manhattan, the financial district faithfully preserves the original dimensions of New York. The narrow and hopelessly chaotic maze of streets traces out what were once 18th-century lanes and paths. During the day, the pavements are crammed with a solid phalanx of office workers who vanish uptown and to the suburbs at night, leaving the area eerily deserted.

Unlike the shopping and cultural heart of the city, which has moved north over the years to the midtown area between 14th Street and Central Park, the financial district still retains its links with the port—New York's traditional reason for existence. Though Manhattan is faced with vigorous competition from New Jersey, the port is still going strong and is easily the busiest in the country. Every year some 20 million tons of cargo pass through its 23 miles of harbour installations.

Yet for the distilleries, oil corporations, car manufacturers, airlines, publishing and broadcasting giants with no historical links with the port, midtown Manhattan acts as another centre of gravity. The broad boulevard of Park Avenue—divided by a neat centre lane of greenery—and the Avenue of the Americas (still called Sixth Avenue by the locals) are lined with the opulent steel and glass monuments that some of the most powerful and influential companies in the nation have built as their headquarters.

Here too is Madison Avenue, the street made famous by the advertizing trade; although few companies now have their addresses here. American advertizing developed the art of selling as big business in its own right; perhaps there is no better measure of its success than the raw figures of what is bought and sold annually in New York—an estimated 100 billion dollars worth of trade. Buying and selling, that is the preoccupying activity of most New Yorkers. Relatively few work in

The claim that 'what is good for business is good for America' is rarely as aptly expressed as in the smoked glass windows of this sleek limousine in the heart of the financial district.

manufacturing. The largest such industry, the garment business, employs about a quarter of a million people. It is easily overshadowed by the four million office workers who staff the financial, trade and service industries.

Yet the true nature of commercial New York is not to be found in the gleaming office blocks of the midtown giants. Tucked away inconspicuously throughout the city are tens of thousands of small, struggling entrepreneurs. The average size of a New York business is 15 people. Small may not be beautiful when compared to the plush elegance of the big and wealthy, but it is still very much the name of the commercial game.

*Above:* The littered floor of the New York Stock Exchange proclaims it the world's busiest. As many as 35 million shares a day have been traded here.

*Left:* If nothing else, the classical columns of the New York Exchange are a reminder that, in the 20th century, it too is very much a temple.

*Right:* Yet another of the great public monuments of the 19th century is the US Treasury Building, again reflecting New York's preference for dressing up financial institutions as classical Greek temples.

*Above left:* Typical of the Seventh Avenue Garment District are the delivery men who shuttle around the neighbourhood towing trolleys loaded with cloth and finished clothes. On the empty return journey, they push-ride the trolleys with a reckless skill that has earned them the name 'Seventh Avenue aviators'.

*Left:* What the Garment District handles today, America wears tomorrow. Nearly a third of all the clothes bought in the United States originate here.

*Right:* The only subject that rivals New Yorkers' preoccupation with getting rich is the problem of staying that way. The protection business is a major industry here. In a city with almost a quarter of a million reported robberies a year (barely the tip of the iceberg), people are obsessed with alarms, locks, safes and burglar defences of every kind.

239

*Above:* Kennedy International Airport is America's third largest port, land or sea, in the value of the goods that it handles. Millions of dollars of small costly items such as bullion shipments, diamonds and works of art pass through here daily.
*Right:* Where else but in the city which claims to be the world's richest would the biggest bank vault be found? The vaults beneath the Chase Manhattan Building are almost the size of a small football pitch and are protected by doors weighing some 40 tons.

# Side by Side

Manhattan is a melting pot of nationalities. As early as the 17th century, more than a dozen different languages were spoken on the island. Undaunted by the arduous sea journey, the appalling food, brackish water, filth and frequent deaths, settlers from all over the world continued to flood into New York in search of a new beginning.

As late as a century ago, more than half the inhabitants of Manhattan had been born outside the USA. Each shipload fed a small community which jealously protected its traditions. These traditions blended together to form the New Yorker we know today, though the original communities still survive in tight groups all over the island.

Emigration to New York first acquired tidal proportions in the 19th century with the large influx of Irish fleeing political unrest and famine at home. By 1870, one fifth of the population of Manhattan was Irish. A little later, waves of Italian peasants arrived from Naples and Sicily, while Jews escaping from persecution in Eastern Europe also helped to swell the throng.

Needless to say feuds soon sprang up between the newcomers and the more established. Most noteworthy were the battles between the Irish, German and black communities. The Italians, on the other hand, tended to stick together; their close family ties engendering the notorious Mafia network. The Jewish community was perhaps the most ostracized, having to suffer both Catholic and Protestant dislike. Today, New York hosts nearly half a million Italians, some 200,000 Irish, 300,000 Germans and Austrians, and a Jewish population of more than two million.

At the turn of the century, the first blacks began to settle in Harlem, so named by Peter Stuyvesant after a town in the Netherlands. Previously a fine residential area, Harlem began to decline with the influx of immigrants from the south who arrived with little money and poor chances of finding decent jobs. The area decayed as unscrupulous landlords allowed apartments to become delapidated tenements in which high rents led to even further overcrowding. Today, violence and discontent is a daily feature in Harlem, and whites are definitely not welcome there. During the 1950s, Puerto Ricans began to settle in East Harlem, a colourful though again poor and badly decaying area of the city known more recently as Spanish Harlem. The combined population of blacks and Puerto Ricans in New York today numbers nearly three million.

Considerable evidence of different cultures can also be seen in downtown Manhattan. Moving north from the financial district, you soon reach Chinatown, crammed with authentic restaurants, tea houses and of course laundrys. Here, even the telephone boxes have pagoda roofs and are adorned with Chinese characters. Though at one time racked by virulent Tong feuds, the community of around 20,000 Chinese today lives in relative peace. The high spot of the year is the New Year celebration, a festival of dragons, lanterns and dancing.

A print of the scene that greeted new arrivals at Ellis Island recalls the hardships of their passage to a new life. At its peak, up to 8,000 immigrants a day, seven days a week, were cleared through the receiving station here.

Nearby in Little Italy, a similar national festival for San Gennaro, the patron saint of Naples, is held every year in September when a statue of the saint, covered in dollar bills, is paraded through the streets. In East Village, you will discover a real hodgepodge of races and creeds with Jewish delicatessens jostling with Greek markets and Italian pasta shops, interspersed with a variety of churches.

There is a small community of Hungarians between 70th and 78th Street along Second Avenue, and a Scandinavian conclave across the East River on Brooklyn Bay Ridge. The Irish are dispersed throughout the city although much in evidence on the green tinted occasion of St Patrick's Day in mid-March. The Greek Independence Day Parade takes place in April and the Puerto Ricans are out in force in June.

Other villages, not solely formed by ethnic groups, also exist in Manhattan. Greenwich Village and Chelsea are havens for artists and students complete with French style cafés and craft shops. The vast warehouses of the SoHo area (South of Houston St) make excellent studios for painters and aspiring film-makers and overspill into NoHo (it had to be North of Houston St!), an area more renowned for its art galleries and chic restaurants. On a more sombre note the Bowery, the 'skid-row' of Manhattan, is a miserable area of alcoholics, drop outs, doss houses and pawn shops.

Each community or village in New York is distinct. They are often closed to outsiders who can only peer at the cultural trappings. Perhaps the melting-pot image is the wrong one for New York. A fruit salad of peoples and cultures is more appropriate where the pieces, although mixed together, manage to stay very distinct.

244

*Left:* Chinatown flourishes in Lower Manhattan like some odd transplant from the Orient; but the pagoda phone box is a distinctly American touch.

*Right:* In recent years, the slums of Harlem have become the almost exclusive preserve of New York's black community.

*Below:* In the Lower East Side, European-style street markets, that once catered solely for the city's immigrant population, continue to flourish.

*Below:* The abandoning of the Bowery for more fashionable areas led this once bustling area to decline and become the last refuge of the city's all too numerous down-and-outs.
*Below right:* The annual St Patrick's Day Parade brings New Yorkers claiming Irish descent out by the thousands for a boisterous stroll down Fifth Avenue.

# Cultural New York

Culture can be measured in many different ways. Switch on a television set in New York and select a programme from one of 14 different stations or turn on the radio and flick through 40 broadcasts, including ten foreign language stations. Or else, walk along Broadway around Times Square through a district that contains more than 30 theatres; for museums and art galleries wander up Fifth Avenue or browse through some 40 odd small, private galleries and dealers along Madison Avenue between 74th and 84th streets and any number of others around the SoHo-Greenwich Village area.

Millions of dollars are made available to the arts every year in New York, most from private subscription. The city is by far the leading cultural centre in the United States. For music lovers, a visit to the famed Carnegie Hall (West 57th St & 7th Ave) is a must. The hall was built by Andrew Carnegie, the Scottish born steel millionnaire and is the former home of the New York Philharmonic. It is famous for its excellent acoustics. The present home of the Philharmonic is the giant arts complex known as the Lincoln Center. The six buildings that comprise it are visited by more than four million people people a year and house the New York State Theatre, the Opera House, the Vivian Beaumont Theatre, the Julliard School and a library and museum of the performing arts.

But New York does not only offer the fine arts. On a more popular level of culture there are also places such as Radio City Music Hall. Built as part of the Rockefeller Center in the 1930s, the main auditorium can seat up to 6200 people. Here, movies are shown along with a spectacular show that includes the Rockettes, a 36-strong precision-dancing chorus line, who to this day are Radio City's greatest attraction.

The New York Public Library on Fifth Avenue and 42nd Street houses more than seven and a half million volumes and has a priceless collection of rare manuscripts, while the Museum of the City of New York (Fifth Ave & 103rd St) traces the history of the city from its Dutch beginnings to the thriving metropolis it is today. A sample of the past can also be enjoyed at the Fraunces Tavern (Pearl St & Broad St) in Lower Manhattan. This tavern, now a restaurant, was first opened in 1762 and was witness to George Washington's farewell to his officers at the end of the War of Independence.

Museums abound in New York. The vast American Museum of Natural History, with more than 40 acres of floor space, is the biggest in the world. It contains an astounding collection of animal life and its exhibits portray each creature in its natural setting. A library, daily lectures and a splendid jewel collection—including the famous Star of India sapphire—are merely added attractions. The museum is a fascinating place showing everything from fossil skeletons to reconstructions of the South American rain forests.

The Metropolitan Museum of Modern Art (Fifth Ave & 84th St) which opened in 1880, is arguably the greatest museum in the country. It houses a collection of more than one million objects of art that span the entire 5000 years of civilized human culture. The Cloisters at Fort Tyron Park, is a branch of the Metropolitan that houses a splendid collection of medieval art.

The Frick Collection (East 70th St & Fifth Ave) is open to the public in Henry Frick's sprawling 19th-century mansion. It is a superlative collection of paintings, furniture and other furnishings. The Whitney Museum (Madison Ave & 75th St) covers the contemporary art scene from 1900 while the Museum of Modern Art (53rd and Fifth Ave) has a

The giant spiral seashell that is the Guggenheim Museum, houses a splendid permanent collection of over 4000 works of modern art.

collection of modern work in every medium from cinema to
photography and design. It is entirely financed by subscriptions and
public donations.

Occasionally, the buildings which house the art treasures are as
intriguing as the works themselves. One such place is the Guggenheim
Museum (Fifth Ave & 89th St) designed by the renowned architect
Frank Lloyd Wright. The museum is a strange looking cone of
concrete, rather similar to a spiral shell. Visitors walk through the
exhibit down a continuous ramp, starting at the roof and making their
way to ground level.

*Below:* The vast foyer of the World Trade Center is an ideal setting for art exhibitions.
*Right:* A view of the cylindrical interior of the Guggenheim reveals the spiralling ramp that winds from the top to the ground. Natural light floods down the central well from the glass-domed roof.
*Below right:* Outside the Chase Manhattan Plaza in the heart of the financial district stands the beautiful sculpture *Trees* by Debuffet. A Japanese water garden lies in the Plaza's sunken courtyard.

*Left:* Overlooking the central plaza and fountain of the Lincoln Center for the Performing Arts are the ten-storey arches of the Metropolitan Opera House. The Lincoln Center houses a philharmonic orchestra, a ballet company, two opera companies, a theatre, a music school and a magnificent library of the arts.
*Below:* The Gallery of Modern Art.

255

*Left:* The South Street Seaport Museum on the East River is one of the all too rare attempts to preserve something of New York's past. Here, a number of 19th-century sailing ships are moored.

*Below:* The vast brownstone front of the American Museum of Natural History, the largest of its kind in the world, overlooks west Central Park. Its exhibits range from natural history to outer space, diamonds, and ancient civilizations.

*Right:* The choice of cinema in New York is next to limitless. Here, in an advertisement for the updated version of King Kong, the great ape keeps abreast of changing times by unhesitatingly choosing the new World Trade Center, as opposed to the original film's Empire State Building.

# A Sporting City

A Sunday stroll in Central Park will go a long way to dispelling the illusion that Americans are a nation of spectator sportsmen. The park roads, which are clogged with traffic during the week, are doubly choked with a swarm of determined joggers and cyclists; up to 50,000 cyclists alone come into the park on a busy weekend.

Physical fitness has, in recent years, become an intense national obsession and the weekend is peak time when the fitness cultists come out in full force. Nor do they go lacking for things to do since the list of sports facilities in Central Park verges on the encyclopaedic.

If jogging and cycling are not to your taste, you can choose boating, soccer, horseshoes, squash, baseball, football, field hockey, bird watching, model yachting, fishing, kite flying, lawn bowling, handball — the list goes on to include some 24 different sports and activities.

In winter, ponds are turned into outdoor skating rinks if the weather is cold enough and indoor rinks stand ready if it is not. Aside from the Central Park rinks, there is also an outdoor one in the Central Plaza of Rockefeller Center where piped music encourages the skaters.

Aside from the 800 acre expanse of Central Park, New York is not well supplied with places of greenery. True, there is the long tongue of Riverside Park running the length of the Upper West Side and Battery Park on the extreme southern end of the island, also the very beautiful Prospect Park in Brooklyn. But for the most part parks are afterthoughts to the city's main development. New York compensates to a degree with a number of so-called 'vest pocket parks'. Dotted around the city are odd little lots that have been set aside for people to sit and rest, and children to play. Here they are benches and potted shrubs; one park on 53rd Street even has an artificial waterfall.

The high temples of American sport are the big arenas such as Shea Stadium in Queens and Yankee Stadium in the Bronx where tens of thousands of fans regularly gather to watch football and baseball games. Of the two sports, perhaps baseball has the greater aura associated with it — although football pulls the bigger crowds. Yankee Stadium, for instance, even has a corner set aside for a monument to Babe Ruth, the homerun king of the 1920s. His record of 60 homeruns in a single season remained unbroken from 1927 to 1961.

Baseball is a relatively slow-moving game during which as much spectator energy goes into abusing the players and chatting with each other as into watching the game. The activity in the stands is nonstop with the fans acting as human chains to pass hotdogs and drinks along the bleacher rows. Halfway through the game an odd ritual occurs known as the seventh inning stretch. As one, the fans rise and begin yawning and stretching in the effort to recirculate the pooled blood on which they were sitting, back to the rest of their body.

Aside from the vast ball parks, there is also the famous Tennis Stadium at Forest Hills where professional and international tournaments are played. The highpoint of the tennis season comes in early September when the US Open Championships are held here. In the middle of Manhattan, at 33rd Street and Eighth Avenue, is the venerable Madison Square Gardens, an arena where every sport from track and field events to indoor bicycling, boxing, wrestling and even

Baseball, described by one English visitor as 'frantic cricket', is arguably one of America's greatest inventions. Here, caught in the act, a swinging batter strikes out.

258

The vast bowls of Shea Stadium *above*, and Yankee Stadium *below*, can each hold the population of a small city. They are the home grounds of New York's professional baseball and football teams.
*Right:* As if the term 'rat race' were not literal enough, New Yorkers by the thousands have donned sweat suits and taken to jogging around Central Park.

circuses are held. New York's professional basketball team, the Knickerbockers, play all their home games here as do the New York Rangers hockey team. Soccer, known throughout the rest of the world as football, has only recently become a popular sport in America. The city's professionals, the Cosmos, play at Downing Stadium on Randalls Island.

New York is also a thriving centre for horse racing. Thoroughbred events are held at the Belmont and Aqueduct tracks in Queens. The most important race of the year is the Belmont Stakes for three-year-olds, held every year in mid-June.

What could be more logical in a city as richly endowed with museums as New York than a museum to sport. Just such a place exists, the Boxing Hall of Fame at 120 West 31st Street. Here are photographs, fightbills and countless mementos of all the great boxers.

Three great American sports;
baseball, football and lifting hotdogs
to the mouth.

MADISON SQUARE GARDEN CENTER

*Left and below:* Madison Square Gardens from outside and within. In this great indoor stadium, professional boxing, hockey and basketball tournaments are regularly staged.
*Below left:* The sunken central plaza of Rockefeller Center is converted into an ice-skating rink in winter.

# New York Off-Duty

Like everything else in New York, the pleasures that can be sampled here are not so much unrestricted as limitless in their range. The answer as to what New Yorkers do when they are not at work is, like the classic Yiddish joke, simply another question; namely, what do they not do?

Everybody loves a parade and few cities enjoy so many as New York. The tickertape procession through the narrow streets of Lower Manhattan is a long-established tradition and a standard welcome accorded to astronauts, sportsmen, popular politicians and returning heroes of every description. As the parade goes by, the windows of every stock-dealing institution in the district are opened to shower down long ribbons of tickertape and general office confetti by the ton.

Aside from these one-off occasions, there are a good dozen major parades that are annual events. The Polish community of the city takes to the streets every year at the beginning of October to proclaim its ethnic virility. The Irish take advantage of St Patrick's Day on 17 March to stage a similar display. However, the Irish presence in New York has acquired a certain legendary status of its own which results in the parade taking aboard a remarkable quota of Jewish, Chinese, Puerto Rican, Italian and even English Irishmen, all happily proclaiming their suddenly remembered heritage with emerald green ties, hats and umbrellas. Even the white line down the centre of Fifth Avenue gets painted green for the day. To paraphrase a famous commercial, you don't have to be a New Yorker to be Irish – but it helps.

Hundreds of thousands of people turn out to watch the Thanksgiving Day Parade late in November that is staged by Macy's Department Store, the city's largest. The parade is a carnival of colour and noise with marching brass bands, vast floats and enormous balloon figures of famous television and children's book characters. This annual event, which began in 1924, has become less a celebration of Thanksgiving than the starting signal for the Christmas shopping season and so it is not unintentional that the parade comes to an end outside – where else – the main doors of Macy's.

One must turn to Central Park, however, to get a real idea of New Yorkers busy relaxing and there is no better way to do it than from the inside of one of the hansom cabs that can be hired at the Grand Army Plaza end of the park. Here on summertime Wednesday and Saturday mornings children's story tellings are held by the Hans Christian Andersen statue. On the other side of The Mall, in Sheep Meadow, the New York Philharmonic plays to crowds of up to 100,000 while at the Woolnan Rink rock concerts offer an equally well-attended alternative. The open-air stage of the Delacorte Theater is the venue of an annual 'pop-Shakespeare' Festival where Elizabethan drama becomes transformed by Brooklyn accents and sharp-tongued urban humour to something trendy but totally 'New York'. And, as if improved Shakespeare were not enough, a small section of the park called the Shakespeare Gardens has been devoted to nothing else but the botanical products referred to in his plays.

The traditional New York greeting for returning celebrities is a tickertape parade through the city streets. Here, Apollo astronauts are welcomed back from their trip to the moon.

*Above:* A scene by The Belvedere, about 1900, when Central Park was still *the* place to be seen taking a walk, or preferably riding or driving a coach. Until 1899 cars were banned from the park.
*Right:* The 843-acre rectangle of Central Park, which has been called New York's 'green lung', is one of the few places in the city where New Yorkers can relax, away from the hustle and bustle of the crowded streets.

Central Park also has a delightful zoo. It is a favourite place of lunching New Yorkers, although strolling and eating is such a widespread habit in the city that it must not be mistaken as having any bearing on the time of day.

More spectacular, and just as enjoyable, is the enormous Bronx Zoo with its 3000 inhabitants and a staggering food bill to match. Here you can thrill to the sight of a real Afro-Bronx game park where the animals are allowed to wander in 'safe-areas' rather than be enclosed in cages.

*Right:* Summertime brings crowds of youngsters flooding to see the marionette theatre in Central Park.

*Below:* The stone chess tables of Central Park attract a steady flow of dedicated enthusiasts seeking fresh air and concentration. Several hundred such tables are scattered in parks around the city.

*Above:* Patches of greenery abound in New York, but they take some finding. New Yorkers make use of every inch of free space to tend their little plots.

*Left:* A perennial favourite for tourists and natives alike is the ferry ride to the Statue of Liberty. The trip across the harbour affords a superb view of the city skyline and a glimpse of the more than 700 miles of dockland.

*Below:* The evening of Independence Day, July 4th, is celebrated with a magnificent display of fireworks over the East River.

# The Lights of Broadway

The pulse of New York quickens at night when the blaze of lights that illuminate the city give it a renewed surge of energy, like some fresh flow of adrenalin. Not only Broadway, but every one of the bustling main avenues becomes transformed into a 'Great White Way' vibrating with life and excitement.

The heartbeat of New York's nightlife pulses — at least in myth — around the entertainment district of Broadway. Here, in the immediate neighbourhood of Time Square are some 36 theatres. In actual fact, very few are on Broadway itself and the majority cluster in the side streets between Broadway and Eighth Avenue and 44th to 53rd streets. Every year, on average, some 70 new productions open on Broadway; quite a staggering figure in these days of escalating costs and shrinking attendance figures. But Broadway is showbusiness — the term very faithfully captures the American approach to entertainment — and like all businesses must have plenty of new products to sell.

In Times Square there stands a statue of the Irish songwriter, George Cohan, who immortalized the entire area with his famous 'Give My Regards to Broadway' melody. The song is an odd blend of the overblown sentimentality that seems to go hand in hand with the brash, glittering face of Broadway and the ruthless and often cynical business practices that prevail behind the scenes. Still, credit must be given where it is due. Cohan, and other writers like him, did manage to give 42nd Street, one of the least romantic names imaginable, a genuine magic of its own. Unfortunately, 42nd Street has come down a long way over the years. Today it is a rather sleazy strip of porn cinemas and related cultural delights.

New York theatre life does not just begin and end with Broadway. A thriving 'off-Broadway' tradition (New Yorkese for Greenwich Village) survives in that part of town where there are some 20 or so well-established theatres presenting a great deal of the most exciting new work to emerge in America. Theatres located elsewhere in the city tend to be lumped as 'Off-off Broadway'. The term tends to describe their place in the financial pecking order as well.

The mid-town theatre district is also filled with dozens of restaurants and clubs that tend to be rather expensive. Yet these are the watering-holes of the rich and the famous who come to New York to be seen from all the world over. The parade of expensive limousines making their way east after the theatres empty is as impressive today as it has always been.

Another style of nightlife flourishes down in Greenwich Village, long the 'Left Bank' or Bohemian district of the city. Here are found dozens of small cafes, restaurants and clubs, each selling its own specialized blend of culture. But whether a place is a jazz, rock or folk club (or any combination of the three) the distinct sound emerges from rather similar conditions. The clubs are cramped, smoky, low, dingy and, for the most part, jam-packed.

The throbbing heart of the night-time beast is New York's famous landmark, Times Square, here ablaze with light and life.

274

New York bars are very much institutions in their own right. In recent years there has been a minor cult in bars for specialist clienteles such as gay bars and singles bars – the latter are sometimes disparagingly termed 'meet-markets'. The typical New York bar, if there is such a thing, as typical, tends to be dark, intimate, somewhat over-refrigerated by the air-conditioning and serves what could easily be the best drinks in the world.

The cocktails are, inevitably, delicious and served by dedicated barmen who work with painstaking care and craftsmanship. Bars range from the very basic neighbourhood variety to the opulent plushness of the best hotels, where, in a time honoured tradition, a pianist will appear from time to time and tinkle the keys – just like a 1940s movie.

*Below:* What watches are to Switzerland, the chorus line of the Rockettes was to America – the ultimate in precision. They were the star attraction of Radio City Music Hall, which closed in 1978 after 45 years of business.

*Above and below:* Broadway, the
'Great White Way' of song and
legend, as it looked at the turn of the
century and as it does today, nearly
80 years later.

The sound of the city – in clubs throughout Manhattan, every variety of music can be sampled; from the new wave sound of Patti Smith to the country and western style of Dolly Parton.

# More than Manhattan

For most of the world, New York is synonymous with Manhattan. To a visitor this may seem logical, but the average New Yorker is quite likely to feel otherwise. For a start, more New Yorkers live outside Manhattan than in it and a great many grudgingly regard it as thriving at their expense.

Manhattan is linked to the outer boroughs by a network of tunnels and bridges and even by ferry. Every morning millions of workers stream across the 16 bridges and through the four tunnels that connect Manhattan to the rest of the world, only to stream back across and through them and desert the island at night.

Brooklyn, an area of more than 76 square miles and numbering some three million inhabitants is virtually a city in its own right. Originally a low-lying marshland of cranberry thickets and birds, it is today a major shipbuilding centre. The borough is not without strife and the appalling slums of Brownsville offer a stark contrast to the elegant dwellings on Brooklyn Heights. Places of interest include the 520 acre, meticulously landscaped Prospect Park, the Botanic Gardens with their section for the blind where plant descriptions are in braille, the Brooklyn Museum and a special Children's Museum.

The longest suspension bridge in the world, the Verrazano-Narrows Bridge, joins Brooklyn to Staten Island. The island lies five miles from Manhattan out in the Upper Bay. It can also be reached by a 20 minute ferry ride from the Battery at the tip of Manhattan which affords a splendid view of the financial district and the Statue of Liberty. This is one of the cheapest ways to enjoy the scenery of the city. The highest point on the 58 square miles of Staten Island is the 410 feet-high Todt Hill. Richmond, once the main town of Staten Island, is well worth visiting to see the authentic 17th-century village which includes one of the oldest schoolhouses in the United States. Also worth a visit is the Conference House at Tottenville where negotiations to end the War of Independence took place between the British and the Americans in 1776, and the house in Rosebank where the famous Italian freedom fighter Garibaldi lived.

To the northeast of Brooklyn lies the borough of Queens, established in the 17th century and patriotically named after the wife of King Charles II. By far the largest borough in New York, it encompasses an area of 121 square miles. Queens is the site of Kennedy Airport, with its 30 miles of runways for international flights, and La Guardia Airport from where domestic flights originate. Queens is also a great centre for leisure activities and is the site of Forest Hill Tennis Stadium and Shea Stadium where up to 80,000 spectators can enjoy football and baseball games. For nature lovers, there are the beautiful Rockaway Beaches in the south and the famous Jamaica Bay Wildlife Refuge, the largest urban nature reserve in the world.

The world's longest suspension bridge, and New York's newest, is the Verrazano-Narrows Bridge that spans the channel connecting the harbour to the Atlantic Ocean.

New York's northernmost borough is the Bronx, named after the
Danish immigrant Johannes Bronck's 500 acre farm that once existed
here. The Bronx, with its population of more than a million and a half,
is a rather delapidated suburb yet it boasts a large expanse of green in
Van Cortlandt Park. Well worth a visit are the New York Botanical
Gardens with their splendid collection of tropical and wild flowers, and
the Bronx Zoo – the largest in the United States with 3000 animals. The
famous Yankee Stadium which accommodates up to 54,000 sports
fans is also of interest if for no other reason than it being the home of
the 'Bronx cheer'.

Of all the boroughs, perhaps the Bronx has the most traumatic
problems. As the middle classes have fled the area and the tenement
sections have been left to decay, parts of the Bronx have acquired an
almost lunar landscape of gutted and abandoned buildings. Arson, the
most recent blight, accounts for some 30 fires a night.

Manhattan, home of the city administration, has often been accused
of self interest by its satellite boroughs. But strong local loyalties
continue to exist, even in the face of the now all too familiar urban
problems, and the outer boroughs still have much of interest for the
visitor to New York.

*Below left:* La Guardia airport in northern Queens today handles all domestic flights, sharing the air traffic with John F. Kennedy International Airport.
*Right:* The sprawling waterfront installations of Brooklyn are the location of one of the world's great shipbuilding industries.
*Below:* The magnificent Bronx Zoo is laid out in an 'open-plan' arrangement that allows animals great freedom of movement.

*Left:* The extensive network of bays and rivers that intersect Greater New York afford plenty of opportunity for boating.

*Right:* Brooklyn and Queens are dotted with housing projects designed specifically for lower or middle income families. Others are purpose built for bachelors or the retired and semi-retired. They are often complete miniature towns in their own right.

*Below:* Jones Beach on the Atlantic Ocean, visible here beyond its open-air marine theatre, is one of a number of superb beaches within a short distance of downtown New York.

# Away from it All

Ringed as it is by an expressway and linked to the rest of the world by some 20 bridges and tunnels and a network of fast roads, escape from Manhattan is a simple matter. An hour's drive from the centre of town can leave you deep in the country or, for that matter, standing in a traffic jam in the endless suburbs of Long Island – you have to choose your route with care.

The Atlantic is within easy reach of New York at a number of places, the nearest of of all being in Long Island. Here there are dozens of beaches. Those to the south are sandy and directly on the Atlantic while the ones to the north are shingle and face the Long Island Sound. Closest to the heart of the city is Coney Island at the southern tip of Brooklyn, and still on the subway line. Here is found one of the most spectacular amusement parks in the country. It is also the home of a hotdog of the same name covered with a delicious spicy sauce.

Further east, on the long finger of land belonging to Queens that borders the Atlantic, are the Rockaway Beaches, the only places in New York City to have good surfing. Continuing in the same direction to Wantaugh on Long Island one arrives at Jones Beach State Park. It has one of the busiest beaches on the entire East Coast with facilities to accomodate more than 100,000 bathers. In addition to swimming and fishing, there is a two-mile boardwalk, numerous restaurants and a Marine theatre where water-show spectaculars are staged.

Many New Yorkers, when they speak of leaving the city, immediately think of making their way to the beautiful rolling countryside that lies to the north. A delightful day's excursion is a trip along either side of the Hudson River Valley

After leaving Manhattan, drive north along the east side of the river toward Lyndhurst, one of the many fabulous riverside mansions that were erected here in the 19th century. Built in 1835 by William Pauling and later purchased by the notorious railway tycoon Jay Gould, this rambling gothic revival castle is today a museum cluttered with expensive furniture and tapestries of every description. The house is set in a magnificent 67 acre parkland of woods, gardens and greenhouses. In July and August every year, outdoor concerts are held here.

To the north one passes the Philpsburg Manor, an early 18th-century manor house and mill. Further on is the Old Dutch Church of Sleepy Hollow, the region where Washington Irving set his famous *Legend of Sleepy Hollow*. Throughout this area are numerous other estates such as Caramoor and Bosobel, although both are surpassed by the extraordinary Dick's Hilltop Castle, an actual model (though unfinished) of the Alhambra in Spain. The money ran out before it was completed, proving that even American millionaires have bottoms to their pockets. The sumptuous Vanderbilt Mansion and Hyde Park, the home of President Franklin D. Roosevelt, are also found in this region.

In summer, the beach and spectacular amusement park at Coney Island draw New Yorkers by the thousands seeking to escape the muggy heat of the city.

The drive along the west bank of the Hudson is less mansioned but equally pleasant. The road leads through Bear Mountain State Park, an expanse of lake and forest wilderness barely 40 miles from mid-town Manhattan. To the north of the park lies West Point, the famous academy for future American military leaders, and Washingtonville, the site of the country's oldest winery. Here too is Duchess County, famous for its long tradition of antique auctions. The dealers here trade almost exclusively in country-style furnishings (called Americana) of every description. Auctions are usually at the weekends.

To the north are the Catskill Mountains, New York's year round playground. This beautiful region abounds with luxury hotels and resorts providing every holiday diversion from sports to big-name nightclub acts. It is even rumoured that one of the best hotels employs a staff psychiatrist for New Yorkers who cannot bear to leave the madness of the city behind.

*Right:* The thoroughbred races at Saratoga Springs, a town also famous for its spa, were once a 'must' event in the social calendar of New York society.
*Below right:* Between the state capital of Albany and New York City, the Hudson River flows through almost Rhine-like scenery.
*Below:* Stifling humidity drives New Yorkers out of the city each summer to the fresh air of the Catskill and Adirondack Mountains.

*Above:* Central New York State, a country of rolling mountain wilderness, is but a few hours travel from downtown Manhattan.
*Right:* To the north of the Hudson Valley lies the meandering expanse of Lake George, long a favourite summer resort of New Yorkers.

# Introduction to Paris

Paris, 'the city of light', is unique, It is a place of wonder and magic and almost unbelievable beauty: a city of the past, with a history that spans 2,000 years, yet a city of the future too, the largest of continental Europe and with the highest population density now of any great city in the world.

No other capital provides such a fascinating amalgam of old and new. Where else is it possible to look up from cobbled medieval streets, with houses untouched from the 12th century, to a skyline which monuments from the ancient Pharaohs share with ultra-modern cloud-reaching structures.

Paris is unique in more than a merely physical sense. For it has an atmosphere, a mystique, that is entirely its own. The city of song, the inspiration of some of the world's finest painting, its fascination is extraordinary. No other city is so revered or longed for. No other across the centuries has so drawn writers, sculptors, musicians, painters and intellectuals from every corner of the globe. They are still there today – at the boulevard cafés, taking a Pernod and watching the non-stop theatre that is the streets of Paris, with their unmatched blend of businessmen and bohemians, students and bourgeois, and the most chic and elegant women in the world.

Above all, perhaps, Paris is a city of synthesis: an intellectual and cultural centre, the meeting place of tourist and pleasure seeker, the capital of high fashion, yet equally a mighty commercial, financial and industrial nexus and the political and administrative hub of France – of which it contains one sixth of the population and reflects all that is most vital and best.

What is the essence of Paris? In the end it is indefinable: a wisp, a scent, a magic that this book will help you experience. For, blending fresh new photographs with succinct and specially written text, this sets out in informed and easy-to-follow sections just what it is that makes Paris so special. Its beauty, glamour, verve...as much as any book can, we have captured them for you here. So, as the French say, come in and be welcome.
'Bienvenue à Paris!'

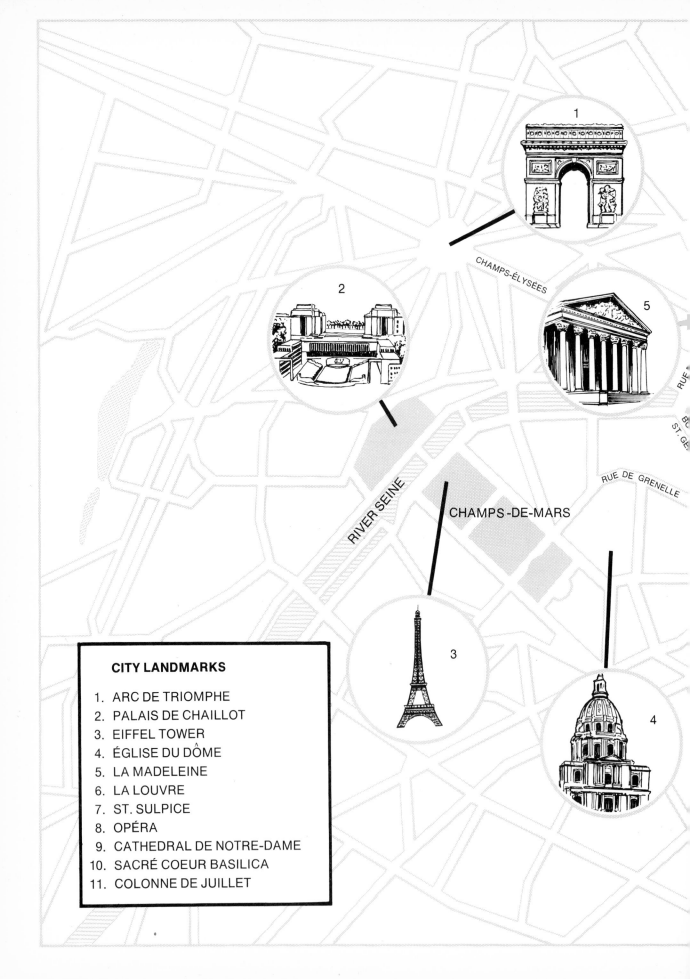

CHAMPS-ÉLYSÉES

RUE DE GRENELLE

RIVER SEINE

CHAMPS-DE-MARS

**CITY LANDMARKS**

1. ARC DE TRIOMPHE
2. PALAIS DE CHAILLOT
3. EIFFEL TOWER
4. ÉGLISE DU DÔME
5. LA MADELEINE
6. LA LOUVRE
7. ST. SULPICE
8. OPÉRA
9. CATHEDRAL DE NOTRE-DAME
10. SACRÉ COEUR BASILICA
11. COLONNE DE JUILLET

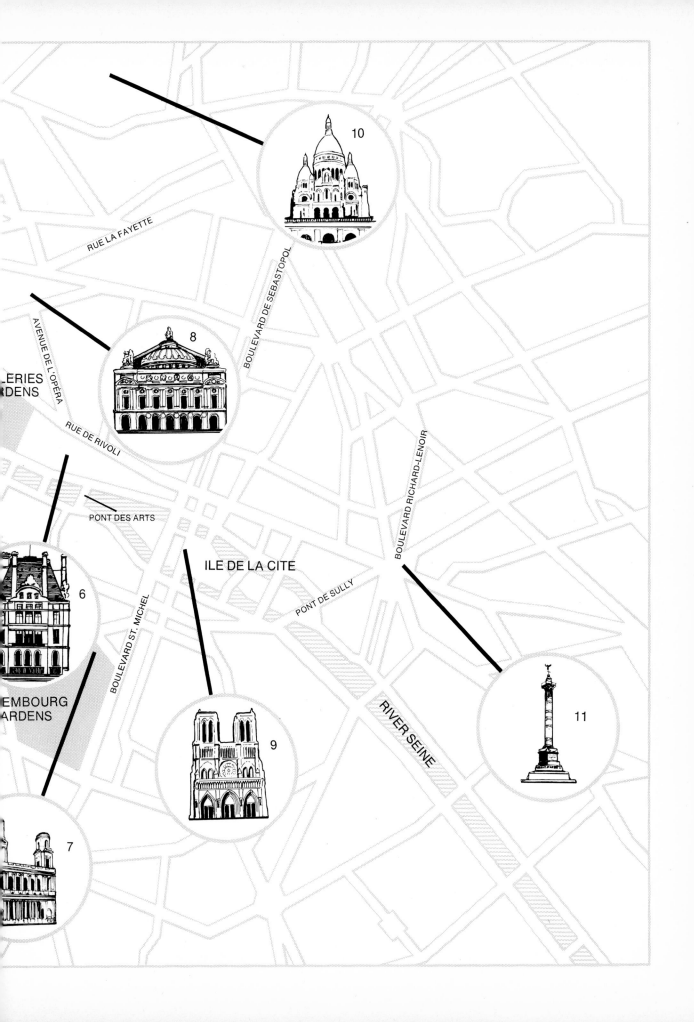

# Setting the Scene

Paris, the capital of France, has a circumference of about 22 miles and a population of some seven million people. The city is situated in northern France, on both banks of the River Seine, 107 miles from the sea. It lies in what is known as the *Bassin de Paris,* a saucer-shaped, once-marshy area between low hills or 'buttes', the highest of which, the *Butte de Montmartre,* is only 423 feet high. Through this basin, in a great loop, the Seine flows for nearly eight miles.

The river is of incomparable importance to the city. Not only does it provide Paris with so much of her character, beauty and charm, it is largely responsible for the city's very existence. For it is here, on an island in the river, that it all began.

Paris dates back into the mists of history, but the first definite mention is made in the *Commentaries* of Julius Caesar, whose troops effortlessly conquered what was then a small village on an island in the Seine. The year was 53 BC. Little is known of that village and almost nothing remains. Marshy land extended to the hills around it and its inhabitants, a primitive Gallic tribe named the *Parisii,* lived by fishing and worshipped the river as a god. Caesar's troops named the island village *Luticia* and formed a settlement there. Although they stayed 400 years, their original name did not last. A military milestone of the year 307 is firmly engraved: 'the city of the Parisians'.

With the Seine providing a ready-made moat, the Romans were not slow to see the commanding position and strategic advantages of their island. They built a fortified camp on it and, where the church of Nôtre Dame now stands, a temple. By the 2nd century, the city had spread from the island—now called the Ile de la Cité—to the south bank and it was here the Romans erected their villas, a forum and baths.

Even in those early days, as a town of around 1,000 inhabitants, Paris was a prosperous place. A focus of highways coming from south and north, on an easily navigable river, there is no doubt that the town's geographical location influenced its future development as a capital city. The plains around it offered good travel routes and rich soils for agriculture and vineyards. A toll was probably charged on passing travellers. And money was brought in by retired officers. But the prosperity of the young city was not to last.

The might of Rome was waning, her empire near disintegration and, towards the end of the 3rd century, the Germanic tribes flowed out across the country—and put much of the city to fire and the sword. The settlement on the south (or Left) bank was destroyed and the inhabitants retreated to the island. This they fortified, using stones from their ruined homes to build a rampart. Life became increasingly precarious and, by the end of the 5th century, the hordes of Attila the Hun were marching directly on the city.

It was then that Geneviève, a young Christian and forerunner of Joan of Arc, rallied the people of Paris and saved the city from destruction—apparently, by the power of her prayers, turning aside the Huns at the last moment, so that they went on to Italy instead. As a result, Geneviève became the patron saint of Paris in her lifetime. And has remained so since.

It seems the prayers of Geneviève, however, were not so strong on a second occasion. In 508 Paris was taken by Clovis King of the Franks, whose kingdom Francia gave its name to all France. Geneviève soon converted him to Christianity and, establishing Paris as his capital, Clovis began the process of building churches and monasteries that was to continue through the centuries.

296

Soaring above the narrow, cobbled streets of Montmartre, the spacious white stone basilica of the Sacré-Coeur, built in the 19th century.

297

The dangers of attack were not over, though, and down the years barbarians subjected the city to periodic raids. In 845 the Norsemen looted it and in 885 they sailed up the Seine again—this time with 700 ships. The Parisians, under Count Eudis, were ready, however. They had repaired the old Roman walls and though the Norsemen laid seige to the city for ten months, Paris did not fall. And when in 911 a treaty was finally agreed with the Norse leader, Rollo, the Parisians were free from the threat of pillage. A new era was about to begin.

In 987 Hugo Capet became king of France. In doing so, he founded a new and powerful dynasty which made Paris its seat and paved the way to the city's future greatness.

In the 11th century Paris expanded onto both river banks: on the Left, schools and colleges scaled the Mont Sainte Geneviève, re-occupying the areas first settled in Roman times; on the Right, a new suburb developed as tradesmen built houses and stores.

*Left:* Sunset over Montmartre, once a small village and now a vital part of Paris.

*Below Right:* Part of the historic market of Les Halles. Dating from the 12th century, the covered part of the market alone once took up ten acres. Much of it has gone now and what is left, given over to modern redevelopment.

In the 12th century, under Louis VI and Louis VII, there were massive transformations. The city now consisted of three parts: the original Île de la Cité with its government buildings, the palace of the king and the cathedral; the Left Bank with its convents, schools and colleges—almost a city in itself with its noisy students, swarming masses of beggars, artisans and thieves; and, finally, the Right Bank inhabited by merchants and seafarers.

By this time, Paris had already developed the same basic structure that exists today: the seat of authority in the old town on the island; the academic and cultural section on the Left Bank; and the commercial and business section on the Right.

Outside the city villages appeared: Montmartre, Saint Denis and the monasteries. A frenzy of building began and it is from then that the oldest churches in Paris date: Saint Germain des Prés, Saint Julien le Pauvre and, most important of all, the incomparable Nôtre Dame.

King Philip Augustus (1180-1223) has justly been called 'The Father of Paris' because of the changes his reign brought to the city. They were many and great. The king built Les Halles as a central market; he built aquaducts to supply water, hospitals to tend the sick; repelled by the stench of the mud of the streets of the Cité, he ordered them paved. In 1190, about to go off on a crusade, and wanting to secure his city's safety, Philip decided to surround it by walls. Outside those walls, on the Right Bank, he built a formidable fortress, the Louvre, to defend the city against attack from the west.

But Paris was a hive of activity in more than just the physical sense. For it was at this time that the schools and colleges on the Left Bank federated themselves into an organization known as the University—and proclaimed self-government. They won royal privileges in 1200 and a university charter (the oldest in the West) was granted by Pope Innocent III in 1215. Throughout the 13th century the University of Paris grew and became the leading academic institution in Europe. As many as 20,000 students lived in the Left Bank colleges, forming within the city an autonomous borough, which, because Latin was its main language, became known as the Latin Quarter—as it is still known today.

It is estimated that during the 13th century the population of Paris rose to an astonishing 100,000 inhabitants. This was an age of expansion in every way. The soaring palace chapel of Sainte Chapelle was built (in only 33 months to house relics already at hand in Paris). And in 1257, under the patronage of St Louis IX, Robert de Sorbon created what was to become one of the world's most celebrated centres of culture and which still bears his name, the Sorbonne.

In the 14th and 15th centuries the growth and prosperity of Paris faded, for this was the time of the *Hundred Years War* (1339-1453).

It was a time too of the weakening of Royal authority—and, led by Etienne Marcel, a rich clothier, the merchants challenged the crown and sought reforms that amounted almost to parliamentary government. When, in 1356, the French army lost the battle of Poitiers to a much smaller English force and King John II of France was taken prisoner, Marcel led a revolt against John's son, the Dauphin Charles. Occupying his mansion as headquarters, Marcel established a form of municipal government there, but it was short-lived. Marcel himself was murdered in 1358.

When Charles duly came to the throne, to guard against further revolts, he moved the royal residence to the fortress of the Louvre which he enlarged and partly rebuilt. He also built round the Right Bank a new and larger belt of ramparts and the greatest construction of that period—the mighty fortress of La Bastille. Despite these efforts, pestilence, the effects of the war and finally capture by the English, did much to deplete the city's wealth and population.

The English held Paris for 16 years and during this time it was virtually abandoned. Joan of Arc tried to eject the invaders in 1429, but was wounded outside the Porte Sainte Honoré. Close by that site there stands a statue of her today.

Perhaps the city's lowest ebb was the year 1430—when Henry VI of England was crowned king of France in Nôtre Dame. But the occupation did not last and within five years the French had won back control of the city. Charles VII returned to the capital in 1436 and began the task of reconstruction. Things were in a sorry state for some time after, though, and a diarist of the year 1439 could note that in one month that winter 14 people between Montmartre and Saint Antoine were eaten by wolves.

*Top Left:* Just one of the many lovely and historic houses that border the Seine on the Ile Saint-Louis.
*Above Right:* The golden statue of the warrior saint Joan of Arc in the Place des Pyramides. Joan died in 1431, but people still make pilgrimages to her statue.
*Bottom Right:* The Petit Palais. The museum here houses a magnificent collection of modern and ancient works of art, including Eastern and Far-Eastern masterpieces.

PAVILLON RICHELIEU

*Left:* The Pavillion Richelieu – just part of the mighty edifice of the Louvre, begun as a fort in the 12th century, but today one of the greatest museums in the world. *Above:* The serenity of the Tuileries gardens, named after a tile factory which once occupied the site.

The hundred years or so to 1572 were on the whole a period of peaceful growth, with the capital spilling out far beyond the walls of Charles V. During this time the Italian Renaissance made its influence felt. The city took on a new look.

The Louvre was rebuilt—transformed from a medieval fortress to a Renaissance Palace; the Tuileries gardens were laid out after the Italian manner; a new and much more splendid Hôtel de Ville was put up. The Pont Neuf was begun and the first stone quays appeared along the banks of the Seine. And on both banks too rose many elegant mansions. Everywhere the spirit of the Renaissance was expressed in the lines of the buildings, in the search for space and light.

The 17th century was the *Grand Siècle,* the great century. During these years grand and regal Paris was born. Towers gave way to Italianate domes that changed the skyline. Large, imposing buildings grew up, wide prospects, magnificent palaces. From 1600 until the Revolution in 1789 Paris was the greatest metropolis on the Continent, a centre of brilliant culture and fabulous wealth. Each new king made his contribution to the city's monuments.

Development went faster on the Right Bank than the Left and the fashionable section extended west to what is now the Place de la Concorde, while the more popular grew out to the east. Under Henri IV and Louis XIII new avenues and boulevards were laid out and lordly mansions mushroomed throughout the Marais district, replacing the old merchants' residences. Upstream from the Ile de la Cité, Louis joined two low islands. These eventually became the Ile Saint Louis.

The Louvre was expanded by each successive king and, to its west, the Tuileries Palace enlarged and joined to it. More stone bridges were built across the Seine. On the Right Bank Cardinal Richelieu built the Palais Royal. Large abbeys and convents covered much of the Left and a new college (now home of the French Academy) was established there by Cardinal Mazarin. On the Left Bank too the queen mothers had palaces built: the Luxembourg Palace for Marie de Medicis, the Val de Grace for Anne of Austria. These palaces had magnificent gardens and increasingly, throughout smart Paris, there was space and light.

The expansion of Paris continued on an even greater scale under Louis XIV though his early years were marred by the civil war named the *Fronde* (after a catapault/sling which was used by urchins in the dry moats of the city).

Incensed by already burdensome taxes the people of Paris revolted and put up barricades in the streets. The nobility sided with them against the crown. Battles were fought inside the capital itself. And intermittently, for five years the conflict went on. It ended with Louis completely victorious—and resulted in two things: an augmenting of royal power; and a widening of the gulf that already existed between the crown and people of Paris.

Indeed, so deep was Louis' distrust of his people, that he transferred the court to Versailles, building a new palace and town. Yet none of this could long halt the development of the metropolis.

Work began again on the Louvre. The Jardin des Tuileries was transformed and, in 1667, the Champs Elysées created. The old fortifications were converted and planted with trees and the first Grands Boulevards were born. Known as the 'Sun King' for the magnificence of his court and reign in which he made France the

*Left:* The dome of Les Invalides, a complex of buildings initiated by Louis XIV in 1671 to house and care for his wounded soldiers. In a crypt directly below the cupola is the tomb of Napoleon.
*Right:* The 17th century Porte Saint-Denis, one of the city's great triumphal arches.

leading nation in Europe, Louis commemorated his victories with the gates of Saint Denis and Saint Martin, the Place des Victoires and the Place Vendôme. In his reign too the great scientific institutions emerged: L'Observatoire, the Collège des Quatre Nations and the Bibliothèque Royale. Near the end of Louis' reign the Hôtel des Invalides was built—to accommodate those wounded in his wars.

But the reign of the Sun King was not all glory. Round the Louvre itself there were slums. The people had no rights and no voice. Their poverty stood out in ugly contrast to the magnificence of so many palaces and gardens. Indeed, in mid-17th century Paris it is estimated that of the population of approximately 600,000 as many as ten percent were either beggars or thieves.

Throughout the 18th century there was a flurry of building. And though Paris did not grow much in terms of population, it greatly increased in area—with many old and ugly sections razed and rebuilt with mansions.

They lined the streets of St Germain on the Left Bank and St Honoré on the Right. This was the great epoch of perspectives, of columns and fountains and grands boulevards. The bridges were cleared of houses, the ramparts broken through, the gates destroyed. The Pont de la Concorde was built to lead to (what is now) the Place de la Concorde. The Rue Royale and the Palais Bourbon were completed. The Ecole Militaire and the Théâtre de L'Odeon came into being—and Jacques-Germain Soufflot began the mighty Panthéon.

But, though the appearance of Paris was of ever-increasing splendour, the condition of many of its inhabitants was still of medieval squalor—a condition exacerbated by the so very visible wealth of the upper strata. And it brought no comfort to the poor of Paris, as they stood barefoot and threadbare with hollow bellies, to see the gilded coaches of the rich roll by.

The people of Paris were appallingly housed, overtaxed, underfed. (In the country there were still serfs.) The contrast between rich and poor, privilege and oppression could hardly have been more acute.

Perhaps what followed could have been avoided by a more perceptive, less inflexible man, but Louis XVI was a fool. With the national coffers exhausted by war in America—and further depleted by the extravagances of his queen, Marie Antoinette—he decided to call a 'States General' (a body roughly comparable to the British Parliament, but which hadn't met since 1614) with the object of raising more money by further taxation. The Assembly consisted of nobles, clergy and commons—or Third Estate. This last group decided that it alone was representative of the people and that no taxation could be levied without its consent.

Louis ordered his soldiers to disperse the Assembly. They refused to act. Pretending to agree to the Third Estate's demands, Louis then secretly called up foreign regiments of the French army. When the news of this reached the people of Paris, they rose.

On July 14th, 1789, in a great symbolic gesture they stormed the grim-looking royal prison of the Bastille, took it after three hours fighting—and destroyed it. Thereafter the insurrection spread through France: châteaux were burnt by the peasantry, their owners driven off or slain. Within a month the ancient system of the aristocratic order had gone and many leading princes and courtiers—those who were lucky—fled abroad for their lives.

*Far Left: Clochards,* the special vagabonds of Paris, live rough but proud, outdoors in the city. These three are taking a midday nap in the Tuileries.
*Left:* The Champs de Mars. In the background, the École Militaire, the UNESCO building, and above them the great Tour Montparnasse.

Now in a position of power, but without the knowledge of how to exercise it, the Assembly found itself called on to create an effective new system for a new age—but was unable to. Events followed each other relentlessly.

A shortage of bread struck Paris and on October 5th a famished people marched on the king at Versailles and forced him to return to the city. Lodged at the Tuileries, Louis dwelt there unmolested for two years and perhaps, had he kept faith with the people, might have lived out his days there as king. Foolishly, though, he attempted to slip away and raise an army—only to be ignominiously captured and returned to Paris. There on August 10th, he was attacked by a commune of the people, taken prisoner with his wife and children and placed in the Temple, while the people of Paris ran riot.

That was the year that the guillotine made its first appearance in the Place de la Grève in front of the Hôtel de Ville. It was later moved to the Place de la Revolution (now Place de la Concorde) and there, on January 21st, 1793, Louis XVI of France lost his life.

From that time the floodgates were opened and there seemed no finer thing than killing royalists. Through the streets of Paris rumbled the Terror with its carts full of the condemned, food for Madame la Guillotine, her appetite insatiable, hour after hour, day after day. In the 13 months before June 1794 there were 1,220 executions; in the seven weeks thereafter 1,376. From first to last there were condemned and executed some 4,000 people and it is no exaggeration to say that the streets of the city ran red and that in that 'Reign of Terror' looting and killing were the law.

308

Revolution is no builder and it was not until internal peace had been secured that Paris and her inhabitants were able to set to work and restore her beauty.

With Napoleon the city continued its evolution. And his love of splendour, of the Egyptian and Greco-Roman styles, left an indelible mark. Bonaparte lived in state in the Tuileries and during his time Paris was constantly enriched: The Arc de Triomphe was begun, the Arc du Carrousel in the Louvre completed. And so too was the church of the Madeleine—as a temple of glory. The Rue de Rivoli with its arcades was built and in the Place Vendôme a great column erected—to Napoleon himself. The Bourse (stock exchange) was constructed, also in temple fashion and the Louvre was enlarged. But Napoleon was a man of the future as well as the past and in his time the first iron bridges of the Pont des Arts and Pont d'Austerlitz appeared—as well as large cemeteries outside the busy quarters of the city, for the many dead of the new regime.

*Left:* The Arc du Carousel. Outside the Louvre at the beginning of the Tuileries, this magnificent triumphal arch was built to celebrate Napoleon's victories of 1805.
*Below:* Commanding the Place Charles de Gaulle, the 165 feet high Arc de Triomphe is one of the most glorious of Paris monuments – and one of the great landmarks of the city.

The defeat of Napoleon led to the reinstatement of the Bourbon dynasty in the person of the ineffectual Louis XVIII. He was succeeded by Charles X, but the people of Paris were conscious now of their power and when Charles started to muzzle the press they rose. And during the three glorious days of July 27-29th, 1830, students and workers, fighting side by side on the barricades, overthrew the Bourbon dynasty.

In its place they installed Louis Phillipe, but after 18 years overthrew him in turn in the February revolution of 1848. Here, once again, the people of Paris spontaneously constituted themselves as a sovereign body and took up the reins of power. The Second Republic was not destined to last long, however, and in October 1850 Louis Napoleon Bonaparte, nephew of the Emperor, secured his election as President of France—taking an oath to the democratic ideal and to regard as enemies all who attempted to change that form of government. Two years later he was emperor of France.

The reign of Napoleon III (1852-1870), even though its end saw the seige, bombardment and occupation of Paris by the Prussians, was a period of extraordinary splendour for the city.

Up to this time Paris, despite its grandeur, was in many ways still a medieval city. But now, with the aid of his prefect Baron Haussman, Napoleon quite literally took large portions of it apart—to recreate them in an image that was modern and new.

To build strategic highways and construct buildings according to Paris's economic need, Haussmann gutted the old city—paying particular attention to those poorer quarters that had in the past bred revolution. The mass of slums and small houses on the Ile de la Cité was demolished. Broad straight streets were cut through slum districts on each bank. Railway stations were built and large rectilinear streets designed around them. In the centre the Boulevards Saint Michel, Sébastopol and Strasbourg; in the west a system of avenues radiated from the Étoile and in the east from the Place de la Nation. The Latin Quarter was pierced by such streets as Saint Germain. The Opéra dates from this period and around the city a series of public parks was formed including the Bois de Vincennes and Bois de Boulogne. Not only this, the Louvre was once again extended and completed in a style to match the existing buildings—and beneath the streets an extensive sewage system built.

In short, a new and finer Paris appeared: more open, regular, comfortable, better lit and policed. By 1870, with a population approaching two million, Paris was the most beautiful and active city in Europe.

The Second Empire crumbled in the quick defeat of the Franco-Prussian War. Outraged at the news of Napoleon's surrender at Sedan (Sept 4th, 1870), the people of Paris decided to fight on alone. And for four months they managed to hold out against the entire strength of the German army who laid seige to the city. But famine finally forced its surrender. A brief occupation by the Prussians followed and then, when Napoleon had abdicated, France elected a new government—that of the Third Republic.

But the Parisians would have nothing to do with it. Independent as ever, they established a revolutionary junta—the Paris Commune. And for three months this body was to rule the city. Then the government forces advanced from Versailles.

Heavy streetfighting followed and, one by one, the barricades were overcome. But as the Communards retreated, they destroyed. They overthrew the Colonne Vendôme. They set fire to the centre of the city from the Tuileries to the Hôtel de Ville, including a good part of the

L'Opera, surely the largest and most lavish operatic theatre in the world. It was founded in 1669 and is now owned by the State.

Faubourg Saint Germain. Over 220 buildings were destroyed, among them the Tuileries Palace (which was never rebuilt) and the Hôtel de Ville, which was.

Finally cornered in the Cemetery of Père Lachaise, the Communards made their last stand where the small and tightly packed stone oratories provided some protection—though not enough. For at the end of a day's fighting 147 of them were captured, lined up against the cemetery wall and shot.

Meanwhile, the Third Republic set about making good the damage, and, in an attempt to restore Paris in world opinion, began to hold great exhibitions. To these are due the Trocadero (1878), the Eiffel Tower (1889) and the Grand Palais and Petit Palais (1900). At the turn of the century too, the great underground railway, the Métro was begun. Not long after that, Paris was once again at war.

In 1914 the German Army reached the Marne River, only a few miles from the capital. The French defended it desperately. For four days more than a million men were locked in mortal combat. As the battle came to a climax, General Gallieni, commander of the city, ordered that every taxi driver take fresh troops to the front. They did. Their action tipped the balance—and Paris was saved. And though it was later shelled by the great gun the Parisians nicknamed 'Big Bertha', the Germans never reached the city.

The post-war period that followed was a troubled one and gave small loveliness to the city. In 1919 the demolition of fortifications had begun and in their place rose rank upon rank of apartment buildings. The suburbs extended in tangles. All over Paris buildings were built of brick or cement, replacing—and much less beautiful than—those previously built in stone. Only one great work of this period can rival anything built before—the splendid Palais de Chaillot (1937). A mere four years later the Germans were occupying the city.

Although it must seem small comfort to those who endured the years of the cold and hunger of that occupation, and to the thousands of Parisians deported and killed, the judgement of history may yet conclude that occupation was a blessing in disguise. For by it the city was preserved from the devastation of modern warfare. And, above all, the bombing that in other capitals destroyed forever so much that was fine of the past.

After the war, Paris quickly resumed its rightful place in the world. Twice she has hosted the General Assembly of the United Nations and has been the seat of such well-known international organizations as NATO and UNESCO.

Although, in central Paris, little new was done in the way of building since the war, in the 1960s under Malraux's Ministry for Fine Arts, a great work of cleaning and beautifying was undertaken. Ancient monuments like the Louvre, L'Opéra and Nôtre Dame now glow with a honey-coloured freshness that belies their great antiquity. More recently too, ultra-modern works like the Tour Montparnasse and the futuristic developments of La Défense have altered the skyline. They show Paris on the move again: a great capital taking a lead once more into the architecture of the future.

This then is the background of Paris. A vital facet in an understanding of the city, for it explains much of the character, the quality, of the place, not just in terms of monuments, but of spirit.

It is a spirit that is piquant, sharp, indomitable. In the last 125 years Paris has known three revolutions, the armies of the Cossacks, the Prussians and of Adolf Hitler camped on the Champs Elysées. Now they are all gone and Paris remains, like the symbol of the eternal flame that burns below the Arc de Triomphe—victorious.

It is a fitting symbol for this city which has shrugged off conquerors, come through so much, yet retained its beauty and its character: rebellious, original, undefeated.

Some things in Paris never change – one of the city's most common sights, a woman shaking sheets from a window.

*Above:* Old comes down to make way for the new in the ever-evolving city. This particular demolition is in Montparnasse.

# Paris of the Past

Every stone in Paris is steeped in the past and the events of her long and mighty history speak out on every boulevard and street corner, through a column, a monument or an arch.

The 17th–century Porte-Saint-Denis, for example, tells of the victories of Louis XIV, who in less than two months conquered more than 40 German strongholds. Napoleon's Vendôme column has its bas-relief cast from the 1,200 cannon the Emperor captured at Austerlitz. The 3000-year-old Obelisk of Luxor in the Place de la Concorde, brought from Egypt by Louis Philippe, stands where the guillotine once stood. And the mighty, soulless mausoleum of the Panthéon is built on the site of a medieval convent – itself occupying ground where there was once a Roman temple to Diana.

Paris is a city of visible, living antiquity. And of all Paris perhaps no building is more representative than the incredible Palais du Louvre.

One of the world's greatest palaces, larger even than the Vatican, the history of the Louvre traces that of the city itself. The very name probable comes from the Saxon *Leovar,* meaning a fortified dwelling. And this is how it started: as a feudal fortress outside the island city in the year 1200. From that time on, like Paris, it grew out in strength and beauty and the massive, two-pronged-fork-shaped complex of buildings one sees today is the result of the work of 17 kings over some 700 years.

In the 14th century Charles the Wise enlarged the fortress; in the 16th, Francois I made it his official residence – and demolished the fortifications, replacing them with a Renaissance-style palace. In their turn, Henri II and Catherine de Medicis constructed the Tuileries Palace and united it with the existing structures. In 1682, however, the court was transferred to Versailles. And gradually the Louvre ran down. Little by little, squatters moved in and by 1750 the palace had fallen into such disrepair that its demolition was considered. But then came Napoleon, ejecting the squatters, restoring splendour; and clearing the slums around the palace. His nephew Napoleon III completed his work. Which left the palace as it is today? Not quite. For in 1870 the Communards burnt down the Tuileries Palace, thus opening out the western side of the Louvre to the long, lovely vistas over the Tuileries gardens and Place de la Concorde.

Nor is the Louvre any longer a royal palace – though never has it held more wealth. Today it is one of the largest, most richly endowed museums in the world, containing some of the most highly prized of paintings and sculptures – not least among which are the *Venus de Milo* and the *Mona Lisa.*

In a way the Louvre defines the very quality of historical Paris. For, despite its long and varied history and the different centuries that have made their contribution to its constuction, there is a sense of unity about it. It seems to come together as a whole. Like Paris herself, an integral and living entity.

The once notorious Palais de Justice. In its huge complex of buildings is the Conciergerie where Queen Marie-Antoinette awaited execution.

*Left:* Statue of Charlemagne, the great Frankish emperor, beside Nôtre-Dame. He died in 814.
*Right:* The 169 feet high July Column in the Place de la Bastille. It stands on the site of the terrible Bastille prison, which the people of Paris pulled down in 1789. The column itself was erected in memory of those who died in the risings of 1830 and 1848.

*Left:* The elegance of the Marais, a district reclaimed from swampland.
*Right:* The Institute of France. It was designed by the renowned architect Le Vau and built in the mid-17th century as the result of a legacy from Cardinal Mazarin.
*Below:* At any moment in the streets of Paris you may encounter splendour such as this.

IVL. MAZARIN S R E. CARD. BASILICAM ET GYMNAS F C A M D C LX I

*Above:* The tomb of the Unknown Soldier with its eternal flame, below the Arc de Triomphe.
*Above Right:* A street of the Latin Quarter – a very old part of Paris and a scholastic centre since the 13th century.

# City of Churches

Paris has been a Christian city for 1500 years and of all its myriad wonders few surpass the churches. Their variety is amazing, spanning the centuries in every conceivable style and position, nestling into the surrounding architecture or standing clear—each one a unique and beautiful jewel.

Of all the great churches of Paris, Nôtre Dame, one of the oldest , is surely the most beautiful. The first of the French gothic churches, begun in 1163 on the Ile de la Cité on the site of a Roman Temple, it is constructed in the shape of a Latin cross: 427 feet long, 164 feet wide and 130 feet high. An incredible structure for the 12th century, it took more than 100 years to complete. Over the ages since, its vast weight has caused it to sink more than three feet.

Almost as well-known, though very much newer, the white-stone basilica of the Sacré-Coeur stands, commanding the hill of Montmartre, one of the great landmarks of Paris. Begun in 1876 and consecrated in 1919, it was constructed as the result of a national subscription, to which three million Frenchmen contributed. A curious mixture of Byzantine and Romanesque styles, the church is 328 feet long, 164 feet wide and 308 feet high. Its bell, the 'Savoyarde', at more than 20 tons, is one of the largest in the world.

In total contrast is Saint-Germain-des-Prés, near the heart of the Latin Quarter, the oldest church in Paris. A fine example of Romanesque architecture, it was originally a monastic chapel of the sixth century. Destroyed more than once by the Normans, it was finally rebuilt in the 11th century. At the time of the Revolution it was used as a saltpetre store. Today St Germain holds the tomb of the great philosopher Descartes.

Far grander is the Madeleine: superbly positioned at the end of the Rue Royale, facing the Place de la Concorde. Designed along Grecian lines, it was built by Napoleon as a temple of glory for the soldiers of his 'Grande Armee' and has neither transept nor side aisles. After Bonaparte's fall, it was considered for several uses — including a railway station — before finally being consecrated a church. With a colonnade of 52 Corinthian columns 65 feet high, the Madeleine is of magnificent proportions: 355 feet long, 141 wide and 98 high.

Built in the 12th century on the site of a sixth century building, the gothic church of Saint-Germain-L'Auxerrois is uniquely famous. For this was the church that signalled the Saint Bartholomew's Day Massacre of Protestants on August 24th 1572. Today, however, its 44 glorious bells play a different tune and the church's interior is a wealth of art and stone carvings and glass from the 15th century. Right outside the Louvre, it was virtually a royal chapel and here were buried royal jesters and many of the artists patronized by the Crown.

Sacré-Coeur by night. The great white dome is visible from almost every part of Paris and dominates Montmartre at its feet.

*Above Left:* Reflections of a city of churches.
*Left:* The cemetery of Montmartre, where many famous men are buried, including Zola, Degas and Stendhal.
*Right:* The Mosque – an unexpected corner of the orient in the heart of medieval Paris.

*Left:* Nôtre-Dame's 12th century door of Saint Anne.
*Right:* Viollet le Duc's 19th century gargoyles on Nôtre-Dame.
*Below:* Nôtre-Dame from the Seine. The great church took more than 100 years to build. It was restored in the 19th century when the central spire was added.

# Gay Paree

Announce that you're off to Paris for the weekend, and people may well smile knowingly. How wrong they would be!

Paris has long had the reputation of being a 'naughty' city: it dates from the 1890s, the time of the can-can, and was confirmed in the 1930s and 1950s, when the city offered ladies shedding clothes with more abandon then anywhere else in Europe. But, alas, standards change – and Paris deserves its reputation no more.

True, the floorshow at the Lido is sumptuously staged; they still do the can-can at the Moulin Rouge; and the Folies Bergères has the longest legs (many of them English) you're ever likely to see. True, the girls at the Crazy Horse Saloon are stunning and disrobe with consummate artistry – but what are these things to the late 1970s? Certainly not 'naughty'. Indeed, in comparison with, say, Amsterdam, Stockholm – or even London – Paris today is decidedly sedate!

And yet – few cities have such an atmosphere of zest, verve, *joie de vivre*. Paris is a living testament to the fact that the French enjoy life – that they respect the right of others to, however individually – and have made of living an art.

The city never stops, never closes. There are 51 theatres, numerous cinemas, cafés, bars, the most glamorous shops, more than 6,000 restaurants. Somewhere or other, one of these is always open and, at any time of the day or night, you can enjoy a drink or meal – and what a meal that will be!

At the famous Maxim's in the Rue Royale, for instance, you will find unsurpassed food in surroundings of an elegance that has not changed since the *Belle Epoch* of the 1890s. In total contrast, the equally famous La Coupôle in Montparnasse, a railway-station-sized restaurant crammed with writers and painters and 'types', will serve you a superb and reasonably-priced meal into the early hours – if you can find a seat!

But perhaps one of the greatest charms of *'Gay Paree'* is its sidewalk cafés. They line the great boulevards; they dot the squares; you find them everywhere – and it is here that the French themselves spend so much of their time: discussing, dreaming and regarding others regarding them. Here you can enjoy at one and the same time the sights of the city and its life. Sip a *petit blanc sec* (dry white wine) or *café arrosé* (coffee with a spot of brandy) and in just a little time you will see the world go by. Indeed, in this mood much of Parisian political, cultural and artistic life has been engendered at its cafés. Those like the *Deux Magots* (magot means grotesque Chinese figure!) have long been a meeting place for philosophers, artists and writers. Even more renowned perhaps, and certainly more elegant, is the *Café de la Paix* on the corner of the Place de l'Opéra – the great original which has provided the name and model for cafés throughout the French-speaking world.

Action at the Crazy Horse Saloon! Founded in 1951 it is the city's best-known night-spot and a must for broad-minded visitors.

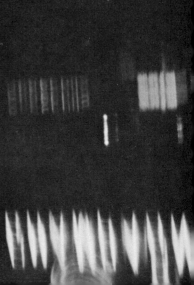

*Left:* The 19th century Moulin Rouge, where the can-can was born.
*Below:* A typically Parisian sidewalk cafe. The city is full of such places.

*Right:* The famous Left Bank cafe and meeting place *Aux Deux Magots.* Situated on The Boulevard St Germain, the cafe takes its name from the sign of a chinese silk screen shop which once stood here.
*Below:* There is always a restaurant or cafe open somewhere in Paris – 24 hours a day.

*Left:* The renowned Maxim's restaurant in the Rue Royale is the well-heeled gourmet's paradise.
*Below Left:* Paris is a city of individuals.
*Above:* French humour: the depressed-looking figure here is saying, 'I'm very funny'.
*Right:* The Parisians love to discuss life. These two old women are outside a famous fish restaurant. The bin on which one of them sits on is full of shell-fish shells.

# Paris Markets

The greatest of all Paris markets was Les Halles, originating in the 12th century, described by Zola as 'the belly of Paris' and in its heyday occupying, in covered area alone, ten acres. Today, it has gone, a victim of modernization, but Paris remains no less a thriving and ebullient trading city, with a multitude of street markets and shops — deep in cellars, in the underground, up twisting stairs, in restaurants — in the most unexpected places!

Starting at the top, in the 1st and 2nd *arrondisements* (Paris is divided into 20 of these administrative zones) you will find a quartier *luxe*. Consisting of the Rue de la Paix, de Castiglione, Saint Honoré, the Place Vendôme and the Rue de Rivoli, this is an area of supreme elegance — probably containing the finest jewellery and luxury items in the world.

At the other extreme, on the quays of the Seine and especially on the Left Bank round the Ile de la Cité, are the famous Parisian *bouquinistes*. With their large wooden book cases perched on the parapets over the river banks, each of them sells very similar-looking, second-hand books and prints.

Across the river on the Ile de la Cité is the Place Louis-Lepine, site of the Marché aux Fleurs. This is the magnificent Paris flower market. And every day of spring and summer it intoxicatingly assaults the senses with hundreds of different scents and blooms. Every day, that is, except Sundays. For then the flower market is given over to birds.

The Marché aux Oiseaux is an upsetting sight, but nonetheless an extraordinary one: for the Place Louis Lepine is filled with hundreds upon thousands of caged birds. (Far too many to a cage sometimes.) They are of every type from canaries to pheasants and of every conceivable colour. Some are even dyed!

Perhaps the most renowned of all Paris markets is the Marché aux Puces, the flea market, at Clignancourt. Here, on Saturday, Sunday and Monday, you can see just about everything imaginable in the way of second-hand goods. Spilling over the pavements, the place has immense 'colour'. Anyone who can find space and the fee can sell here. The vendors range from tramps with rubbish-dump junk, to polished professionals. It's said you can't find a bargain in the flea market, but it has been done and the thing to remember is – haggle!

As well as this, Paris has a Dog and Donkey Market; a Stamp Market; a Wine Market; a Gingerbread Fair and a Ham Fair (which also features scrap iron!). Indeed, in a sense, the city herself is one great market, for each district has at least one weekly market day and everywhere, clothing, food, flowers, and bon-bons are temptingly displayed.

The shop windows of Paris are a minor art form in themselves. The simplest *boulangerie* calls with its fresh-bake smell and appetising stacks of long loaves. And even at the most modest *boucherie* you are quite likely to see an entire pig's head — with a flower in its mouth!

A Paris street market. This one is in Montparnasse, and is typical of many throughout the city.

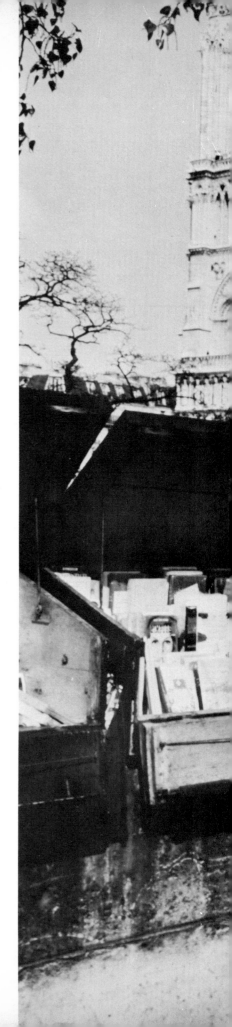

*Above:* Marché aux Puces, the most famous of all Paris markets, the Flea Market at Clignancourt.
*Right: Bouquinists* by the Seine. And just across the river, the stately pile of Nôtre-Dame.

*Left:* The Marché aux Oiseaux in the Place Louis-Lépine. This notorious bird market sells every imaginable kind of bird as pets or for the pot!

*Above Left:* A butcher and his assistant contemplate his handiwork.

*Above:* Part of the beautiful Marché aux Fleurs, or flower market, on the Ile de la Cité. On Sunday the flowers give way to the birds.

Two sides of Paris fashion:
*Below:* The vast selection of ready-to-wear clothes ın a Paris store.
*Below Right:* A mannequin displays a couturier's collection at one of the city's innumerable fashion shows.

# Cultural Paris

A harmony of old and new, of function and design, a city where on any street corner you may encounter a minor masterpiece, Paris is itself a living work of art.

From the statues of the Tuileries to the triumphs of the Musée Rodin; from the pavement artists of Montmartre to the Leonardos of the Louvre; from the Left Bank *bavardiers* to the masters of the Comédie Francaise, Paris's cultural life is unbelievably rich. And as French culture finds its quintessence in the visual and dramatic arts, it is only fitting that, in this her prime city and its environs, there should be no less than 51 theatres and 107 museums.

Indisputedly foremost among these is the Louvre. Repository of works of art from ancient Egypt and the Orient and Greece and Rome, through medieval right up to modern times, this one museum holds 400,000 treasures in all.

Then? Everyone will have their preference. The Musée du Jeu de Paume in the Place de la Concorde has a staggering collection of Impressionists; among them, Manet, Monet, van Gogh, Renoir, Degas, Cezanne — many of whom of course lived in Paris. Other museums not be missed are the Carnavalet; the Musée de Cluny; the Palais de l'Alma and the Musée Rodin. Les Invalides, where Napoleon is buried is also a museum of armour and regimental relics. The Palais de Chaillot which was built for the exhibition of 1937, also houses the Musée de l'Homme.

From the time of Napoleon III one of the great cultural centres of Paris has been the Opéra. The largest theatre for opera in the world (covering an area of 120,000 square feet) it is a spectacle in itself: even more ornate inside than out, with its sumptuous, onyx-balustraded grand staircases, multi-coloured marble foyers, magnificent chandeliers and, since 1966, a fresco by Chagall.

No look at cultural Paris would be complete, though, without a mention of the Comédie Francaise. The most important of the five Paris theatres subsidized by the State, in its foyer one can see the statues of the great dramatic writers: Voltaire, Molière, Victor Hugo, Dumas and many others. Here at reasonable prices one can 'assist' at the great classics of French theatre, the works of Molière, Racine and Corneille. Here too are performed the great moderns such as Claudel and Anouilh. But as well as all this, the Comédie Francaise has an extra importance in French culture. For more than any other institution, it enshrines ideals that are integral to French civilization, the classical ideals of patriotism, courage, courtesy, virtues of living and of language that the French esteem.

The glorious Chagall ceiling at the Opéra, the Paris home of State-subsidized opera and ballet.

*Left:* Just part of the vast architectural complex of the Louvre, the city's most important museum and art gallery.
*Below Right: Le Penseur* or *the Thinker* by Rodin, France's best-known sculptor.
*Below Left:* The École Militaire – the military academy – at the end of the Champs de Mars, where Napoleon studied.

*Right:* A portrait of Racine, the 17th century poet and dramatist, at the Comédie Francaise.
*Below:* The exterior of the Comédie Francaise, formed in 1680.
*Far Right:* A typically Parisian apartment building of the 15th *arrondisement*.

1639    J·RACINE    16

# Parks and Gardens

Paris does not have a large, centrally situated park, such as Hyde Park in London or Central Park in New York. In terms of green metres per capita, it offers less than many other capitals. Yet, wandering down its chestnut-lined streets, there is no sense of this; strolling through its glorious gardens one is amazed to find such ordered beauty and tranquility in a city. In Paris' two great parks with their lakes and woodlands, there is a feeling of being in the countryside itself.

Most used by Parisians and probably most loved of her gardens is the Jardin de Luxembourg. Elegantly stretching away in front of the Palace of Luxembourg, it extends for 57 acres of lawns, terraces, trees, fountains, fine statues and even playing fields. A public park since the 17th century, it has long been a meeting-place for students from the nearby university and the serenity of its Medici fountain has proved the inspiration of countless writers and poets.

Next is the Jardin des Tuileries, a garden of order and elegance, covering half a mile betwen the Place de la Concorde and the Place de la Carrousel, outside the Louvre. Superbly laid out in the later half of the 17th century by Le Nôtre, it consists of long sides with high, tree-planted terraces, flanking a wide central area of lawns, chestnuts,

limes and beautiful geometric flower beds. There are ponds (with trout!) a shaded children's playground, and statues absolutely everywhere: by Cosysevox, Coustou, Pradier, Le Poultre.

On the east of the city is its great park – the Bois de Vincennes. At 2,308 acres, this is the largest park in Paris. A private park since the 13th century, it was given to the people by Napoleon III and today contains the zoo – one of the finest in Europe – and several museums, woods, three lakes with islands, an Indochinese temple, a tropical garden and a floral park, displaying hundreds of different types of flowers.

More elegant than Vincennes and almost opposite on the west of Paris, is the Bois de Boulogne. Until 1852 it was part of a forest with several châteaux. In that year, though, it was given to the city by Napoleon III, who commissioned Haussmann to replan it. The wood became a vast park, inspired, it is said, by Hyde Park.

Today, with its woods and lawns and waterfalls and gardens, the Bois de Boulogne covers an area of more than 2,200 acres. The park is a favourite recreational area for Parisians, with boating on the larger of its two artificial lakes, a zoo in the Jardin d'Acclimation, horse-riding in the woods and two racecourses, the famous Longchamps and Auteuil.

Just one of the scores of glorious statues throughout the Tuileries. The gardens were laid out in the 18th century.

*Below:* This avenue in the '15th' is typical of the charm of so much of the city.
*Right:* The ubiquitous game of boule – played here in the Luxembourg gardens.
*Bottom Right:* The Jardins du Luxembourg, leading down to the Luxembourg palace, built in 1615 by Marie de Medici, wife of Henri IV.

*Left:* The famous Medici Fountain by
Salomon de Brosse.
*Below:* Statue of student resistance
in the Luxembourg Gardens.

AMI SI TV TOMBES VN AMI SORT DE L'OMBRE A TA PLACE

AVX ETVDIANTS RESISTANTS

*Left:* The fountain of the four corners of the world in the Jardins du Luxembourg.
*Below:* The early 17th century Place des Vosges is perfectly square – 354 feet long on every side – and encompassed by picturesque mansions. It is the city's oldest square.

# Modern Paris

Paris quite possibly contains and consists of a greater multitude of treasures of art and architecture than any other city. For this reason, it has been likened to one vast museum; but the comparison is invalid. For Paris is a living entity – and as such is constantly evolving. In the process a new Paris rises round the old, evoking the criticism of traditionalists for its striking modernity, yet incorporating architecture of superb design, as advanced and beautiful as any in the world.

Built for the Exhibition of 1889, the Eiffel Tower began modern Paris and in its way has still not been equalled. Some 984 feet high (except in warm weather when it can rise up to eight inches) it is composed of 12,000 metal parts fastened by two and a half million rivets. Yet it weighs only 7,000 tons and with its four 'feet' covering an area of more than two acres, is calculated to exert no greater pressure on the earth per square inch than a man does seated in a chair.

There are three floors: the first at 190 feet; the second at 380; and the third at 905. This top floor provides an unrivalled view of all Paris. On a clear day the view carries as far as 40 miles.

Much more recent, and in their way quite as striking, are the high-rise futuristic buildings erected in the 1960s and 1970s in the Quartier de la Defénse. Most notable feature among these is the vast hall of the Centre National des Industries et des Techniques, for its extraordinary swooping vault covers an area of no less than 980,000 square feet, with only three points of support.

The airport of Charles de Gaulle deserves mention, too, as the most modern in Western Europe. A triumph of logical design, it incorporates a central body, from which radiate octopoidal arms. Served by moving walkways, each of these ends in a 'satellite' hub, with which the appropriate airplane is able to make direct contact.

The massively functional high-rise housing development around the Gare Montparnasse is something of a bugbear for the critics of modern Paris. They might well have a point—were it not for the grace of the Tour Montparnasse, which soars above it all, lifting the entire complex. A slender and elegant 58 storey building, (with at its summit the most scenic restaurant in Europe, the Tour Montparnasse has, since the 1970s, become a feature of the Paris skyline, loved by some Parisians, grunted at by others. It is undeniably impressive by day and by night dramatic, seeming to glow black against the sky, with a darkness that is only intensified by the horizontal strips of red light set at intervals along its great sides.

The most recent arrival on the Paris scene and completed in 1976, is the controversial Beaubourg. Erected on the site of part of the ancient market of Les Halles as a museum for modern art and culture, it is a vast, box-shaped, steel and concrete structure with convertible floor space, served by enclosed and moving walkways outside the building. From a distance they have the appearance of huge coloured tubes.

Third floor roof garden by the Sheraton Hotel in Montparnasse. In the foreground a pedestrian walkway crosses high above the Rue René Mouchotte.

358

*Left:* The Palais de Chaillot (1937), as seen from the first floor of the Eiffel Tower. It houses an underground theatre and various museums.
*Below:* Most famous of all the landmarks of this great city – the Eiffel Tower. Built in 1889, it soars 984 feet above Paris.

*Below Left:* 19th century appartment building in Montparnasse.
*Right:* Changing the skyline: construction in the 15th *arrondissement.*
*Below Right:* The Pompidou Centre in the Beaubourg.

# Along the Seine

Paris began on the Ile de la Cité in the River Seine. It is the river to day, as it has always been, which provides the city with so much of its character and grace.

More central to Paris then the Thames is to London, or the Tiber is to Rome (and probably more beautiful and atmospheric than both) the Seine flows clean through the city in a long majestic loop for some eight miles and divides it into two almost equal parts, the Rive Droite (Right Bank) and the Rive Gauche (Left Bank).

Very much an inland river, too far from the sea for any tang of salt or cry of seagull, the Seine is slow-flowing and at Paris only about 100 feet above sea-level. Throughout the centuries it has become controlled by man and is very much a tamed river now, little wider than the great Parisian avenues and dredged as far as Rouen to a constant depth of 10 feet. Walled in along its length by stone quays, frequently lined with trees, the river is crossed in Paris by no less than 33 bridges, the oldest being the Pont Neuf (meaning 'New Bridge'), which was begun in 1578.

With its two tributaries, the Marne and the Oise, the Seine has to drain the whole of the low-lying plain of Northern France, and however tamed it may be, still has its angry moods. In the past it used to rise to flood tide and in 1448 and 1590, when it was almost possible to cross the summer river on foot, winter saw terrible floods that wrought havoc in the city. Even as recently as 1910, the water level rose an astonishing eight metres and the city was flooded as far as the Gare St Lazare. Parisians mark the rise of the river by its relationship to the Zouave soldier at the foot of the Pont D'Alma. At the height of the 1910 flood he was standing in water up to his neck!

The borders of the Seine provide some of the loveliest views in all Paris: changing, colourful, panoramic. On the Right Bank, the Quai de la Rapée is lined with great trees that shade calm alleys. Further west, over the ancient stones of the Pont Marie, is the haven of 17th century houses on the Ile Saint-Louis. And downstream, at the furthest point of the boat-shaped Ile de la Cité, there is the sense that it is almost the island which moves, not the river. Further downstream the quays are lined with *bouquinistes* and extend to the Carrousel and Les Invalides. Upstream, between the Pont d'Arcole and the Pont d'Austerlitz, is the commercial Port of Paris and to this, through a network of river and canals, come goods from all over France.

Parisians have always made the most of the Seine. Along its banks they sit, stroll and meditate. Lovers find an idyllic rendezvous, fishermen idle away the hours (and sometimes even catch a perch or two) and the famous Parisian *clochards* (tramps) find a resting place beneath the bridges. Constantly changing, bringing a band of sky to the earth and everywhere spreading varying shades of light, the Seine reflects the great city that it refreshes and renews. It is the balm and one of the great joys of Paris.

The Ile de la Cité – where Paris began around 2000 years ago.

*Right:* Fishermen at the Quai de La Megisserie.
*Below:* Nôtre-Dame seen from across the river.
*Below Right:* A *clochard,* or tramp, finds a little comfort on the Right Bank of the Seine.

*Below:* The Pont Neuf, built
between 1578 and 1606 and the
oldest of the city's 33 bridges.
*Below Right:* On the Left Bank, a
painter finds his inspiration by the
river.

*Left:* 'Down by the bridges of Paris . . .'
*Above:* The Ile de la Cité as seen from Ile St Louis.
*Right:* On the furthermost point of the Ile de la Cité, a man meditates by the calm waters of the Seine.

# Paris Underground

The wonders of Paris do not end with her streets or the Seine, but continue way beneath both.

When Haussmann first built the sewers of Paris in the Reign of Napoleon III, they were considered one of the triumphs of the emerging city. They are still of interest today. A virtual city underground, the sewers cover no less than 12,600 acres and carry, as well, water, gas and electricity mains, telegraph and telephone. From their inception they have exerted a fascination. The writer, Victor Hugo immortalised them in *Les Misérables;* they were one of the most fashionable of tourist attractions at the turn of the century (along with the morgue); and even now, in the season, conducted tours leave from the Place de la Concorde four times a week.

In their grim fashion, the Paris *catacombes* are of even greater interest than the sewers. They extend under the Left Bank from the Place Denfert-Rôchereau all the way to the Jardin des Plantes, a honeycomb of ancient quarries some 60 feet below the surface, the result of stone mining that was going on as far back as Roman times.

When the Cîmetière des Innocents was demolished in 1786, the bones were disinterred and brought to the *catacombes* in carts. At first this was done reverently, but as numbers grew and the contents of still further cemeteries were added, the reverence faded. In the end the grisly remains were treated as just so much rubbish to be dumped. And so it was—in these tunnels and quarries—all that remained of three million people.

In the 19th century, someone with a grim sense of order had the bones rearranged: in patterns of skulls, rib-cages, etc. and the *catacombes* today consist of a labyrinth of galleries lined with bones and skulls. It was in this setting in the last war that the opposition to the Germans had its headquarters in August of 1944. And here too that those Communards who escaped the massacre at Père Lachaise were finally caught by government troops—and slaughtered among the skeletons.

A far more cheerful side of Paris, without which no book on the city would be complete, is the Métro: the city's underground railway, which is often overground too! One of the most efficient, and surely the most attractive, systems of its kind in the world, the Métro provides the fastest, cheapest and least strenuous way of getting round the city. A train arrives approximately every two minutes. Many of the trains are quite silent, running on rubber wheels. The whole thing has been thought through with typical French logic: the same fare takes you to any station (though you can travel first or second class). And, as it's impossible to get in without paying, you don't lose time bothering to surrender your ticket on the way out.

As much as anything in Paris their subway exemplifies the French love of beauty. For the stations are not merely clean; each is distinctive, light, individually decorated. Many are downright attractive and stations such as Louvre, for instance, even exhibit antiquities and

The Louvre station in the Métro: so lavish, one feels the train has actually arrived inside the museum itself.

*Left:* The station at La Defénse.
*Below:* A typical art nouveau
entrance to the Métro.

*Below Left:* One of the more bizarre of Paris tourist attractions, the sewers.
*Right:* Some of the machinery that keeps it all going.
*Below Right:* The *Catacombes* – once the macabre repository of some three million skeletons.

# Taking a Trip

Paris is a superbly compact city which, with a little help from the Métro, can be comfortably covered on foot. And she is equally well-placed for outings. For the countryside is quickly reached and of all the many excursions one can enjoy, none requires travelling more than 15 miles from the centre of the city.

The flea market at Clignancourt, the park of Vincennes, the Bois de Boulogne, all are easily accessible – and even racing at Longchamps, you are still within sight of the Eiffel Tower. So are you too at the park of Saint-Cloud, a favourite resort of Parisians. Once containing an old château which was burnt down by the Prussians, a fountain and terrace remain and from here the view is magnificent: with the Tour d'Eiffel seeming to rise from the very trees of the Bois de Boulogne.

Other parks worth visiting, too, are: the Parc des Buttes, Chaumont, with its artificial waterfall and high island crowned by a Greek temple; and the Jardin des Plantes – which features a botanical gardens, a maze and zoo.

Not far from the Jardin des Plantes is the Arènes de Lutèce, the remains of a Roman arena. Not a great deal is left, but you can still see the names of spectators carved in the stone of the benches. Today the arena itself, where once Christians were martyred, is a favourite place for the omni-popular French game of boules.

But most gratifying of all the excursions from Paris is Versailles. One of the wonders of France, a quarter-mile long palace of pink and cream stone in the style of the classical period of the French Renaissance, Versailles has to be experienced to be believed. Originally a modest hunting-lodge, Louis XIV moved his court there from the Louvre, transforming it into a vast and splendid palace with heroic-sized statues and sumptuous state appartments. The finest of these, the Galerie des Glaces, is 240 feet long, 43 high, and has walls ornamented with green marble Corinthian pilasters and mirrors of Venetian glass. Created by Le Vau and Mansart and Le Brun, with its gardens exquisitely laid out by Le Nôtre, Versailles in its day accommodated in luxury Louis' household of no less than 20,000 people. With its vast size, lavish stuccos and frescoes and tapestries, it presents a vision of wealth and splendour that is quite staggering to the modern mind.

After such opulence, it is salutary to visit the cemetery of Père Lachaise. On the east of the city, this is the largest of Paris's cemeteries, the one to which the French themselves make pilgrimages, and which is literally crammed with the graves of the great. Oscar Wilde, Chopin, Molière, la Fontaine and many other famous men and women are all buried here. And the place presents as well one of the strangest sights of Paris. For it is packed with monuments, little oratories – row upon row of them – that look rather like stone telephone kiosks – and it was firing from these that the ill-fated communards made their famous and fatal last stand.

The beautiful gardens of Versailles. Designed by Le Nôtre in the 1660s, they cover, in all, an area of almost 250 acres.

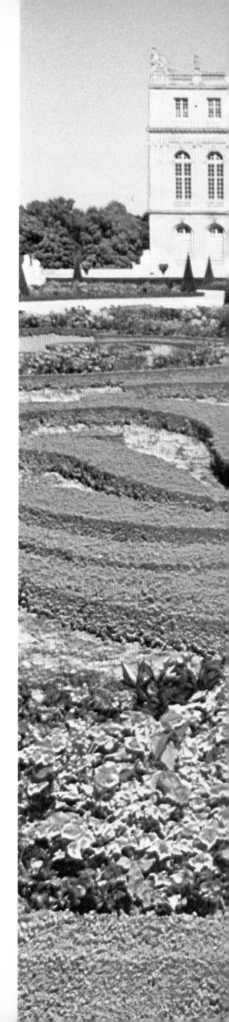

*Far Left:* A fraction of the great exterior of the palace of Versailles.
*Left:* One of the scores of sumptuous state appartments inside the palace.
*Below:* Panoramic view from the palace terrace over the gardens.

*Left:* Boating in the Bois de Boulogne. Once a royal hunting park the area was given to Paris in 1852 by Napoleon III.
*Below Left:* With more than 2200 wooded acres, the Bois offers a wealth of places to picnic.
*Below:* These luxuriant woods are only minutes from central Paris.

*Left:* The racecourse at Longchamps, where one can lunch while watching the racing – with the finish directly below.
*Below:* The Eiffel Tower soaring above the Longchamps car park.

*Below Left:* The Parc des Buttes Chaumont with its Greek temple.
*Below:* The grave of Edith Piaf, France's famous singer who became known as the 'little sparrow'. She died in 1963.
*Below Right:* Oscar Wilde's grave in Pere Làchaise cemetery, where so many of the great are buried.

# Introduction to Rome

About 3000 years ago groups of shepherd-farmers settled on the semi-circle of hills overlooking the Italian coastal plain of Latium. Later, these early settlers started to move down onto the plain. Fifteen miles from the mouth of the River Tiber they found a deep valley containing seven hills: the Palatium, Cermalus, Fagutal, Oppius, Cispius, Aventine and Caelian. This site attracted the newcomers because it was well-watered and protected and commanded a possible river crossing midway between the coast and the hills. From the wattle and daub village of these early Latins arose what was to become the mightiest city in the western world.

During the course of the next 28 centuries, Rome earned its title as the Eternal City. As the co-founder with Ancient Greece of western civilization, it enjoyed a great Silver Age of poetry and prose, and painting and sculpture. Its master architects produced the incomparable Forum Romanum and the splendid palaces of the Palatine. As the home of the Popes it became the religious centre of western Europe, adorned with a breathtaking collection of great churches and religious art: the Rome of Michelangelo, Bernini and so many others, still lives and breathes. In the same way, Rome is still the city that attracted the 18th-century travellers on their Grand Tour and the reluctant capital of the newly founded Italian state.

This book illustrates all these aspects of Rome's history, as well as creating a lively picture of the city as it is today: the Rome of great crowded squares and fountains; of romantic bridges; of noisy markets and chic shops; of delicious food and *la dolce vita*. Like all great cities, Rome has as many faces as a multi-faceted diamond.

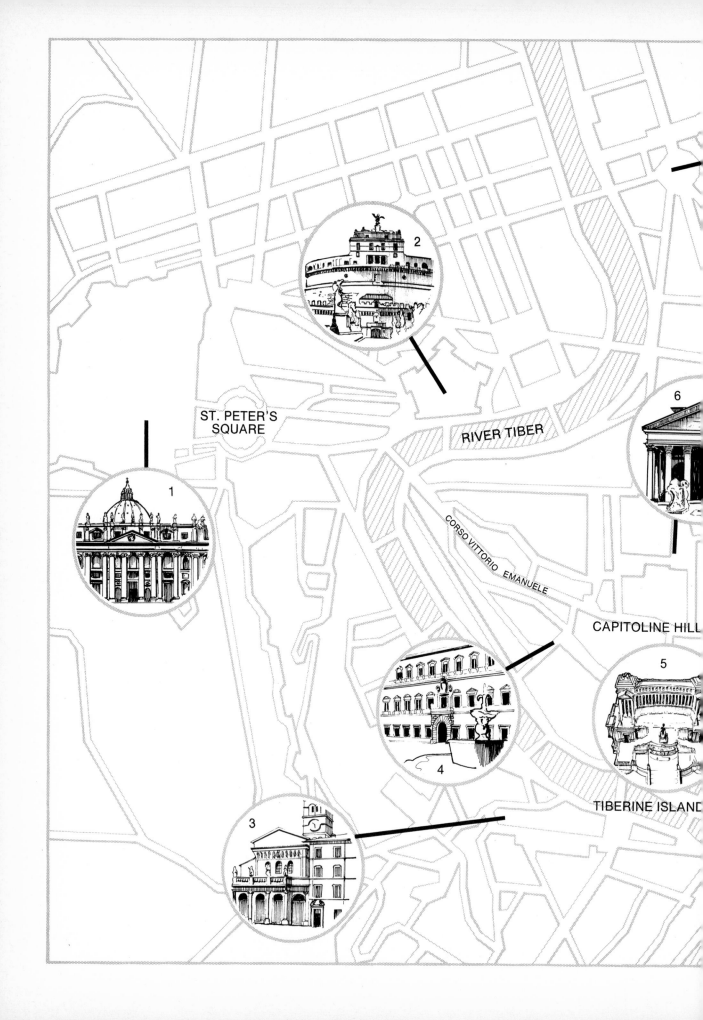

ST. PETER'S
SQUARE

RIVER TIBER

CORSO VITTORIO EMANUELE

CAPITOLINE HILL

TIBERINE ISLAND

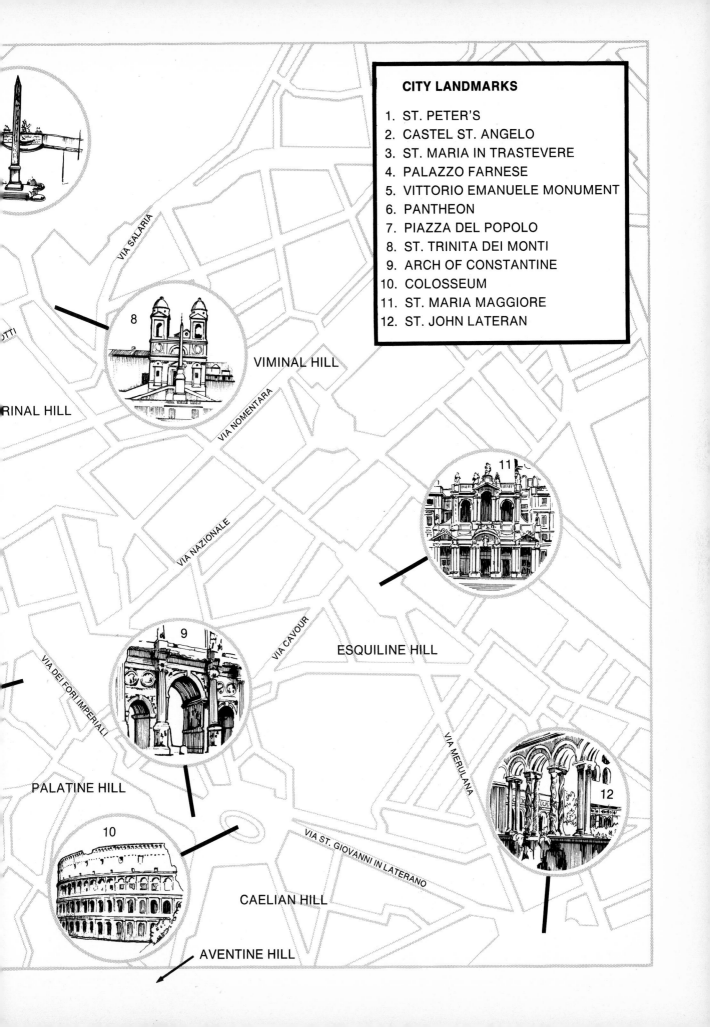

**CITY LANDMARKS**

1. ST. PETER'S
2. CASTEL ST. ANGELO
3. ST. MARIA IN TRASTEVERE
4. PALAZZO FARNESE
5. VITTORIO EMANUELE MONUMENT
6. PANTHEON
7. PIAZZA DEL POPOLO
8. ST. TRINITA DEI MONTI
9. ARCH OF CONSTANTINE
10. COLOSSEUM
11. ST. MARIA MAGGIORE
12. ST. JOHN LATERAN

VIMINAL HILL

RINAL HILL

VIA SALARIA

VIA NOMENTARA

VIA NAZIONALE

VIA CAVOUR

ESQUILINE HILL

VIA DEI FORI IMPERIALI

PALATINE HILL

VIA MERULANA

VIA ST. GIOVANNI IN LATERANO

CAELIAN HILL

AVENTINE HILL

# The Eternal City

Rome has been the focal point of the western world for most of its 2700 year history. Its origins are lost in myth and legend. Was the city founded by the twins Romulus and Remus, in about 753 BC and occupied by a colony of Latins? Or was it created by a mysterious band of exiles from Asia Minor, as Virgil suggested in his epic poem, *Aeneid?* As yet there is no clear-cut answer to this question.

What we do know, however, is that during Rome's crucial formative years it was dominated by the Etruscans. Very little has been learned about these superb soldier-craftsmen, their language has yet to be translated. However, their artefacts suggest a people of great sophistication and power. The Romans owed this ancient race an enormous debt because their triumphs were built upon a culture and technology acquired, at least in part, from them.

After the expulsion of Tarquin the Proud, the last of Rome's kings, in 510 BC, the city became a republic, ruled by the Senate and people as the legend on its famous seal proclaims: SPQR – *Senatus populusque romanus.* While a complicated constitution and body of law slowly evolved, the Roman army rapidly grew in power. The dynamic city state quickly extended its frontiers to include the Latins, Etruscans, Samnites, Lucanians and the Greek settlers in southern Italy. No sooner had the Italic peoples been absorbed than the Romans turned their restless attention to the conquest of Sicily, Carthage, Spain and Greece in the period between 340 and 133 BC.

In the early days of the Republic the city consisted of an assortment of evil-smelling hovels perched on the Palatine Hill, in the Suburra and along the left bank of the River Tiber. The basis of Roman society was the ancestor-venerating family, ruled by an all-powerful paterfamilias. The families were divided into clans (gentes) with common names, gods and burial places. Cattle ranching on the rich pasture land by the river gave way to agriculture and the rise of the peasant farmer. Gradually, Roman society became divided into Patricians and Plebeians; the latter had already compelled the former to recognize their representatives, the tribunes of the people, by 450 BC.

In Republican times, the hub of Roman life was the Forum, an oblong space of about two and a half acres surrounded by shops. The Temple of Vesta, the goddess of the hearth and family, and the House of the Vestal Virgins stood on one side of the complex in the shadow of the Capitoline Hill. On the other side loomed the imposing shape of the Regia, the house of the Pontifex Maximus, the High Priest. The Senate building stood in the north-east corner. Traversing the area was the Via Sacra, a winding road along which triumphal processions passed on their way to the Capitoline.

The Via Veneto with the Excelsior Hotel and palm trees in the foreground. This street is famous for its hotels, cafes and nightspots.

The most dramatic developments on the Palatine Hill took place during the Imperial Period when the early emperors competed with each other to build the most impressive and extravagant palace complex. The summit was covered with the houses of Augustus, Tiberius, Caligula, Domitian, Hadrian, and most magnificent of all, that of Septimus Severus. His rose in seven massive stages along the southern flanks of the hill. In addition, the Palatine possessed a beautiful stadium, several temples set in gardens, the Halls of Justice and a barracks for the Praetorian Guard. Across the valley, the Oppian Hill was almost completely covered by Nero's Golden House.

*Below:* The Via dei Fori Imperiali runs in a straight line to the Piazza del Colosseo. This magnificent street, lined with trees and flower gardens, was opened in October 1933 as the Via dell' Impero. On its right lies the Roman Forum and other Imperial Fora.

*Right:* Part of the aqueduct built by Domitian to provide water for his palace on the Palatine Hill. It was an extension of the Aqua Claudia which ran from the Caelian to the Palatine.

As the city grew in wealth and power, the Campus Martius became covered with baths and places of entertainment like the Theatre of Marcellus, much of which still stands as a splendid example of Roman monumental architecture. It was started by Julius Caesar and completed by Augustus in 11 BC; he named it after his nephew Marcellus, the son of Octavia. Further south on the site of part of Nero's demolished masterpiece, the Golden House, arose the Colosseum, the longest lasting testimony to Rome's greatness. Started by Vespasian, dedicated by Titus in AD 80 and completed by Domitian, it rang with the clash of gladiators' weapons, the roars of animals and the victims' screams throughout the Imperial Period.

By the reign of Constantine (306-337), Rome had a population of one million — 190 granaries and 250 corn mills supplied the city with flour; 150 fountains and eleven aqueducts provided it with water. There were eleven market-places, eleven baths, ten basilicas, two circuses, two amphitheatres and 28 libraries. The city was divided into quarters, criss-crossed by paved streets and deeply rutted by the wheels of heavy wagons and chariots, except where modern looking bollards barred the way. At the busy intersections, there were brightly coloured niches containing statues of the gods. In spite of the ever encroaching slums and the surprisingly modern looking apartment blocks, the city contained many beautiful gardens, rich with statues and fountains.

The rich still enjoyed life: working or receiving clients in the cool of the morning, taking a siesta at midday and exercising in the Campus Martius or one of the city's many gymnasia in the afternoon. On completing their exercises, young and old made their way to the baths to enjoy the sensual luxury of an elaborate cleansing rite. The baths were enormous architectural masterpieces equipped with brightly decorated reception rooms, steam rooms and a variety of water plunges ranging from the scaldingly hot to the icy cold. Clean, massaged, oiled and dressed in clean clothes, the Romans were ready for their main meal and social event of the day. This good life was only made possible by the toiling hordes of slaves. Some were abused and maltreated while others were prized for their skills. A few were even allowed to open their own businesses.

*Left:* The Appian Way, called by Stalius 'the Queen of roads', was built in 312 BC and joined Rome to Capua. Later, it was extended to Benevento and Brindisi.
*Right:* Horse-drawn buggy rides are still a popular way to see Rome. Often whole families squeeze into their capacious seats.
*Below:* The Theatre of Marcellus was founded by Julius Caesar and completed by the Emperor Augustus. Its severe lines and elegant proportions have inspired many artists. The exterior was restored in 1932.

The ordinary people, who lived in the city's crowded tenement blocks and slums, worked in the busy fora, the narrow streets full of tanners, butchers, sword makers, barbers and numerous wine shops and eating houses, or on the busy wharfs of Ostia. The poor and destitute were reconciled to their lot by the provision of the proverbial bread and circuses. At night, the rich kept to their houses or the well-lit thoroughfares. The streets of Rome were infested with robbers and kidnappers, species of criminals that have flourished throughout the city's long history. Heavy carts rumbled through the streets, rocking from side to side, occasionally trapping the unwary against the walls.

By the time Constantine became Emperor in AD 306, the days of Ancient Rome's greatness were numbered. The vulnerability of the city to the attacks of the barbarians had already forced the Emperor Aurelian to build a great enclosure of fortified walls between AD 270 and 275. The authority of the old gods had been undermined by the spread of Christianity whose persecuted members were buried in the catacombs outside the city. Following Constantine's recognition of the Christian faith, churches sprang up on the sites of St Paul's outside the walls, St Sebastiano, St John Lateran and St Maria Maggiore. Long before Alaric the Visigoth's hordes appeared beneath the walls of Rome in 410, the city had been supplanted as the focus of political and economic power by Constantinople, Constantine's new capital, built on the site of the old Greek town of Byzantium on the Black Sea.

For several centuries Rome remained a magnet for the barbarian invaders. Each in turn hoped to find the world's accumulated wealth stored there. In the sixth century, the Byzantine Emperor Justinian made a spirited attempt to restore the western empire. All he succeeded in doing was creating a beleaguered province based on the city of Ravenna in north-east Italy, not Rome. During this period, as the once mighty city declined into a regional backwater, a new power arose within its crumbling walls, the power of the Papacy. Building assiduously upon the rock of its Petrine foundation, the Pope gradually established his supremacy over the bishops of western Europe. Then the Papacy looked round for a political defender to take the place of the defunct Roman Empire. First Pepin the Short and then Charles the Great were chosen for this role. After many years of vacillation, Charles, or Charlemagne as he was known, appeared in Rome in 800 and was crowned emperor in St Peter's on Christmas Day. A new empire, the Holy Roman Empire, had been born.

By the tenth century, Rome was a town of some 60000 souls, dominated by noble families who struggled with each other for control not only of the town but of the Papacy itself. Much of the vast area within the dilapidated walls was filled with orchards and fields where sheep and pigs roamed freely. The Forum had become a stone island in a sea of vegetation; plants pushed their way up between the flagstones and wrapped themselves around the cracking pillars, now stripped of most of their marble. Nevertheless the power of the Papacy continued to increase. During a titanic struggle over the right to appoint bishops, Pope Gregory VII first excommunicated, then humiliated Emperor Henry IV at the castle of Canossa where he begged the Pope's forgiveness. Even though Gregory later had to suffer the indignity of flight from the imperial armies closing in on Rome, and ended his life in exile among the Normans of southern Italy, he had established the Papacy as an independent force and had laid the foundations for even greater claims to authority over the laity.

The strengthened Papacy reached the apogee of its power during the reign of the subtle pontiff Innocent III, (1161-1216). He played a key part in launching the Fourth Crusade and then diverted its soldiers to the conquest of Constantinople and the Byzantine Empire. From this pinnacle of power, the Papacy steadily declined during the next two centuries into disrepute and relative impotence. Following bitter struggles among the Roman nobility, Clement V, in 1308, moved the Papal seat to Avignon in southern France, unintentionally inaugurating the period known as the Babylonish Captivity which lasted until 1378.

*Below:* Throughout the Middle Ages, Swiss pikemen were in great demand. In 1506, the Pope formed the Swiss Guard which retains its striking uniform, which is said to have been designed by Michelangelo.
*Right:* An altar in the Catacombs. The Catacombs are subterranean tufa quarries where the early Christians worshipped, took refuge from their persecutors and buried their dead.

While the Papacy was enduring these tribulations and slowly recovering from them, Italy was experiencing the first stages of the so-called Renaissance or rebirth of learning. The last years of the 15th and the first years of the 16th centuries were the golden age of Papal Rome. The city became the cultural centre of the western world once more, attracting the great artists of the period like Leonardo da Vinci, Michelangelo and Raphael. The Sistine Chapel was built and although decorated by a number of renowned painters remains dominated by Michelangelo's magnificent ceiling frescoes and the *Last Judgement.* St Peter's was rebuilt, its famous dome being the work of Bramante and Michelangelo, and a new city laid out. The Capitoline Square was dramatically altered. Michelangelo refaced the Palazzo Senatorio and the Palazzo dei Conservatori and built the Palazzo Nuovo to complete the unity of the complex. To emphasize the importance of the star patterned pavement, Michelangelo placed the equestrian statue of what was then thought to be Constantine the Great (actually Marcus Aurelius) at its centre.

*Below left:* The Church of St Maria in Cosmedin is distinguished by its bell-tower. Romanesque in style, this is one of the finest in Rome.
*Right:* Ponds and fountains were to be found everywhere in Ancient Rome as it was the custom for the rich to provide such amenities for all to enjoy.
*Below:* The Villa Guilia was built in 1550–1555 for Pope Julius III and houses a collection of pre-Roman antiquities. The courtyard contains this superb loggia.

While Rome was being transformed and beautified by the artists of the high Renaissance, the Papacy made its last attempt to play a dominant role in the political life of Europe. The era of the Italian Wars saw Italy invaded in the north by the armies of France and in the south by those of Spain. The Renaissance Popes tried desperately hard to maintain the balance of power and to preserve their own lands and influence by creating leagues and alliances. The result of this meddling in European politics was the devastating sack of Rome in 1527 by the unpaid and mutinous imperial troops.

A century later the Popes threw themselves into even more ambitious building programmes than their Renaissance predecessors. As a result the centre of Rome took on its present, distinctly baroque character. Under Paul V's patronage the great nave of St Peter's was added while the sculptor Bernini designed a tomb for Urban VIII (1623-1644). This became a model for all funeral monuments for more than 100 years. Bernini also covered the tomb of St Peter with the superb baldacchino or canopy, for which the Pantheon temple was stripped of its bronze ornaments. With the accession of Innocent X in 1644, Bernini fell from favour and Francesco Boromini and Alessandro Algardi became the dominant artistic influences. Innocent's greatest achievement was the Piazza Navona with its brilliant fountains. The Sienese Pope, Alexander VII (1645-1667), reinstated Bernini whose career reached its climax with the construction of the Cathedra Petri.

After the death of Clement IX in 1669, papal patronage declined rapidly, partly at least as a result of Urban VIII's profligacy. However, the 18th century saw the Papacy once more taking a vigorous interest in the arts. Various famous projects were set in motion: the Spanish Steps were built by De Sancti, the facade of the Lateran was created by Alessandro Galilei, and the Trevi Fountain brought to triumphant completion by Nicola Salvi. The Capitoline Museums were founded and the bases of their unique collections of Roman statuary laid down.

*Left:* The Piazza San Pietro was Bernini's masterpiece. The stupendous colonnade and fountain were completed for Alexander VII (1656–1667).
*Below:* The Spanish Steps are a popular area for artists and salesmen. Jewellery, leatherwork and paintings are the most popular commodities.

Music, drama and painting flourished under the enlightened
patronage of Cardinal Pietro Ottoboni. Mid-century Rome was
swamped by the rising tide of neo-classicism stimulated by the
discovery of the ruins of Pompeii and Herculaneum in the 1730s and
1740s. The Villa Albani was built in the 1750s as an Imperial villa
suburbana and lavishly adorned with antique marbles. The Borghese
Palace was modernized by Antonio Asprucci. Throughout the 18th
century more and more foreigners made Rome the focus of their
Grand Tour. On their visits to the city, they not only imbibed the
teachings of neo-classicism but laid the foundations of their own
private collections of *objets d'art*. Rome became Europe's largest
market for antiques and works of art.

The French Revolution in 1789 and Napoleon's later conquests upset
the settled pattern of Italian and Roman political life. The Pope and the
Italian royal families were exiled, at least for a time, and their people
given some experience of self-government before they were absorbed
into various Napoleonic systems. Although, on Napoleon's defeat,
their old masters were reimposed upon the Italians, the forces calling

*Above:* The monument of Victor
Emmanuel II, sometimes known as
the wedding cake, is built of
dazzling white Botticeno marble
from Brescia and dominates the
Piazza di Venezia. It was
inaugurated in 1915.
*Right:* Trajan's Column was
dedicated in AD 113 to the memory
of the Emperor's conquest of the
Dacians, the inhabitants of present-
day Rumania. The Emperor's
statue was replaced by one of St
Peter in 1588.

for the Risorgimento had been released. After abortive revolutions in 1830 and 1848, an Italian state without Rome was established by a formidable triumvirate made up of Victor Emmanuel II of Piedmont-Sardinia, Count Camillo Cavour and Giuseppe Garibaldi. The Papacy remained secure within its walls as long as Napoleon III continued to garrison troops in Rome, but following their defeats in the Franco-Prussian War the French withdrew and Garibaldi's legion breached the walls and took possession of the city in the name of the new Italian state. Unhappily, this led to the severing of relations between the Papacy and the new regime: a state of affairs which continued until 1929 when Mussolini's Lateran Treaties at last healed the breach.

*Below:* The EUR, or Esposizione Universale di Roma, is twelve minutes' train journey from Rome. It was started in 1938 to the designs of Marcello Piacentini as a memorial to the achievements of Fascism. It was not completed until 1952 when various government offices were moved to the site and many museums were opened.
*Right:* A modern obelisk in the EUR.

From 1870, Rome became what she had never really ceased to be, the capital of Italy. Now, Piedmontese influence was added to those of Ancient Rome and the Papacy. A new quarter sprang up around the Piazza Vittorio Emmanuele II, a porticoed square which forms the hub of a series of straight thoroughfares intersecting at right angles. The unification of Italy was commemorated by the controversial Victor Emmanuel monument, or the wedding cake, as some irreverent Romans call it. It was the outcome of an architectural competition won by Giuseppe Sacconi in 1884, and took more than 25 years to complete. Opinions differ as to its architectural and artistic merit but there is no doubting its monumental size and message. At the beginning of the 20th century, the grey structures along the Via Vittorio Veneto were built and set the pattern for many pre-war building projects.

During the Fascist era, a renewed interest in archaeology led to the excavation of many architectural treasures. These in their turn stimulated a new neo-Roman style of which the Foro Italico and the Piazza Augusto Imperiale are typical examples. Under pressure from the growing population, more and more buildings appeared on the right bank of the Tiber in the Prati di Costello and Monteverde quarters and outside the walls in St Giovanni and St Lorenzo. The expansion of the city beyond the walls continued after the Second World War when its population reached two millions.

407

# Classical Rome

The Forum Romanum, the centre of Ancient Rome, can be entered through clusters of stallholders and ice cream sellers on the Via dei Fori Imperiali. The Forum was probably first occupied in the sixth century BC after the valley between the Palatine and Capitoline Hills had been drained by the construction of the great sewer called the Cloaca Maxima. Gradually, the shops were removed and the Forum became solely the civic centre of Rome.

Immediately to the right of the entrance are the remains of the Basilica Emilia (179 BC) with its huge central hall. Next door is the Curia where the Roman Senate met from about 650 BC until the fall of the empire. During the Republic, the citizens gathered in the Comitium, the square outside, to make important decisions. At the north-west corner is the Arch of Septimus Severus and in front of what was originally the main square stands the Rostra, a raised dais from which orators like Cicero harangued huge crowds. On the opposite side of the square to the Curia and Basilica Emilia stands the Basilica Julia, which was commissioned by Julius Caesar and served as a court of justice and the Temple of Castor and Pollux (484 BC). The Temple of Julius Caesar forms the fourth side of the square; this was where Caesar's body was burned and Mark Antony gave his famous oration to the people.

From this main square the Via Sacra, the ceremonial thoroughfare, makes its way east, bordered by the Temple of Vesta and the House of the Vestal Virgins on the right and the ruins of the Basilica of Constantine on the left, before passing under the Arch of Titus.

Turning right before the Arch, the visitor can ascend the Clivus Palatinus to the Palatine Hill where, it is said, the first city was laid out by Romulus. Keeping to the left one comes upon the beautifully proportioned Stadium and the ruins of Augustus' and Domitian's great palaces and the House of Livia with its famous murals. From all these sites, there are splendid views out over the Circus Maximus. Immediately to the north lies the Cryptoporticus, a long vaulted passageway which used to connect Nero's Golden House with the Palaces of Augustus, Tiberius and Caligula; the foundations of the last two now lie beneath the Farnese Gardens which can be reached by staircases from the Cryptoporticus.

Outside the Forum Romanum lay five other fora. Nowadays, the Via dei Fori Imperiali on its way to the Colosseum passes the ruins of the Fora of Trajan and Augustus on its left and that of Caesar on its right while crossing over the sites of the Fora of Nerva and Vespasian. At the end of the avenue lies the Colosseum, the greatest testimony to Rome's grandeur and blood lust, with the Arch of Constantine on the right and the remains of Nero's Golden House on the left.

This splendid model by I. Gismondi shows Rome in the days of the Emperor Constantine. On the left, the Circus Maximus stretches alongside the Capitoline, while the Colosseum can be seen on the right.

*Left:* Originally named the Flavian Amphitheatre, the Colosseum was first referred to by its modern name by the Venerable Bede (673–735) who quoted the prophesy: 'While the Colosseum stands, Rome stands'.
*Below:* The Palatine seen from the Circus Maximus. Little remains of the giant stadium where crowds numbering 300000 watched chariot races, athletic contests, wild animal shows and sea battles.

*Left:* These are the remains of the magnificent polychrome marble pavement belonging to the Flavian Palace, part of the Imperial residence on the Palatine.
*Right:* These three lofty columns are all that remain of the pronaos of the rich and elegant Temple of Vespasian.
*Below:* Statues of Ancient Rome lining an inner wall just off a busy street.

# The Great Basilicas

The basilicas of the Ancient Romans were large buildings used for judicial and other public business. They usually occupied a large site in the Forum. Their design became more or less standardized: a long nave divided by columns into aisles with an apse at the end opposite the entrance. Down to about the end of the tenth century Christians adopted the basilican form for their churches. Among the earliest churches to be erected in Rome were the five great basilicas: St Peter's, St Maria Maggiore, St John Lateran, St Paul's beyond the Walls, and St Lawrence beyond the Walls. These quickly became associated with the Pope and are known as the Five Patriarchical Churches.

St Peter's was built on top of an extensive cemetery on the slopes of the Vatican Hill. Excavations in 1940-1949 uncovered the remains of a pre-Constantinian shrine containing human bones, which appears to have been the object of great veneration. Although this cannot yet be positively identified as St Peter's tomb, it does prove the continuous sanctity of the site from earliest Christian times. The present building is a magnificent concoction produced by Bramante, the first architect, Michelangelo who created the dome and Maderna who designed the nave. Important contributions were also made by many other great artists. The walls and floor of the nave are covered with marble decorations by Giacomo della Porta and Bernini. Among a plethora of splendid works of art, Michelangelo's remarkable Pieta, executed during his early years, is one of the most outstanding.

St Maria Maggiore contains fine fifth-century mosaics above the colonnades of its nave which is decorated with the first gold to have come from America. The baroque facade is by Fuga (1743).

St John Lateran is the metropolitan church of Rome and was rebuilt several times as a result of fires and other disasters until it assumed its present baroque form. The bronze for the great central doors came from the old Roman Senate House in the Forum. Borromini, who refashioned the nave, is responsible for its imposing rather coldly mathematical proportions. The church also contains a statue of Constantine which used to stand in his baths. Adjoining the basilica is the Palazzo del Laterano, the Pope's official residence until the Babylonish Captivity.

According to tradition St Paul is buried beneath St Paul's beyond the Walls. This with the exception of St Peter's, is the largest church in Rome. The original structure was almost completely destroyed by fire in 1823, only the choir and the cloisters escaping the flames. The choir contains 13th-century mosaics and a magnificent altar canopy.

St Lawrence beyond the Walls is the smallest of the Patriarchical churches and is really two churches, one built in the sixth century, the other in the 13th. It contains a fine episcopal throne and excellent pavements in the nave and choir by the famous Cosmati school of Roman artists.

Part of the two semi-circular colonnades which partly enclose the Piazza San Pietro. Each colonnade consists of a quadruple row of Doric columns, forming three parallel covered walks.

*Below:* The main facade of St Maria Maggiore was designed by Fuga in 1743. It is approached by steps and consists of a portico with a loggia of three arches.
*Right:* The Basilica of St John Lateran was built in 1574 and is the cathedral of Rome. Until 1870 the Popes were crowned here.

The immensity of the interior of St Peter's is disguised by the symmetry of its proportions. The eye is drawn to Bernini's superb baldacchino which is bathed in light from the great dome.

*Left:* The facade of St Peter's Basilica. The ballustrade supports statues of Christ, St John the Baptist and eleven of the Apostles – the statue of St Peter is inside.
*Below:* St Paul's Cloisters were finished in about 1214 and were the work, at least in part, of the Vassalletti. In the centre is a beautiful rose garden.

HIERVSALEM

*Left:* Fine mosaics decorating the sanctuary arch are a striking feature of the interior of St Maria Maggiore. They show lively biblical scenes including the Annunciation, the Visit of the Magi and the Flight into Egypt.

*Below:* The most famous of Michelangelo's Pietas was completed by the artist in his twenty-fifth year (1499). It is perhaps the most moving of his sculptures and is the only one inscribed with his name.

# Bridges Over The Tiber

By the end of the Classical Period, five or six bridges had been constructed across the Tiber. Only one now remains more or less intact. The oldest, the Ponte Rotto or the broken bridge, was built in 181 BC but has been extensively restored following serious flood damage in the 16th and 19th centuries. In spite of the constant danger of flooding, it was not until the 19th century that the Lungotevere embankments were built to contain the river and straighten its course.

Further upstream, one comes to the oldest surviving intact bridge, the Ponte Fabricio. It was built in 62 BC and faces the Theatre of Marcellus, one of the finest examples of Roman monumental architecture. The bridge joins the mainland to the almond shaped Isola Tiberina. This island contains the Fatebenefratelli hospital; a tall medieval tower, formerly part of an 11th-century fortress; and the church of St Bartolomeo, which was erected on the site of the temple of Aesculapius. The island is linked to the Trastevere or right bank of the Tiber by the Ponte Cestio which may have been built by the Emperor Gratian. Following the serious 19th-century floods, it had to be entirely rebuilt although the central arch retains its original design and measurements.

The Pons Aelius, now known as the Ponte St Angelo, was built by the Emperor Hadrian in AD 135 as a fitting approach to his great mausoleum. This contained the bodies of many of his successors as well as his own. Only the three central arches of the bridge actually date from this time. Since 1925, the Mausoleum or the Castel St Angelo as it is better known, has been a museum containing a fine collection of weapons dating from the Stone Age to the present day. In addition, the museum boasts some well-known paintings, antique furniture and tapestries.

Some of the finest views in Rome can be seen from the Ponte Umberto, particularly in the early morning light. From the point where the bridge joins the left bank, one can enjoy a magnificent panorama including the Ponte St Angelo, the Castel St Angelo, the Borgo (the walled Leonine city which has been the stronghold of the Papacy since AD 850) and the dome of St Peter's.

The Ponte Cavour joins the main city to the Prati quarter. From it can be seen the Mausoleum of Augustus on the left bank. Augustus, Rome's greatest emperor, and many other members of his family were buried here. Archaeologists unearthed an outer ring of twelve compartments surrounding an inner sepulchral *cella* containing three niches. In the central niche they discovered the cinerary urns of Augustus and his wife Livia with those of his nephews Gaius and Lucius Caesar on one side and that of his sister Octavia on the other. During the Middle Ages, the Colonna made the tomb into a fortress. After various vicissitudes, it became a concert hall and remained as such until 1936.

The last of Rome's great bridges, the Ponte Vittorio Emmanuele, also offers fine views of the city and river, especially at sunset.

The Vatican City lies on the right bank of the Tiber and has the status of an independent state. This is one of the finest views of St Peter's, rising behind the St Angelo Bridge.

*Left:* Across the bridge lies the
Castel St Angelo which was
originally the Emperor Hadrian's
Mausoleum. Since 1925, it has
housed an important collection of
military treasures.
*Right:* The Ponte St Angelo has
statues of St Peter and St Paul at
the Castel St Angelo end and is
lined with ten other statues.
*Below:* The Ponte Cestio, first built
in AD 152, was rebuilt in 1892. It
joins the south side of the Isola
Tiberina to the Trastevere quarter
of Rome.

ASPICIANT·AD·ME
QVEM·CONFIXERVNT

*Left:* A single stone arch of the
Pons Aemilius, the first stone
bridge across the Tiber, remains in
the river bed. Since its final
collapse in 1598, it has been known
as the Ponte Rotto.
*below:* The Ponte Umberto I
crosses the Tiber between the
Castel St Angelo and the
Mausoleum of Augustus. It leads
to the Palace of Justice on the right
bank.

*Above left:* An elegant new bridge across the Tiber.
*Below left:* The Ponte Fabrico joins the Isola Tiberina to the left bank of the Tiber.
*Above:* Another of Rome's many bridges. This one is near St Peter's Square.

# Holy Week

The highest point of Rome's year is Holy Week. This is an important family holiday as well as a great religious occasion. For weeks before, the shops are full of gigantic Easter eggs, some fully five feet high and weighing 150 pounds. These spectacular masterpieces of the confectioner's art are usually for decoration rather than for sale – once the festivities are over, they are rendered down into more easily disposable bars.

In the last few days before Easter, pilgrims and tourists pour into the city by car, bus, rail and air. There is usually not a bed to be had in the whole city. On Maundy Thursday, the ceremonies begin with the Mandatum when the Pope washes the feet of twelve old men or twelve young boys, recalling Christ's washing of the disciples' feet. On Good Friday, the service of Tenebrae commemorates the three hours of darkness that fell over the earth following the Crucifixion. One by one the candles in the churches are extinguished until only one bright flame remains alight, representing Christ, the Light of the World. The first Easter Mass is held on Holy Saturday, marking the end of Lent and the churches are full of the pungent smell of incense and crammed with worshippers. On Easter Monday, a quarter of a million people push and shove their way into the Piazza St Pietro, obscuring Bernini's famous fountains to hear the Pope give his traditional blessing, *urbi et orbi,* and to give his Easter message in a variety of languages.

Pilgrims make their way to the five Patriarchical Basilicas and the many other churches, all with their own precious relics. Many visit the Scala Santa, the Sacred Stairs, reputedly those from Pontius Pilate's residence in Jerusalem, down which Christ passed after his condemnation. Thousands ascend these famous 28 steps on their knees, stopping on each to say a prayer. The steps lead to the Chapel of St Lawrence which contains a mozaic of Christ and, protected by a silver tabernacle presented by Innocent III, the relic which gives the chapel its peculiar sanctity.

Meanwhile, many Roman families take the opportunity to set off in cars and buses for their first picnic of the year either at the seaside or in the country. Easter is an exciting time for young children with the giving of presents and sweetmeats. Doting parents take their little ones to see the Punch and Judy shows in the Piazza Navona or the Pincio Gardens.

Pope Paul celebrates Easter and delivers the famous sermon, *urbi et orbi,* from a balcony overlooking St Peter's Square.

*Left:* Pope Paul being carried through crowds of worshippers to celebrate Mass on Palm Sunday. *Above:* A religious co-fraternity leads a procession during Lent.

*Below:* The Pope washes the feet of choir boys in imitation of Christ's cleansing of his disciples' feet before the Last Supper.
*Right:* Palm sellers doing good business outside St Peter's on Palm Sunday.

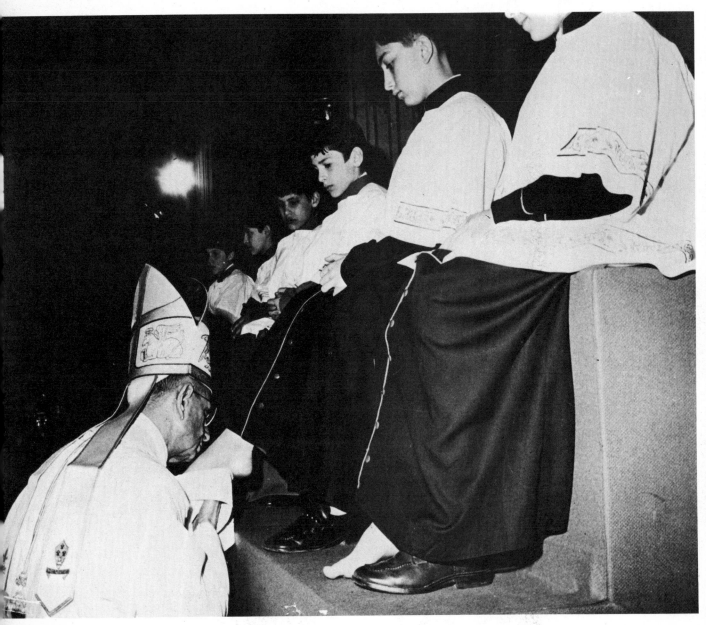

# Roman Food and Eating Houses

Food and drink are of absorbing interest to most Romans. Everywhere one goes the streets are full of eating houses: pizzerias, rotisseries, luncheonettes, trattorie and ristoranti offering an amazing variety of meals for every taste and pocket.

Breakfast for visitors usually consists of rolls or crisp bread, butter and conserves although this may be varied at times by the appearance of bomba, excellent jam doughnuts. The Romans usually make do with coffee. The main meals of the day are *pranzo* or dinner, usually eaten between 12.30 pm and 2.30 pm and *cena* or supper, taken at 8.30 pm to 10.30 pm. However, the eating houses and cafes never seem to be empty, just more or less full, as the Romans, like all Italians, are very partial to snacks and glasses of wine, aperitif or liqueur between meals. Certainly, there is nothing more enjoyable after some vigorous sightseeing than sitting in the shade of an awning, sipping a drink and watching the world go by.

Romans' meals are serious, lengthy affairs introduced by antipasti or delicious hors d'oeuvre, soups or pasta. As one would expect every kind of restaurant prides itself on the quality of its spaghetti, cannelloni (rolled pasta pancakes filled with meat, cheese and tomato sauce), lasagne (layers of pasta with a similar filling) and ravioli. Most *trattorie,* the smaller restaurants, offer superb vegetable soups at a very modest price. One of the most popular entrees is paper thin slices of Parma Ham with honey-dew melon or ripe figs.

Probably the best loved of Latin main courses is *Agnello all'aretino,* succulent lamb roasted with rosemary and basted with oil and vinegar, red wine or Marsala. It is cut into thick slices and served in a sauce made from its own juices, with saute potatoes and a green salad. *Porchetta* (roast pork) and *Saltimbocca alla Romana* (slices of veal wrapped around fine strips of prosciutto and sage leaves) are also popular. The main course is usually followed by cheese and fruit although there is normally an extraordinary range of mouthwatering desserts available as well.

Good wines are produced by the neighbouring hill towns. Frascati, Grottaferrata, Albano and Genzano are excellent white wines while Marino and Velletri are the most popular red wines. Most restaurants provide pleasant house wines at reasonable prices. Caffe-espresso, believed to be an aid to digestion, completes a feast fit for a gourmand if not a gourmet.

Although visitors may find the prices charged by the *trattorie* more suited to their pocket, it is well worth paying extra to dine at one of the more expensive restaurants in, say, the Piazza Navona to enjoy the interplay of Italian social life.

Finally, there are a great variety of shops selling sweets, confectionery and ice cream (*gelato*). Without doubt Rome offers a variety and range of food to suit the most discriminating or jaded of palates.

A chef proving, with the help of the maitre d'hotel, that his pasta is good enough to eat.

*Below:* Music while you eat: small groups of musicians make the rounds of the local restaurants and cafes every lunch and dinner time.
*Right:* A typical pavement cafe situated in the sidestreets near the Piazza Navona.

*Left:* Although the way in which meals are presented varies from place to place, the quality remains excellent. The Cafe de Paris in the Via Veneto caters for the smart set.
*Below:* On a hot summer's night there is nothing quite like a long leisurely dinner in an open-air restaurant.

*Right:* There are cafes everywhere in Rome. This one is situated in the Piazza del Pantheon.

*Above:* Eating is a serious business for the Romans. It is a time for conversation and a time for meeting friends.

*Right:* An empty open-air restaurant is a rare sight in Rome. Only in really cold weather do the regulars take refuge in the interiors of the cafes.

# La Dolce Vita

The nature of *La Dolce Vita* in Rome depends very much upon one's financial position. For the rich, the Via Veneto is the centre of Rome's night life, with its nightclubs, bars and restaurants. Otherwise it might be the more intimate parties given in the fashionable residential areas by film stars, politicians and successful businessmen. For them, the winter is a time for visiting fashionable skiing resorts; the summer an opportunity to get away from it all either in their houses up in the hills around Rome, or in their yachts cruising around the Mediterranean. This life is, however, confined to the very few.

For the average Roman, eating-out is an important pastime and there are more than 5000 restaurants to accommodate him. In the suburban quarters, the residents meet at their local cafe to gossip and watch the rest of the world pass by.

For the young Roman the 'passeggio' is the thing. Dressed in their best clothes, they promenade up and down the fashionable piazzas and streets eyeing their contemporaries and criticizing their outfits. The more fortunate young Romans also indulge in the newest version of the passeggio, 'cruising' through the brightly lit streets in their highly polished and decorated cars.

Brought up to believe that the Italian male is probably the world's greatest lover, the young Roman spends a considerable amount of time and money at the barbers – another important Italian meeting place – and the tailors. Dressed to kill, he indulges in the national sport, the pursuit of girls, especially foreigners. Their activities vary from the amusing, for accompanied women, to the frightening for those who are unescorted. Solitary or even group window-shopping and sightseeing is not to be recommended for female visitors at night.

The Roman spends a good deal of his time either watching or playing sports of one kind or another. Blood sports are still popular. Important boxing matches are held in Rome and the Romans like nothing better than watching two big brave modern-style gladiators thumping each other. Roma, the local football team, inspires fanatical support and the roars of the crowd reach an ear splitting crescendo whenever a match is played.

Betting is a national passion. Billions of lire are spent each week on the football pools, horse and greyhound racing and the national lottery. Betting plays an important part in the life of the poorer Roman: it offers him an opportunity to escape from the mundane day-to-day struggle of work into the elegant and sophisticated world described by gossip columnists and depicted in glossy magazines. As well as all this there are the customary discos and dance halls and more than 200 cinemas, loudly proclaiming their wares from enormous hoardings covered in luridly coloured posters.

The Piazza Barberini is one of the most important squares in Rome. In the centre is Bernini's masterpiece, the Triton Fountain, completed in 1643. The Via Veneto leads from here to the Porta Pinciana.

*Left:* Two priests on a motor scooter, by no means an unusual sight. The Romans' love affair with all forms of motor transport is as strong as ever.

*Above:* The open-air Punch and Judy show is a popular attraction during the Easter celebrations with adult and child alike.

*Left:* Youth waits for age at a street water pump. Signs of poverty can still be seen in what is one of the world's great cities.
*Below:* A priest talking to a policeman – the law and the Church are important strands in Roman life.

# City of Culture

Rome possesses such a treasury of museums and art galleries that it is difficult to know which to mention and which to leave out. Without doubt the Vatican Palace houses an incomparable series of museums and art galleries. The Museo Paolino contains collections of Roman and neo-Attic sculpture, Christian inscriptions and artefacts from a wide variety of primitive and more recent cultures. The Vatican Picture Gallery covers the whole history of western painting and sculpture from the Byzantine era to the present day. In addition there is the Gallery of Tapestries, the Raphael Rooms and the Sistine Chapel built by Sixtus IV between 1478 and 1481. This, the private chapel of the Popes where the cardinals used to meet to elect the pontiff, is dominated by Michelangelo's masterly ceiling frescoes (1508-1512) telling the Genesis stories from the creation of the world to the adventures of Noah and his vast *Last Judgement* covering the altar wall (1534-1541). The latter became the model for the school of Mannerist painters. Scholars from all over the world visit the Library which contains more than a million printed books and 60000 manuscripts.

The Capitoline Museums contain fine collections of Roman portrait busts, the *Capitoline Venus* and the famous *Dying Goth or Gladiator.* The Picture Gallery of the Palazzo dei Conservatori displays major works by Bellini, Lotto, Veronese, Peruzzi and Titian.

The Galleria Borghese boasts Canova's famous statue of Paolina Borghese, Napoleon's sister, and Bernini's even more renowned *Apollo and Daphne.* The Picture Gallery includes Titian's celebrated *Sacred and Profane Love* among many other masterpieces.

It is not for nothing that St Cecilia, the patron saint of music, was a Roman. Rome has a great reputation for the study and performance of music. Its renowned Academy of St Cecilia was founded by Palestrina and the Rome Opera competes with Milan and Naples for the operatic palm of Italy. During the summer, selections of operas by Verdi, Puccini, Rossini and Donizetti are brilliantly staged at the Baths of Caracalla before huge appreciative crowds. Famous for their stage effects, nothing is more exciting than the chariot charge to the front of the stage in a flash of tossing plumes and shining harness in *Aida.* The ballet and orchestral music are equally popular and open air concerts are often held in the floodlit Basilica of Maxentius in the Roman Forum during the summer.

Rome is also the capital of the Italian film industry – more films are made in Rome than in Hollywood. Forty years ago, the Fascists built a grandiose film city called Cinecittà. In these studios, and the more modern ones on the Via Latina, the likes of Vittorio da Sica, Pier Paolo Pasolini, Dino de Laurentiis, Ponti and Zeffirelli have produced some of Italy's finest films.

Rome possesses Italy's largest university and attracts students and scholars from all over the world because of its excellent facilities and high academic standards.

Michelangelo's statue of Moses in St Peter's in Chains. This powerful figure was one of several planned by Michelangelo for Julius II's tomb, but the rest were never finished.

454

*Left:* Trajan's column is 97 feet high and made of 18 drums of marble. A spiral frieze winds around the column covered with 2500 figures illustrating the Emperor's Dacian campaign.

*Above:* Hundreds of ancient statues have been unearthed during excavations. In spite of many years' work, there is still a wealth of artefacts to be discovered.

The School of Athens by Raphael in the Vatican Palace represents the triumph of philosophy. Plato and Aristotle dominate the scene and are surrounded by groups of the world's greatest scholars.
Overleaf: The Creation of Adam, perhaps the most famous scene from Michelangelo's frescoes on the ceiling of the Sistine Chapel. They were painted between 1508 and 1512.

# Squares and Fountains

Rome is a city of squares which resound to the lapping and bubbling of water and whose walls reflect its myriad lights. The building and adorning of fountains is an old Roman tradition. It is claimed that Imperial Rome contained no less that 1352 fountains. Their greatest post-classical creator was Lorenzo Bernini. It is believed that he was responsible for the original plans of the Trevi Fountains which form one whole facade of the Palazzo Poli and represent the royal residence of Neptune, god of the sea.

The River Fountain in the Piazza Navona is one of Bernini's finest works, and was executed by the master and his students between 1647 and 1650. The four magnificent statues represent the rivers Danube, Ganges, Nile and Rio de la Plata. The Piazza has retained the shape of the Emperor Domitian's stadium and racecourse upon which it is built. Throughout Rome's history, festivals, jousts and open air sports have been held here. From the 17th to the 19th century, the Romans crowded to the square on every Saturday in August to see it turned into a shallow lake of sparkling, prismatic coloured waters. It is still the most animated piazza in Rome and contains some of its finest and best loved ristoranti.

The Piazza Barberini is one of the most important squares in Rome. In its centre stands Bernini's masterpiece, the Fontana del Tritone (1642-1643). Four dolphins support a shell upon which a triton is seated blowing water out through a conch shell held between his hands.

The Piazza del Popolo, designed by Valadier in 1814, forms the most noble and impressive entrance to Rome. At its centre stands an ancient Egyptian obelisk which is guarded by four lion fountains, created by Valadier. The hieroglyphics on the obelisk tell of the bloody victories of the Pharaohs, Ramses II and Merenptah in the second millenium BC. Augustus brought the monument back to Rome and set it up in the Circus Maximus, the great racetrack lying in the shadow of the Palatine Hill. It was removed to its present site in the 16th century as part of the ambitious urban plans of Sixtus V.

Another renowned centre is the Piazza di Spagna containing the Spanish Steps where, in the old days, artist's models used to ply for hire. This was the heart of romantic Rome when it was frequented by people like Gogol, Stendhal, Liszt and D'Annunzio, the poet-soldier Mussolini modelled himself upon. In 1821, John Keats died in the red house at the bottom of the steps; this is now a museum in his honour. Every day, the foot of the steps is covered by a gorgeous selection of flowers for sale. But they are seen at their finest at the beginning of May when they are decorated with tubs of magnificent azaleas.

Every visitor to Rome will carry away his own kaleidoscope of memories of the many squares and fountains he has encountered in the course of his travels through the city. He will probably agree with the Ancient Romans who said that *Murmure suo fons canit vitae laudem* – by its murmuring the fountain sings the praise of life.

The Spanish Steps. This famous flight of 137 steps was built in 1721–1725. On top of the steps, the Piazza della Trinita dei Monte is dominated by an ancient obelisk and the church of the same name.

*Below:* The Fountain of Rivers by Bernini has a colossal statue at each corner representing the rivers Danube, Ganges, Nile and Plate. Here, the Nile covers its face.

*Right:* A view of the Piazza Navona. In the foreground, Neptune struggles with a sea monster, surrounded by nereids and sea horses, in a fountain designed by Leone della Bitta and Zappola in 1878.

From the roof of St Peter's one can see the full glory of Bernini's colonnades which open so that the eye looks down the Via della Conciliazone to the Tiber and the Castel St Angelo.

465

RES...RATA
ANNO ... ...CCIV

*Above:* The splendid fountains at the centre of the Piazza della Rotonda emerge from this elaborate base. Above it rises the obelisk of Rameses the Great which used to grace the Temple of Isis.

466

*Below:* Steps leading to the Capitoline Hill or the Campidoglio, the smallest but most famous of the Seven Hills of Rome. The Palazzo Senatorio, behind, was the official seat of the Governor of Rome.

*Left:* The Fountains of Trevi were completed in 1762. Two giant Tritons lead Neptune's winged chariot while the figures of Abundance and Health stand in niches on either side.

*Below:* The Piazza della Bocca della Verita occupies part of the ancient cattle market of Rome. In the background stands the Temple of Vesta.

# Stores and Markets

Rome's most famous shopping areas are not as dominated by great department stores as those of Paris or London. The Romans prefer smaller, more personal, specialist shops. Where department stores exist in the centre of Rome they still exude a faint aura of better days with their rather opulent, faded style of exterior decoration. The memory of these rather Edwardian structures vividly contrasts with the bright and sometimes rather tawdry department stores and supermarkets of the new residential quarters.

Although the Via del Corso stretching from the Vittoriano to the Piazza del Popolo and the Via Veneto are reputedly the best shopping areas, the finest and indeed the most expensive shops are to be found in the little streets off the Corso especially the Via Condotti which leads to the Piazza di Spagna and the Spanish Steps. Here window shoppers can see the finest and most expensive goods produced in Italy and the rest of the world. Particularly attractive are the jewellers with their collections of rings, bracelets and necklaces set with crystals, corals, ivories and jades as well as the more conventional precious stones. Every shop has in addition a wide selection of cameos. For the visitor, the best buys are leather goods – the shoes, sandals and gloves are particularly good – and the splendid silk shirts, ties and scarves which are available in every shade of colour and style.

Excellent small shops can also be found in the Piazza del Parlamento and the Via della Scrofa near the Piazza Navona. Fine clothes for children and adults are readily available at a price. It should not be forgotten that Rome is one of the great fashion capitals of the world and is well known for its well cut and often daring creations. Genuine and astronomically expensive antiques are for sale in the Via del Babuino and the Via del Coronari.

Rome is not short of markets. Every day, in one quarter at least, there is a full scale market as well as the permanent ones at the Piazza Vittorio Emmanuele II, the Campo dei Fiori and the Porta Portese. The latter is the site of Rome's Flea Market where almost anything can be bought from junk, genuine antiques, cheap clothes, flowers from the Alban Hills and fish from Ostia. These open air markets are dominated by the bawling of the street vendors and the hubbub of the traffic.

Every square has its own food and vegetable stalls and flower sellers who sprinkle the dusty pavements in summer with cooling water; the scent of whose produce sweetens the otherwise rather rank smell. The best place to buy flowers is still the Spanish Steps in the Piazza di Spagna. Everywhere one goes there are ever-ready ice cream and mineral water sellers.

A sausage stall. Everywhere one goes in Rome, there are food stalls, festooned with mouth-watering delicacies.

*Left:* A shoe shop in the Via Veneto.
Even Rome's smartest streets
cater for all pockets.
*Above:* A clothes stall in an open-
air market. Like every great
European capital, Rome has its flea
market.

*Left:* During the summer, flower stalls provide a welcome patch of colour and a source of sweet scents in many a dusty Roman Street.
*Below left:* Some Romans insist on doing all their shopping in the open markets where they can enjoy the delights of haggling over every price.
*Below:* A vegetable stall offering a comprehensive selection of Mediterranean produce.

*Above:* The Campo dei Fiori is an
attractive market with old stalls and
canvas shades. At one time, this
was where public executions were
held.
*Right:* Ready for the pot. Live
chickens in an open-air market.

# Roman Excursions

Many places of interest lie within easy reach of Rome. One of the most beautiful is Hadrian's Villa, situated on hill slopes planted with olives, stone pines and cypresses some three miles from Tivoli. Little is now left of the vast palace the emperor built as a refuge from the cares of office. Originally it contained copies of many of the buildings he had seen and admired on his journeys around the empire. Of these all that remains are fine examples of the Roman theatre and baths, giving the visitor some idea of the luxury and grandeur that Hadrian enjoyed.

Tivoli itself is a pleasant summer resort, chiefly famous for the Villa d'Este which dates from the 1550s and is situated in a magnificent terraced garden containing 500 fountains. At the lower end of the town on the banks of the River Anio, one of the chief tributaries of the Tiber, stands the Temple of Vesta, which was admired by the Renaissance masters including Bramante whose Tempietto was, it is argued, inspired by its study.

Frascati, on the vine clad slopes of the Alban Hills, was once the home of Henry, Cardinal of York, the younger brother of Charles Edward Stuart, Bonnie Prince Charlie. The town's main attractions are its baroque cathedral and its famous white wines. The next villages along the road, Montepozio and Montecompatri, command fine views over Tivoli to the Sabine Hills. From the motorway and from the old Roman track beneath it, visitors can enjoy magnificent panoramas of the Monti Prenestini to the east.

Tusculum, another fine hill town, older than Rome itself, offers fine prospects of the whole of the Campagna to the capital and the sea beyond, the Sabine Hills and Monte Cavo, the highest of the Alban Hills. During the Middle Ages, the town served as a fortress for the local counts who made the mistake of espousing the cause of the Hohenstauffen Holy Roman Emperors from Germany. This led in 1191 to the whole town being systematically destroyed by order of the vengeful Roman senate. Hardly anything remains of the medieval and classical buildings that once lined its streets.

A short bus ride away from the capital lies Ariccia and Bernini's church, St Maria Assunta. Further along the road, the traveller comes upon Lake Albano at whose southwestern corner, high on the slopes of the hills and approached by a great avenue of ilex trees, stands a Capuchin monastery. From this vantage point, one can look across the lake to the site of prehistoric Alba Longa. It is only a short journey from here to Castel Gandolfo which contains the Pope's summer residence and St Tommaso, another beautiful domed church by Bernini.

Within easy reach of Rome by the Metropolitana (the local electric railway) or by bus are the ruins of Ostia, the ancient port of Rome. Here one can see one of the most complete ground plans of a Roman town ever excavated.

Ostia Antica is the ancient port of Rome. It is named after the ostium or mouth of the river Tiber.

*Above:* The villa d'Este has
incomparable gardens and 500
fountains. They contrast vividly
with their parched surroundings.

*Below:* The Pope's summer residence at Castel Gandolfo overlooks Lake Albano. The palace, its gardens and the former Villa Barberini enjoy the privilege of extra-territoriality.

*Left and right:* Ostia once supported a population of 100000 devoted to satisfying the needs of the capital. Excavations have revealed its complete ground plan. It was divided into housing blocks by straight streets which intersected at right angles. There are good examples of fora, temples, theatres and even a fire station.
*Below:* Many fine mosaics in black and white stone have also been discovered at Ostia.

# Introduction to Tokyo

Tokyo, the capital of Japan, is an endless display of fireworks; the sparks fly in every direction but never last long enough to be recalled in detail – an oriental firecracker ignited by the ultra-modern electronic lighter.

The city is a unique blend of leisurely eastern philosophy with western materialism. It is a place of contrast, a place of surprise. Where else would one find traditionally kimono-clad passengers relaxing in 125 mile-an-hour trains? Where else would a classical 1,000 year old theatre compete for audiences with a punk rock disco?

Custom may die hard in latter-day Tokyo but bricks and mortar seem to change as rapidly as the days themselves. The repeated devastation of fire, earthquake and the Second World War air raids have made Tokyo probably the world's most up-to-date city. Scarcely an old building remains: every office block, every store, every apartment, proclaims Tokyo's brash modernity. The steel, glass and concrete of the new age are indeed generations away from the rapidly dwindling relics of ancient Tokyo.

Tokyo is now estimated to be the most populous city in the world; any rush hour commuter will fervently agree, although wishing it were otherwise. It is also fast-moving, exhilarating and mysterious.

This book captures the excitement and the wonder of the Tokyo of the 1970s. Informed, succinct text married to a breathtaking series of photographs make it essential reading for anyone wishing to learn more of this enigmatic city.

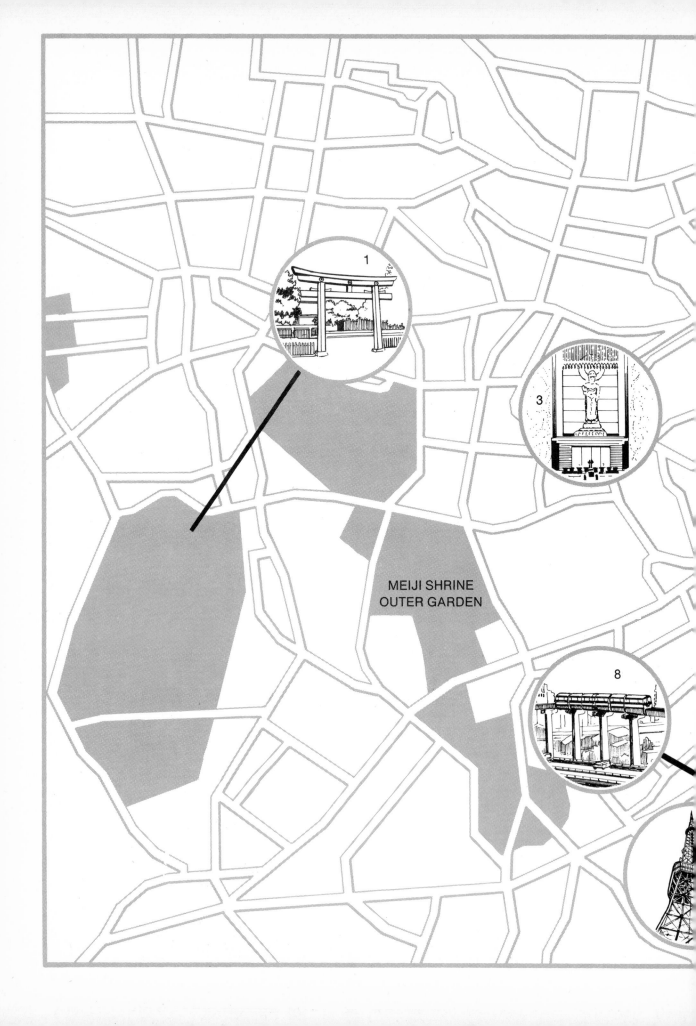

MEIJI SHRINE
OUTER GARDEN

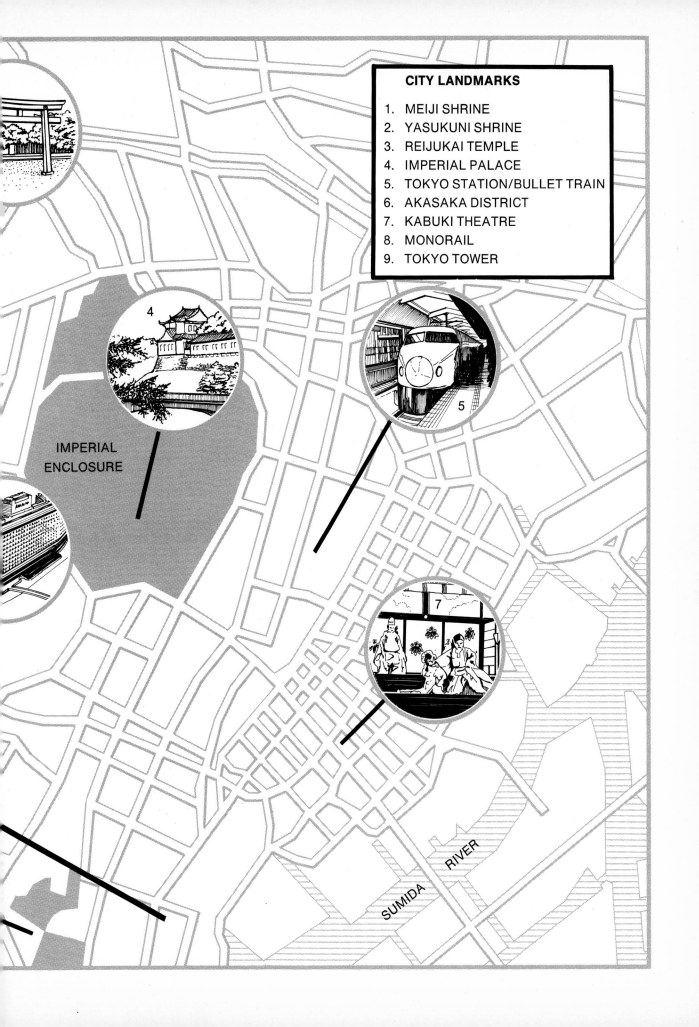

**CITY LANDMARKS**

1. MEIJI SHRINE
2. YASUKUNI SHRINE
3. REIJUKAI TEMPLE
4. IMPERIAL PALACE
5. TOKYO STATION/BULLET TRAIN
6. AKASAKA DISTRICT
7. KABUKI THEATRE
8. MONORAIL
9. TOKYO TOWER

IMPERIAL
ENCLOSURE

SUMIDA RIVER

# Past and Present

In 1457 a warrior and poet called Ota Dokan built a castle in the Toshima district of Japan. The castle stood on the site now occupied by the Imperial Palace and overlooked the marshy lowlands of the Sumida River. Ota took the name of his castle from the scattered fishing village which lay at its feet.

That name was Edo – later to become Tokyo – and it means estuary or literally, 'a place which juts out'.

By the end of the 15th century Edo still numbered no more than 100 houses. But in 1603 the castle was taken over by Tokugawa Ieyasu. This marked the beginning of the area's development. Ieyasu, founder of the Tokugawa Shogunate, turned the castle into a military garrison, considerably extending and altering the existing structure.

Two and a half centuries later the Shogunate was overthrown and the monarchy restored. In July, 1868, Edo's name was changed to Tokyo and it became the capital of Japan. The following year Emperor Meiji moved his court there from Kyoto.

This signalled the start of a flood of western ideas and culture into the country – Tokyo in particular. The Japanese called this process of civilization and enlightenment *Bunmei Kaika.* They were obsessed with catching up with Europe and America: anything western was emulated, admired and whenever possible, shamelessly copied.

The general leaning towards western influences made Tokyo the Japanese centre of modern culture. New literary movements sprang up in the universities; Shakespeare's plays were translated by Tsubouchi Shoyo; Russian literature was introduced as well as German, English and French. In 1887 the Tokyo University of Fine Art and the Tokyo University of Music were established in Ueno, becoming the centres of artistic and musical training.

Freedom of speech and of the Press was also highly regarded. Many newspapers (shimbun) were founded in the first decades of the Meiji Era, mainly for the purpose of supporting certain political parties. Among these were the noteworthy *Nichi-Nichi Shimbun* and the *Tokyo Asahi Shimbun,* founded in 1872 and 1888 respectively.

Around the turn of the 20th century, a commercial centre was built in the Marunouchi 'inside castle', which was in fact situated in the outer moat zone of the castle. Although Osaka was still Japan's largest commercial centre, Tokyo was about to take over.

The growth of Tokyo was drastically checked by the great earthquake of September, 1923. The subsequent fire killed more than 100,000 people and destroyed 360,000 houses. A short time later, however, Tokyo was reconstructed; its streets were widened and new steel-and-concrete blocks put up. The city's growth continued until the Second World War.

Sakura, or cherry blossom, is the Japanese national emblem and has long been regarded as the flower of flowers. There are more than a dozen species of which Yamazakura, Someiyoshino and Higanzakura are the most popular.

The war changed everything, demolishing the old and giving birth to the new: the system of government; the constitution and laws; social structure; people's lives, morals, thoughts and manners. Tokyo was reborn as the centre of democratic government and of capitalism. What followed became known in the west as the Japanese economic miracle.

Tokyo is divided into 23 administrative wards and has a population of 11,373,000 (approx. a tenth of that of the whole country) within its 796 square miles. The city lies at the mouth of the Sumida River, facing Tokyo Bay which opens out on the Pacific Ocean. The whole metropolitan area, bordering on the Chiba Prefecture to the east, on the Saitama Prefecture to the north, on the Yamanashi Prefecture to the south-west and on the Kanagawa Prefecture to the south, stretches westward across the still developing residential district into the steep Okutama and Chichibu Mountains.

All international flights to Tokyo operate to and from Haneda Airport or Tokyo International Airport, in Ota-ku, about eight miles south-west of the city centre. A new international airport was built several years ago in Narita, Chiba Prefecture, to help control the ever increasing air traffic. However, a continuing dispute over compensation for those who live in the neighbourhood has made it impossible to use. Consequently, Haneda is, for the time being, Tokyo's only airport.

There is no international seaport in Tokyo. Ocean lines to the capital region operate to and from Yokohama, Kanagawa Prefecture, while some domestic services like Oshima and/or the Hachijojima line are operated to and from Takeshiba Pier near Hamamatsu-cho.

*Above:* Ice cream is very popular among the younger generation and ice cream sellers are found all over the city.
*Right:* Although Japan's biggest opposition party, the Socialist Party and middle-of-the-road parties like Komeito (Clean Government Party) and the Democratic Socialist Party are making steady gains in seats, the ruling Liberal Democrats have been in power for the past 30 years.

*Left:* In this overcrowded city a great many people are still forced to live and work under the elevated railway. Happily, though, their numbers are steadily decreasing. *Above:* Tokyo's radio mast, situated in the Shiba Park is about 1,000 feet high – over 100 feet taller than the Eiffel Tower in Paris. It has been in operation since 1958. *Right:* Instant photos! If you are a busy tourist, you can take a picture here, or have one taken for you.

Japanese National Railways (J.N.R.), helped by several private railways on outlying lines, maintain an efficient rail network throughout Japan. Where necessary, services are supplemented by ferries and buses, many of them owned by J.N.R. Shinkansen or bullet trains run from Tokyo to Hakata, Fukuoka Prefecture, covering the 730 miles in six hours 56 minutes.

The over-ground rail network of J.N.R. and the private railways are efficient and economic, as well as being ideal for exploring the metropolitan area. In the heart of the city the Yamanote line, (light green trains) runs in a complete circle, connecting all the chief termini to one another. The Chuo line (pink trains) runs between Tokyo Station and Takao right across the Yamanote line and through the old residential area in the west, with its branch one line operating between Tachikawa and Okutama. The Keihin-Tohoku line (light blue trains) operates between Ofuna, Kanagawa Prefecture, and Omiya, Saitama Prefecture, running alongside the Yamanote line between Shinagawa and Tabata. The Sobu line (yellow trains) operates between Mitaka in the west and Chiba in the Chiba Prefecture, running parallel to the Chuo line between Mitaka and Ochanomizu. The Joban line (green trains) runs between Ueno and the developing residential area in the north. The majority of the trains, which are designed for commuter traffic, with seating capacity being much less than their standing room, are fast, clean and not overcrowded, except during peak rush hour times. The underground rail network run by the Tokyo Subway Corporation and the City of Tokyo also covers the whole metropolis and is very convenient.

Tokyo's main roads are either circular or radial concentric loop roads which are numbered consecutively from the nearest one to the centre. They are designed for access north or east from south or west, particularly in the suburbs, without coming into the centre of Tokyo. The roads radiating from the city run out to the densely populated satellite towns scattered outside the metropolitan area. Nowadays the central area has what they call the Metropolitan Motorway, which has served to ease the heavy traffic a little. But Tokyo's roads are still a nightmare for drivers and families living nearby.

To the east of the Sumida River stretches an area of thick alluvial soil. It has settled as deep as 13 feet in some places as the groundwater has been drawn off for industrial purposes. This lowland area is called Zero Metre zone because it is below sea level; the area used to suffer heavily from typhoons, flood tides and earthquakes.

Higher land in the west of the metropolitan area consists of volcanic layers on top of sand and gravel, leading to the fertile soil of Kanto plain. To the south of Tokyo lies hilly land, varying in height from 164 to 656 feet. Since the 1960s it has been developed as a residential area for an expected population of 500,000. Further to the south and west stretch the highlands of Okutama and Chichibu, part of the Chichibu-Tama National Park, consisting of old geological formations separated by the Tama River and its tributary valleys. The steeper slopes are wooded and the foothills are terraced with cultivated fields; the river supplies Tokyo's water.

*Below:* Geisha girls, dressed in their colourful and traditional costume. They are trained, from an early age, to entertain men in Japan's tea houses. The girls also perform at social functions where they sing, dance and play musical instruments.

*Right:* This geisha girl is carrying out ikebana, the Japanese art of flower arranging. It is learned by most women, usually as a qualification for marriage.

The climate of Tokyo is generally mild, although the summers are extremely hot and humid. The mean annual temperature is 14.7°C (58.5°F). As in the monsoon zone, Tokyo has two windy seasons: in summer masses of warm, humid air from the Pacific which causes the rainy season, tsuyu or baiu as the Japanese call it, in June; in winter a flow of cold, dry air from Siberia, which causes strong freezing winds (karakkaze). Tokyo is usually visited by a few typhoons every year between June and October. The average annual rainfall is 62 inches compared with that of London, 25.32 inches, and of New York, about 40 inches.

*Left:* Like all Japanese cities, Tokyo is liberally dotted with shrines. This one is dedicated to Jizo-son, a bodhisattva who is believed to save suffering human beings in the world of 'no Buddha'.

*Below:* Chochin, or paper lanterns, is a form of lighting used more for nostalgic and commercial reasons than for religious and practical ones. These particular lanterns are lit by electricity and hang outside a restaurant.

Tokyo is situated in the Fuji volcanic chain and has two or three earthquakes of medium scale each year. It used to be said that it was impossible to build skyscrapers in Tokyo due to possible major earthquakes. The great Kanto earthquake in 1923, which caused vast damage to the eastern area of Tokyo, proved however, that the five storey wooden pagoda of Ueno and the stone walls of the Edo Castle moat had remained standing because they were built in such a way that the shockwaves were dispersed in various directions. Traditional wooden buildings did not use nails but tenon-and-mortice joints which because the timbers had dried out and become loose absorbed the external energy. The stone walls of the moat, on the other hand, were coarsely laid for the same reason.

496

Tokyo's first skyscraper, the Kasumigaseki building, was designed to have the same flexible structure. So far it has survived several medium scale earthquakes and nowadays other skyscrapers are being built in the busiest areas, such as Shinjuku and Ikebukuro.

Theoretically, a great earthquake will occur around Tokyo any time within the next 20 years, unless the accumulated earthquake energy beneath Tokyo Bay is somehow dispersed. If it were to hit central Tokyo, the casualties would be exceptionally high and the city's function as the nerve centre of Japan paralyzed. In 1973 Komatsu Sakyo, the country's leading science fiction author, wrote a book entitled *Nihon Chinbotsu* (The Sinking of Japan), in which he showed how the earthquake following a great volcanic eruption would destroy Tokyo. In fact, Tokyo is sinking year by year, especially in the eastern areas, the Zero Metre zone, partly because of mass consumption of groundwater and partly because of dangerous movement of the crust.

*Above:* The koto is a traditional musical instrument with 13 long silk strings, played mostly by kimono-clad women.
*Left:* The interior of Asakusa Kannon Temple. The worship of Kannon, or the goddess of mercy, became popular with the rise of the Buddhist Hokekyo sect. The temple is thought to have been founded in the seventh century.
*Right:* Meiji-Jingu, the most important Shinto shrine in Tokyo, is dedicated to the Emperor Meiji (1852–1912) and his wife the Empress Dowager Shoken (1850–1914).

About three quarters of the dwellings in Tokyo are made of wood with fire-proof concrete and steel houses gradually becoming more common. The style of these houses is a mixture of east and west. They have two or three living rooms furnished with tatami (reed mats) and shoji (paper sliding doors) separated by fusuma (sliding screens), and a lounge in European style. Throughout the whole metropolitan area, there are many housing developments being undertaken by the Japanese Housing Corporation, the City of Tokyo and also by private building concerns.

*Left:* Children going into the Meiji-Jingu (jingu means shrine). The huge Inner Garden is thickly covered by old trees.
*Below:* A Shinto ceremony for a newly born baby at the Meiji-Jingu. Shinto is unusual in that it has no special doctrines or teachings.

All the large newspapers, publishers and broadcasting companies have their head offices in Tokyo. *Asahi Shimbun* which achieved the highest circulation in the world of 11,171,790 copies in March 1976; *Mainichi Shimbun* and *Yomiuri Shimbun* are the so-called Big Three of the Japanese newspapers. A daily economics journal called *Nihon Keizai Shimbun,* several papers in English and Korean and many popular sports and entertainments papers are all published in Tokyo. Dozens of other daily and weekly papers are also printed and distributed, as well as various kinds of weekly magazines. Tokyo has about ten television channels of both V.H.F. and U.H.F.; almost all programmes are televised in colour. N.H.K., the Japanese Broadcasting Corporation, is the only public broadcasting authority. There are also more than 60 radio stations.

The language of Tokyo is generally regarded as standard Japanese, although this is not strictly correct. In fact the Tokyo dialect is the basis of the common Japanese, or Kyotsu-go which is a form of speech designed for people throughout the whole of Japan. The famous accent of downtown Tokyo, the Beranmee, is appreciated as clear and lively by the people of Tokyo, and at the same time thought coarse and unrefined by the people of Osaka. It is possible to say, however, that the Tokyo dialect has served as a nucleus of the common Japanese, providing the country with political unity and a standardized education.

*Left:* A traditionally clad Japanese girl advertising a theatrical performance.
*Above:* Barges on the Sumida River. In old days the river was also called Ookawa (Big River) and carried heavy traffic. It was once so polluted that no fish could survive

in it for long. Now, however, it has been cleaned up considerably. *Right:* A father carrying his baby like this is a fairly rare sight in Tokyo.

# Festival City

In the hustle and bustle of city life, a series of New Year's celebrations are a good opportunity to remind people of the old days. Like many other cities in Japan, the streets of Tokyo are gaily decorated and the girls wear colourful kimonos and display traditional hairstyles.

The most exciting event during the first seven days of the New Year is the Dezomeshiki, or parade of firemen. Tokyo has always been troubled with fire and the firemen have long been regarded as heroes. During the parade they dress in traditional costumes and perform acrobatic stunts on tall bamboo ladders.

At the beginning of summer, festivals or feasts, or matsuri as the Japanese call them, are held: traditional pageants with huge covered litters parading through busy streets. One of the largest and most exciting is Sanno Matsuri which originated in the Edo Era. Bon festival is a good occasion for family reunions. During the festival lanterns are lit for souls who, according to Buddhist belief, come back to this world

As amusement on summer nights, people have enjoyed firework displays since the Edo Era. The firework show at Keio Tamagawa on the Tama River during August has taken the place of the almost legendary one of Ryogoku on the Sumida River. It was abolished because it was thought too dangerous.

Among other historical festivals, the Tokyo Festival held in October is a newcomer which started only about 20 years ago. It celebrates the establishment of the autonomous municipality of Tokyo in 1898. A number of events such as the Tokyo Harbour Festival and the Miss Tokyo contest are featured.

During November, the Tori-no-ichi or Cock Fairs of Otori Shrine, Asakusa, are held on the cock days according to the Chinese animal calendar. People buy kumade, or bamboo rakes, for their happiness and business prosperity. The bigger the kumade they buy, the more prosperity they achieve. Therefore, people spare no expense.

With the approach of the New Year, Toshi-no-ichi or year-end markets are held at the Asakusa Kannon and Yagenbori Fudo Temples; various kinds of New Year decorations are arranged on every stall.

Tokyo's streets are hung with coloured banners to celebrate the festival of Tanabata on July 7th. This is the Star festival when, according to Japanese folklore, the cowherd Altair meets his lover, Vega the weaver, in the Milky Way.

504

*Above:* Children's Day is celebrated on May 5th. Families with little boys festoon their houses with paper or cloth carp strung on bamboo poles.
*Right:* A street full of people in traditional dress taking part in the Nebuta Matsuri festival.

*Below:* Shrine palanquins, or covered litters, are paraded through the streets during the Ningyo Kuyo festival.
*Right:* Traditionally clad men celebrating a Shinto festival.

# Cultural Tokyo

Tokyo has fewer cultural legacies than Kyoto and Nara. But it is impossible to ignore the inheritance from the Edo Era, when a unique culture flourished under the policy of seclusion. And, since the opening up of Japan, Tokyo has been the gateway to western culture. During the Meiji Enlightenment Period, for instance, Rokumei-kan, situated in central Tokyo, played the role of a social club where evening parties and balls were held for foreign diplomats and the aristocracy. Western manners and customs were rapidly introduced among commoners too. Since then Japanese culture has been greatly influenced by the west.

People in Tokyo have more opportunity to come into contact with western culture than elsewhere in Japan. Western music and dance are performed in various places. Many public institutions, such as the National Museum of Western Art, the Metropolitan Gallery of Fine Art, and department stores, hold various kinds of art exhibitions. The Bridgestone Gallery, owned by the Bridgestone Tyre Company, boasts a collection of 18th and 19th-century paintings of international renown. Another large private collection of unusual oriental *objets d'art* and antiques can be seen in the Nezu Art Museum. The largest museum in Japan, of course, is Tokyo's National Museum.

A taste for traditional culture, such as flower arranging and tea making, can also be satisfied. Lovers of traditional theatre are also catered for. The No, a highly stylized and abstract masque with dance and song, is regularly performed at Suidobashi Nogakudo and Yarai Nogakudo. Kabuki, a popular drama with dance and song, is performed by men only at Kabuki-za. Bunraku, a puppet drama with Joruri song, is performed at the National Theatre near the Imperial Palace.

There are numerous universities and colleges in Tokyo: among them the state-owned Tokyo University, the main buildings of which are situated in Bunko-ku. It is not only an academic symbol but also the epitome of the social structure of present-day Japan.

More than 50 per cent of high-school leavers go on to university or college and almost half of them gather in Tokyo. In addition to the 100 year old Tokyo University, there is Tokyo Kogyo University (engineering); Hitotsubashi University (trade and commerce); Tokyo University of Education and Tokyo Geijutsu University (music and art).

Besides these state-owned universities, there are many noteworthy private ones with their own unique method of study and/or education in some scientific field. These include Meiji, Chuo and Nihon in the so-called Latin Quarter near Kanda, Waseda and Keio.

Kabuki is a highly regarded art form which originated during the Edo Era in the latter half of the 16th century. This shows a scene from a performance in Tokyo. All the parts are played by men.

*Above:* Tokyo's Kabuki-za theatre, home of Kabuki. The theatre is situated in Ginza and was opened in 1889. It seats 2,216.
*Right:* Dance and music play an important role in Kabuki's highly stylized drama. The musicians mainly use a three-stringed balalaika-like instrument called a shamisen.

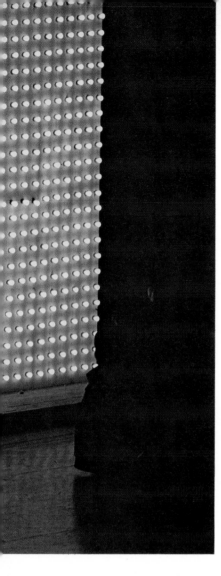

*Left:* A bird dance. The performers are imitating cranes – sybols of longevity.
*Above:* A revue at the Kokusai Theatre in Asakusa. In contrast with Kabuki drama, both men and women take part.
*Right:* The humble umbrella is being used as a prop in this ancient Japanese folk dance.

*Below:* A folk dance with a fan and a wand for exorcising evil spirits.
*Right:* The Tokyo National Museum is the largest museum in Japan and contains approximately 86,000 exhibits associated with the history and culture of Japan, China and India.

*Right:* The Meiji Memorial Picture Gallery in the Meiji Shrine Outer Garden. The approach road, designed so as not to damage the beauty of the garden, has been said to remind the British of The Mall in London.

# The Economic Miracle

The Marunouchi-Tokyo station-Nihonbashi district, stretching to the east of the Imperial Palace, is the city's main business and financial area. Important trading companies known as sogo shosha, banks, insurance companies, stock brokers and similar establishments are all concentrated in this district, the nerve-centre of Tokyo, which epitomizes the Japanese economic miracle after the war.

Nihonbashi was the centre of trade even in the Edo Era: from here radiated the five high roads like Tokaido and Nakasendo. Echigoya, the present Mitsukoshi Department Store, was running a business as a clothing and dry goods store. The rivers and canals were crowded with boats coming from Osaka and other major coastal regions. Before and since the war the place has been a centre for department stores and wholesalers.

Around the turn of the century a commercial centre was built in the Marunouchi district, consisting of red-brick buildings of three or four storeys. After the war, with rapid economic growth, the area has become swollen; Maru-biru, an eight storey building, was the forerunner of Japanese economic growth. Many companies moved their head offices here from Osaka, which had previously been the largest trading town in Japan. Nowadays rows and rows of solid western-style buildings are competing in size and magnificence. At the same time the business district itself is expanding towards the neighbouring section, Kasumigaseki, the political centre of Japan.

During the daytime the district is crowded with white-collar workers who commute enormous distances, from as far away as Gunma and Yamanashi. The shortage of housing has driven people far from the city. Every morning thousands of people travel in packed trains. During the rush hours at every junction students, hired for the purpose, push passengers into the trains. In spite of these uncomfortable conditions, people want to work in the district. At night, in striking contrast to the day, it becomes a kind of no-man's-land peopled only with night-watchmen.

Japan is now the world's leading shipbuilding nation. In 1972 the *Globtik Tokyo,* then the world's largest oil tanker (483,000 tons), was launched from one of her 1,000 shipyards. This shows an aerial view of Tokyo's busy dockland.

*Below:* Marunouchi is Tokyo's
nerve centre. Almost all the major
banks and companies have their
headquarters in this district.
*Right:* Kasumigaseki Building, the
first earthquake-proof skyscraper in
Japan, is modelled on an ancient
five storey pagoda in Ueno Park,
which withstood the great Kanto
earthquake of 1923. So far, the
Kasumigaseki Building has
survived several earthquakes of
medium scale.

*Left:* A pinball fanatic's paradise – one of Tokyo's amusement arcades.

*Below:* The Tokyo Securities Exchange in Kabuki-cho. It was reorganized in 1949 according to the Securities and Exchange Act of the same year.

*Right:* Every street in the city centre is busy with traffic all day long. The narrow road network causes congestion throughout Tokyo.

*Left:* Those citizens who cannot afford to, or who are unwilling to live near their place of work, are forced to travel from neighbouring districts, spending hours in the overcrowded trains.

*Below:* The main station at Shinjuku, a young and expanding outlying Tokyo district. As the terminus of two major private railways and the junction station of the National Railway, Shinjuku is rapidly becoming a thriving shopping and business centre.

# Tokyo Sports

Judo, karate, aikido, kendo, sumo: these are the Japanese traditional sports. Sumo, Japanese wrestling, has been established as a national sport for centuries. Its origin springs from a legend that two gods wrestled in order to decide the ownership of a region. Sumo attained its position as a professional sport in the 1750s. Now, more than two centuries later, it is still one of the most exciting spectator sports.

The Kokugikan Hall, sumo's home base, has a seating capacity of 10,000 and is always full, especially on the final day of a 15-day tournament. Outside the hall colourful flags are lined up bearing the names of the wrestlers. Sumo has undergone only minor changes in rules and form throughout its long history and has maintained its great popularity, especially in downtown Tokyo, where people live in a more traditional and conventional manner.

Before each match both wrestlers stamp on the ring and bend their knees into a half-sitting posture. They then bow to each other and clap their hands. Afterwards they scatter a handful of salt over the ring – the old custom of purification – and toe the mark. This is repeated several times in a modified Shinto ritual. The fight is usually over in seconds.

It is more than a century since baseball was introduced from America. Now it has grown into the most popular participant and spectator sport for all ages. There are twelve professional teams in Japan, divided into two leagues, the Central and Pacific. Each team has its own stadium. The Mecca for baseball fans is the Korakuen Stadium, situated in central Tokyo. The stadium is owned by the Yomiuri Giants, probably the most popular team in Tokyo.

Apart from the professional teams, there are many baseball teams in the high schools, universities and the non-professional organizations.

Other traditional sports, karate or judo, for example, can be best seen in the Budokan Hall – an attractive building constructed in the traditional Japanese style at the time of the 1964 Tokyo Olympics.

A sumo wrestling match at the Kuramae Kokugikan stadium. Tournaments last up to 15 days and are televised live. The stadium seats 10,000 and is nearly always filled to capacity.

*Left:* Nippon Budokan Hall, modelled on the ancient Japanese style of architecture, stands in the vicinity of the Imperial Palace. It was used for the judo events in the Tokyo Olympic Games of 1964 and has been the centre of Japanese martial arts ever since.

*Below:* Japanese characters spelling karate – empty (kara), hand (te). Karate is a system of unarmed combat using the hands, feet, head and other parts of the body as weapons.

*Below:* A judo match between fathers and sons at the Kodo-kan Judo Hall. Here hundreds of Japanese and foreigners daily practise the art of self-defence known as judo (gentle way).

*Left:* Swimming, as is obvious here, is a popular Japanese pastime.
*Below:* Mr Kono, a black belt sixth dan, demonstrating the sometimes awesome art of karate by splitting a wooden block with his foot.
*Right:* Kendo, or ritual fencing, is another martial art which is practised by the majority of Japanese males. Here boy fencers are waiting to take part in a kendo competition.

530

# Consumer Paradise

There are a great many department stores in Tokyo selling a wide variety of goods, from necessities to luxury articles. But there is another aspect. Throughout the year the stores hold exhibitions, sometimes of famous works of art from abroad. On Sundays or national holidays the crowds flock into the department stores to shop or just to see these exhibitions.

It is nearly ten years now since certain streets were designated pedestrian areas on Sundays. Ginza, the most fashionable avenue in Tokyo, teems with people strolling around the department stores and boutiques. It is the same in Shinjuku, although this is more popular with young people. The shopping streets run in all directions from the station; there is also the metro-promenade where all sorts of shops are found. If you don't want to go further than the station, you take a lift or escalator to the station building where anything you want can be bought. This is the same at all main stations.

The only thing missing is the sort of street markets which are so popular in London. But you can enjoy the lively downtown life in Nakamise Street at Asakusa. The long shopping arcade from the Kaminarimon Gate to the Sensoji Temple, is lined with souvenir shops. Here you will sense a different atmosphere from fashionable Ginza or the modern and youthful Shinjuku. Life is more traditional. Sometimes young people who are a little tired of the modern streets come here on a nostalgic visit.

Ameyoko Street is very lively. All sorts of goods are arranged casually in front of the shops. Just before the New Year, the street swarms with people looking for cheap provisions for the celebrations.

The recent big increase in living standards has given young people more to spend. Much of their money is spent on hi-fi equipment and the audio departments in the stores are always busy.

The bright lights of the consumer paradise. The narrow streets are festooned with numerous advertising signs and boards of every kind. No special restriction is imposed on the colour and method of street illumination in Tokyo.

*Below:* Asakusa Nakamise is one of the oldest and busiest shopping arcades in Tokyo. Many of the shops specialize in kimonos, their accessories, zori (sandals) and handbags.

*Right:* A window display in a kimono shop. Kimono, literally and in practice, means clothes of any kind. However it also describes the traditional costume of long, loose robes with wide sleeves.

*Left:* Artificial cherry blossom at Kannon Temple, Asakusa. Technology, it seems, is taking over everywhere!
*Below:* Most Japanese are gadget-crazy. The electrical shops are always crowded with customers buying anything from a miniaturized television set, to the latest, automatic washing machine.

*Below:* Ginza teems with extremely expensive general shops and stores selling a wide variety of high-quality goods. They include three major department stores, Mitsukoshi, Matsuzakaya and Matsuya.
*Right:* Akihabara is Tokyo's electrical appliance quarter.

# Tokyo's Nightlife

Sakariba is a word which describes a district of bars, tea houses, restaurants, night-clubs, strip-clubs, discos, cinemas and theatres where nightlife is enjoyed in direct proportion to the money in your pocket.

In the Ginza area there are any number of bars noted for their expensive and exclusive atmosphere. Japanese-distilled Scotch costs more than £1 for a single measure: real imported Scotch is priceless! Street after street is crowded with department stores, tea houses, boutiques, haberdasheries, shoe shops, fruit shops and restaurants: every shop boasts of the fact that they are in Ginza. To satisfy their pride, therefore, you sometimes have to pay £2.50 for a single dish of avocado.

Politicians and company executives who are connected with the government frequent a place called Akasaka. It is more exclusive than Ginza; Akasaka contains many traditional restaurants or ryoutei as the Japanese call them. They are reserved for V.I.Ps. Money is important in Akasaka but not as important as position and influence.

Roppongi has two different faces: one is just like that of Akasaka, symbolized by exclusive and traditional restaurants, the other is more youthful and less exclusive. Restaurants and coffee shops, more European and/or seemingly more revolutionary, swarm with the so-called Roppongi-zoku (Roppongi-clique), some being intellectuals like writers, or university students.

Shibuya, Shinjuku and Ikebukuro, having rapidly developed after the war, have many common features: they are all termini of private railways with huge department stores owned by the same railway companies. There are a lot of 24-hour-open restaurants, tea houses, coffee shops and discos.

Asakusa is one of the oldest and most popular Sakariba in Tokyo. Once it was the main centre for all amusements: revues, light plays, comedies, films and even prostitution.

Ginza, Tokyo's most fashionable area, takes its name from gin (silver) and za (foundry), as 350 years ago, a silver foundry stood here.

*Left:* Endless night in Tokyo. Although many of the tea and coffee houses and restaurants close at eleven o'clock, the lights of Tokyo never quite go out.

*Above:* Night at Shinjuku, the city of the young which never sleeps. The 24-hour discos and coffee houses are crowded with students, hippies, artists and, as can be seen here, women plying the world's oldest trade.

*Below:* A crowded street in Asakusa. Asakusa Rokku is still loved by those people who remember the time when life was not quite so hurried.

*Right:* Pornographic productions saved the Japanese film industry from the slump it had fallen into as a result of the rise of television. There is a Japanese version of Linda Lovelace's *Deep Throat,* as well as one of *Emmanuelle!*

*Below right:* A cinema at Asakusa Rokku.

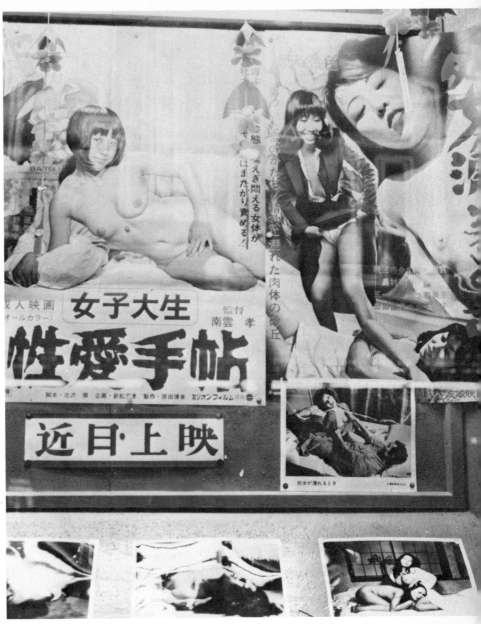

# The Imperial Family

According to mythology the Japanese Empire was founded in 660 BC by Jimmu Tenno, a great-grandson of the Sun Goddess, Amaterasu, from whom all emperors were subsequently to claim descent. The myths were handed down and, until 1945, successive generations were taught that the present emperor, Hirohito, was the 124th emperor in direct descent from Jimmu Tenno.

The emperors were, in fact, worshipped as gods until Emperor Hirohito renounced his divinity in 1946. The emperor, in his capacity as the representative of the Sun Goddess on earth, was a reigning sovereign without power during the Shogunate. Successive emperors were to reign in Kyoto while the government of the country was carried out by the Shogunate in Edo, present-day Tokyo.

After the overthrow of the Tokugawa Shogunate and the emperor had been restored to power, Tokyo became the imperial centre of Japan. The emperor moved his court to the present Imperial Palace, formerly the castle of the Tokugawa Shogunate, from Kyoto in 1869. During the Meiji era, literally meaning enlightened government, the tenno system was established; in other words, the emperor was given almost absolute power, although it was the bureaucracy that actually ruled.

The present emperor is the third occupant of the throne since the Meiji Restoration. Under the terms of the new constitution, Hirohito is the symbol of the state and national unity. Apart from public duties, he spends his time studying biology and is noted for his researches into moss.

In spite of Hirohito's present, more ordinary existence, he was brought up in traditional seclusion, although his children have been given more freedom. When Crown Prince Akihito married a bride of his own choosing, in 1959, a commoner, of neither imperial extraction nor of aristocratic birth, people showed their approval: the wedding was broadcast throughout Japan and the streets swarmed with people who wanted to see the beautiful bride. Now the crown prince and his family, living in Akasaka Palace, lead a more or less ordinary family life. Despite this popularization of the monarchy, it is still said to be secluded compared with the British monarchy.

The Imperial Palace with the Nijubashi, or Double Bridge, in front. The palace, once the castle of the Tokugawa Shogunate, is surrounded by a series of moats and covers an area of 250 acres in the heart of Tokyo.

*Below:* Tourists visiting the Imperial Palace. The palace consists of two separate buildings – one reserved for official royal functions and the other as an Imperial residence.

*Right:* The Music Pavilion, an impressive modern, tiled building in the grounds of the Imperial Palace.

*Top, above and right:* The main
buildings of the Imperial Palace
were destroyed during the last war.
Reconstruction was completed
only as recently as 1968. The
palace has been in official use since
April 1969. These parts are those
specially designed for official
functions.

# Parks and Gardens

There are altogether 250 parks in Tokyo, the largest of which is Ueno Park with an area of 210 acres. The statue of Saigo Takamori, hero of the Meiji Restoration, stands there wearing a kimono with his dog on a lead beside him. The park also includes museums, galleries, zoological gardens and a library.

A cultural, as well as an historic atmosphere is engendered by the Toshogu shrine, built in the 17th century in memory of Shogun Ieyasu, founder of the Tokugawa Shogunate. The five storey pagoda in front of the shrine, survived the great Kanto earthquake of 1923 and dates back to 1639. In the south-west of the park, there is the Shinobazu Pond which is famous for lotus flowers.

In the vicinity of the Ueno Park, there are two famous landscape gardens: the Korakuen Garden and the Rikugien Garden, built by feudal lords. They feature stone lanterns, ponds, arched bridges and beautifully displayed plants. Next to the Korakuen Garden, there is the Korakuen Sports Centre which consists of a baseball stadium, swimming pool and amusement park.

Most of Tokyo's parks were laid out as private gardens for feudal lords and have become open to the public throughout the decades. Typical is the Shinjuku Gyoen National Garden, transferred to the state in 1949 and now a recreation ground. The garden, situated to the south-east of Shinjuku, which is a large shopping and amusement centre, is now a popular outing spot. After the garden is closed, people may wander towards the Meiji Shrine Outer Garden or Inner Garden. The former consists of a gallery and various sports facilities, including the National Stadium, the main stadium for the 1964 Olympics. The latter is thick with old trees and the southern part of the grounds is famous for an iris garden. It contains more than 80 varieties.

In spring, the gardens and parks are full of people who come to see the cherry blossom. In autumn, chrysanthemums bloom in every park and garden. One of the best known parks for chrysanthemum shows is the Hibiya Park, near the business centre.

Happo-en ornamental garden is famed throughout the world for its planned and delicate design.

*Above:* A fountain in Hibiya Park, inaugurated in 1903 as the first park in the much-admired European style.
*Right:* A waterfall in Otani Gardens. Many of Tokyo's better, high-class restaurants have their own landscaped gardens.

*Left:* The Koishikawa Botanical Gardens in Bunkyo-ku.
*Right:* Ueno Zoological Gardens, with an excited group of school children taking a walk with a baby ostrich. Among the zoo's other attractions are two giant pandas – Ran-ran and Kan-kan.
*Below:* Tokyo's pigeon population has increased dramatically thanks to the amount of food they are fed by tourists.

*Below:* Shinjuku Gyoen National Gardens, five minutes walk from Shinjuku station. The gardens were transferred to the State from the Imperial household to be a public recreation ground.
*Right:* Carp are admired by the Japanese for their strength and persistence. They are also considered very good to eat!

# Old Tokyo

When Tokyo was known as Edo, it was a city of craftsmen and skilled workers whose livings were guaranteed by the state. Around the Edo Castle were distributed craftsmen's districts, each of which formed an exclusive society similar to the European guilds. The name of Ginza, for instance, means literally the foundry of silver and originates from the silver mint established there in 1612.

The engineers, carpenters, plasterers, tilers and other craftsmen who took a hand in repairing and remodelling Edo Castle (built in 1457 for Ota Dokan) in 1603, were not men of science and technology in a modern sense, but by heritage and their own experience were familiar with the best building methods. Today you can still see the beautiful parabolic curve of the outer layers of moat-stones as well as that of the roof of the castle. This curve serves to disperse external pressure or energy and protects the buildings from earthquakes.

To the south-east of the Imperial Palace there stands the Imperial Hotel. In contrast to the traditional beauty of the Edo Castle, that of the huge brick hotel is more European, reflecting the cultural trend of the Enlightenment Period of the early Meiji Era.

To the north of the Imperial Palace stretch old streets full of second-hand bookshops from Kudan-Shita to Surugadai-shita: people in Tokyo call this quarter Jinbo-cho. You would be lucky to find any really ancient books. Even a ten year old book is regarded as antique in Tokyo. However, the musty atmosphere which pervades each shop is a constant reminder of the nostalgia of the days of the Meiji Enlightenment and Taisho Democracy.

Nowadays there is virtually nothing old left in Tokyo: it is, of course, possible to come across some architecture, streets and parks which seem to proclaim their age, but they mean virtually nothing – just skeletal oldness, mere nostalgia. It is true that the Japanese in general tend to reject and exclude anything old or traditional as old-fashioned, but Tokyo's drastic reformation and modernization is due to two ruinous factors; the great Kanto earthquake of 1923 and the perpetual air-raids during the Second World War, which destroyed more than 700,000 buildings.

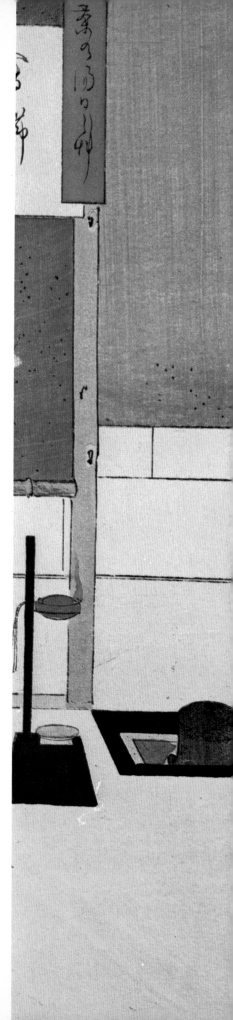

An old print of a Japanese tea ceremony. The art of cahnoyu (tea making) was perfected by Sen-no-Rikyu (1522–1591). Nowadays many young girls acquire the skill as a qualification for marriage.

*Below:* Times past in Ginza. The trams and rickshaws have long since vanished and are now more usually to be found in novels and stories of old days.
*Right:* A performance of ancient music and dance dating back to the seventh century.

*Overleaf: The Three Horsemen,* a print by Katsushika Hokusai (1760–1849). Hokusai was a famous Ukiyoe, or woodcut exponent, together with Hiroshige and Utamaro. His genius can be seen mostly in landscape prints.

563

*Left:* An old engraving of a cash-and-carry shop dating back more than 100 years.
*Above:* An old photograph showing an Asakusa street market as it once was.

# Away From it All

Musashino is an area which extends from Kawagoe City in the Saitama Prefecture down to the Tama River and then eastward to the Ara River. It was once thickly covered with woodlands but has been developed with such speed that only a few patches in the west have been left for recreational purposes.

Old Musashino, or traces of it, can be found in the Chichibu-Tama National Park. Several reservoirs, like Okutama-ko, Tama-ko, and Sayama-ko are not only sources of water supply for Tokyo, but suitable places for a one-day excursion from the city.

Mount Takao is a popular hiking spot, convenient transport being available. On the mountain top there is a small temple among old trees. Fresh green in spring and scarlet-tinged in the autumn, the area attracts many hikers.

Tamagawa Recreation Park, Toshima-en and Yomiuri-land are just a few examples of the numerous parks outside the city. Seibu-en is also a well organized park, noted for the Unesco village, where you can find replica houses from all over the world. Another suitable place for a family outing is the Tama Zoological Garden and safari park, where lions and other animals are kept in the open.

In the western region of Tokyo, traces of Musashino are found: Inogashira Park, Shakujii Park and Jindaiji Botanical Gardens.
The Izu-shichito or Izu-Seven-Islands, situated in the Pacific Ocean to the south-west of Tokyo Bay, are beautiful resorts, washed by the warm Black Current. Oshima, the largest island, is noted for Japanese camellias blooming in the early spring; red flowers, seen among dark green thick leaves, attract tourist's eyes. Another spectacle of this island is Mount Mihara, the active volcano.

Further south, but still within an hour's flight from Tokyo, is Hachijo-jima. This was an island of the banished in the Edo Era, known as Hachijo-jima where even the birds dared not fly. Many sad songs of the banished, yearning for their loved ones have been passed down from generation to generation. Today Hachijo-jima is a happy place with blue seas and clear skies.

A beautiful tiered pagoda with the snow-capped peak of Mount Fujiama rising in the background.

*Left:* The camellia tunnel of
Oshima. The biggest of the Izu-
Seven-Islands, Oshima is noted for
its active volcano Mihara-yama and
tsubaki, or Japanese camellias,
which are not only beautiful to look
at, but produce a cosmetic oil.
*Below:* Meoto-iwa, or 'wedded
rocks', in Ise-Shima National Park.
The new Tokaido bullet train makes
the journey from Tokyo in less than
three hours.

*Above:* Mount Shirane in the Nikko National Park. Nikko is particularly noted for a magnificent 17th-century shrine which is dedicated to Tokugawa Ieyasu, the founder of the Tokugawa Shogunate and for its natural beauty. It is less than two hours from Asakusa by train.
*Right:* Mount Zao in Tohoku, is a well-known winter sports resort.

# Changing Tokyo

Change in Tokyo is sudden and rapid. The people are quite accustomed to relinquishing the out-of-date and the impractical for the sake of modernization and economic growth.

Until just 20 years ago all the main streets in Tokyo were covered with a network of trams which have now been replaced by buses and the underground railway. Although the trams were slow and noisy, they never polluted the city. Now motor cars, the symbol of the Japanese economic miracle, kill trees with their exhaust fumes.

Large parts of Tokyo were destroyed by air raids during the Second World War but afterwards the city grew rapidly. Shinjuku, Shibuya and Ikebukuro are now large shopping and amusement centres, when once they were the dreary outskirts of Tokyo. The formerly bleak Shinjuku area has prospered and become the city's second largest commercial district, with skyscrapers like the 46 storey Keio Plaza Hotel which stands on the demolished site of a filtration plant. There is a splendid view of the city from the observation platforms of the 1,000 feet high Tokyo Tower, a multi-purpose radio tower on a rise of the Shiba Park.

With the rapid development of the city, its population has increased year by year. The shortage of housing has driven people out of the city and at the same time the improvement of various commuting facilities has dispersed them even further. Tokyo's eastern and north-eastern suburbs have, therefore, been growing into residential areas. The suburbs show the results of a rather short-sighted housing policy: seemingly crushed houses ranging from tiny shacks to huge blocks of flats. Woods and forests are being destroyed and replaced by housing lots. Nowadays wild animals are only to be found, in the mountains.

Everything in Tokyo changes rapidly; window displays of the department stores are altered every week. Even a piece of ten year old furniture can be regarded as a rare antique. Amidst rubbish piled up by the roadside you will find refrigerators and television sets that are still in good condition.

Everyone seems to believe that waste is a virtue. The economic miracle has changed not only the city itself but the people's morality. Whoever visits Tokyo after a short absence will find himself to be a *Urashima Taro* who, according to Japanese folklore, became an old man when he returned to his home town after spending a cheerful three years in the sea god's palace.

The west gate of Shinjuku station. Shinjuku's west side is expanding rapidly and is often referred to as fuku-toshin, the second city-centre.

*Left:* The monorail running between Hamamatsu-cho and Haneda Airport is the fastest way to reach the airport. The motorways are almost always blocked with lines of traffic.
*Below:* The monorail speeding to its terminus at Hamamatsu-cho.

*Left:* The Akasaka Hotel is one of Tokyo's many top-class hotels.
*Below:* This bullet train covers the 730 miles between Tokyo and Hakata in 6 hours and 56 minutes. The service between Osaka and Okayama, inaugurated in 1972, claims to be the world's fastest point-to-point schedule. The 110 mile journey takes just one hour.

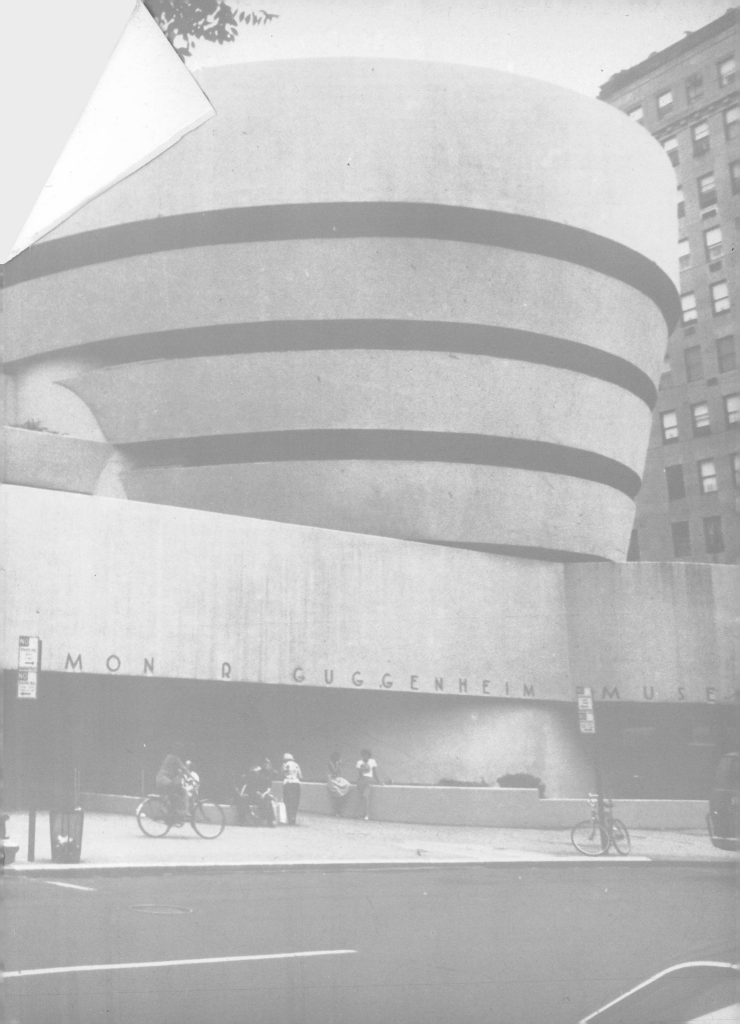